Practical Tools for Youth Entrepreneurs

Thea van der Westhuizen

Practical Tools for Youth Entrepreneurs

An Applied Approach for South Africa and Beyond

Thea van der Westhuizen
University of KwaZulu-Natal
Westville, South Africa

ISBN 978-3-031-44361-9   ISBN 978-3-031-44362-6 (eBook)
https://doi.org/10.1007/978-3-031-44362-6

This work is based on research supported in part by the National Research Foundation of South Africa (Grant Number: 122002-Shape).

© University of Kwazulu-Natal 2024. This book is an open access publication.

Open Access This book is licensed under the terms of the Creative Commons Attribution 4.0 International License (http://creativecommons.org/licenses/by/4.0/), which permits use, sharing, adaptation, distribution and reproduction in any medium or format, as long as you give appropriate credit to the original author(s) and the source, provide a link to the Creative Commons license and indicate if changes were made.

The images or other third party material in this book are included in the book's Creative Commons license, unless indicated otherwise in a credit line to the material. If material is not included in the book's Creative Commons license and your intended use is not permitted by statutory regulation or exceeds the permitted use, you will need to obtain permission directly from the copyright holder.

The use of general descriptive names, registered names, trademarks, service marks, etc. in this publication does not imply, even in the absence of a specific statement, that such names are exempt from the relevant protective laws and regulations and therefore free for general use.

The publisher, the authors, and the editors are safe to assume that the advice and information in this book are believed to be true and accurate at the date of publication. Neither the publisher nor the authors or the editors give a warranty, expressed or implied, with respect to the material contained herein or for any errors or omissions that may have been made. The publisher remains neutral with regard to jurisdictional claims in published maps and institutional affiliations.

Cover illustration: Andriy Popov/Alamy Stock Photo

This Palgrave Macmillan imprint is published by the registered company Springer Nature Switzerland AG
The registered company address is: Gewerbestrasse 11, 6330 Cham, Switzerland

Paper in this product is recyclable.

Foreword

Delivering a student-focused interaction that blends theory, industry practice and community consciousness, to help an individual find meaning and success in life, is the challenge of teaching entrepreneurship in an experiential mode. The targeted student is nurtured and oriented to be an economic driver through the cultivation of creative and innovative thinking. This is critical in an environment of high unemployment and increased social inequalities, where solutions are not easily generated or are probably not well applied.

Often, we fail to recognize the tremendous amount of innovation that educators bring to solving an array of challenges in today's classrooms. It is the teaching philosophy of; "learning from and learning by experience" that empowers the entrepreneurship student to construct his/her own knowledge from previous and current experiences, being guided by future expectations. A futuristic orientation embeds in the student, a questioning and envisioning mind-set. This principle is anchored in the work by Kolb (1984), who espoused that knowledge is created through the transformation of experience, and that holistic approaches are therefore needed to provide bridges across life situations.

Thea's experiential pedagogy which find expression in this book, provides these bridges. Effective youth entrepreneurship is transformational. This is in line with what scholars on experiential teaching believe, that students learn best when they are engaged in hands-on activities and are involved in a process of enquiry, discovery and interpretation. They interact with practicing entrepreneurs, business leaders, government agencies, and other business networks, that are an integral part of the learning ecosystem. Thea has always believed and applied this approach from the time she started her own business, initially as a student and later as a fulltime entrepreneur to the present time she is sharing these practices in this book.

She has lived and worked in the Middle East where she applied many aspects of the experiential entrepreneurship ecosystem model as a Local Economic Development Strategy in the Al Gharbia region, Abu Dhabi, United Arab Emirates. Through the approach a desert landscape was successfully transformed into a thriving economic hub. She later initiated (in the KwaZulu-Natal province of South Africa) a very successful systemic action learning and action research programme called SHAPE (Shifting Hope Activating Potential Entrepreneurship), a refinement of an experiential entrepreneurship teaching ecosystem model I had developed earlier. She developed this approach and validated it through practice. The SHAPE became a successful programme financed by the National Research Fund, the EThekwini Municipality and The University of KwaZulu Natal. The programme won the "Global Innovative Youth Incubator Awards" in Washington DC, in 2018. It has become a youth development flagship programme at the University of KwaZulu Natal.

She shares experiences accumulated over the years, in different geographical settings and business roles, such as project management, entrepreneurship, academia and youth empowerment; all interwoven into thoroughly researched and clearly articulated topics. These different attributes on the scholarship of teaching and learning, covering action learning, experiential learning, and youth development, are found in this book; ***Practical Tools for Youth Entrepreneurs: An Applied Approach for South Africa and Beyond***.

Thea and I share the underlying principles on the scholarship of teaching and learning of Entrepreneurship. This book is an invaluable contribution to youth empowerment and development. Youth entrepreneurship is the future of our country and the continent.

Shepherd Dhliwayo
Professor of Entrepreneurship
University of Johannesburg
South Africa

Acknowledgements

This work is based on research supported in part by the National Research Foundation of South Africa (Grant Number: 122002-Shape).

Riaan Steenberg (Ph.D.): co-investigator and research member to SHAPE; Director of the Stellenbosch Graduate Institute. Contributions are evident in Chapters 1 and 4–7.

Technical Contributions

R. Klopper: Graphic design and illustrations
F.B. Green: Initial language editing and manuscript formatting
D. Griffin: Secondary data quality assurance
R. du Plessis: Manuscript formatting

Peer Review Declaration

The publisher, Springer Nature, endorses the South African 'National Scholarly Book Publishers Forum Best Practice for Peer Review of Scholarly Books'. The manuscript was subjected to a rigorous two-step peer review process prior to publication, with the identities of the reviewers not revealed to the authors or contributors. The reviewers were independent of the publisher and/or the authors in question. The reviewers commented positively on the scholarly merits of the manuscript and recommended that the manuscript should be published. Where the reviewers recommended revision and/or improvements to the manuscript, the author responded adequately to such recommendations.

Organisation of the Book

The book is divided into three parts and nine chapters.

Part I (Chapters 1–3) introduces youth entrepreneurship, provides a background to the SHAPE ecosystem strategy for developing youth entrepreneurship, and illustrates the SHAPE YES (youth entrepreneur support) Network for youth entrepreneurs.

Part II (Chapters 4–8) provides suggestions for enabling entrepreneurial action and mapping momentum in youth entrepreneurship.

Part III (Chapter 9) the final chapter, concludes with a reflection from the author, a youth entrepreneur for twenty years and currently working in the higher education space to transfer skills-of-life lessons learned to youth entrepreneurs. Thea van der Westhuizen founded the SHAPE social innovation and social technology in 2013.

Clarification of Concepts

Barriers to Entrepreneurship

As mentioned in the Introduction, we use the word 'barrier' to describe challenges or obstacles that hinder or prevent youths from making progress in seeking to become entrepreneurs. Personal barriers (concerning systemic intermediaries) experienced by the individual are included because they are perceived as external influences. Identifying these barriers provides useful knowledge to assist youth entrepreneurs.

Various authors have described external barriers to entrepreneurship. Among these are business environmental barriers, such as tax burden, unfair competition, and inadequate finance, as well as external environment dynamism, technological opportunities, industry growth and demand for new products.[1]

---

[1] Krasniqi (2007).

Ecosystem

An ecosystem is a complex whole whose functioning depends on its parts and the interactions between those parts[2] where systemic elements affect the whole, rather than just parts, and refers to the interrelatedness and integration of systems.[3] An approach can be described as 'the process of going towards something'. The term 'ecosystemic' in the context of this study signifies an emphasis on enablers and barriers of a whole (systemic-connectivity)[4] rather than to disparate entities (systemic-dysconnectivity). An ecosystemic approach was adopted in this research to provide information on the seven constructs listed in Chapter 1.

Entrepreneurial Heartset

The entrepreneurial heartset refers to the neurological processes that occur within an individual, shaping and cultivating their entrepreneurial mindset and behavioral actions.

Entrepreneurial Mindset

An entrepreneurial mindset is the end product of thought and a state of mind characterized by a focus on entrepreneurial activities and outcomes. It represents a specific mindset that drives individuals to seek opportunities, foster innovation, and create new value. Those with entrepreneurial mindsets possess a natural inclination towards entrepreneurship, demonstrating a propensity for identifying and capitalizing on opportunities for growth and success.

---

[2] Jackson (2003).
[3] Leonard (2010).
[4] Jackson (2003).

Entrepreneurial Handset

Entrepreneurial handset refers to the observable behavioral actions taken by individuals in pursuit of entrepreneurial activities and goals.

Intermediaries to Student Entrepreneurs

The external barriers encountered by student entrepreneurs concerning systemic intermediaries were examined by expert and experienced scholars,[5] using a systematic approach towards the six categories mentioned in the Introduction.

Learning a Living

Young people will need to be developed not only to earn a living but to 'learn a living'.[6] Learning a living relies on the quality of relevant skills and competencies of learners. Globally, mobile labour, competition and increasingly sophisticated technology pressurise learners to be well-equipped with skills and self-efficacy to perform successfully in the demands these new trends bring.[7]

SHAPE

SHAPE, an acronym for Shifting Hope Activating Potential Entrepreneurship, is an academic concept designed to foster entrepreneurship within South African Higher Education Institutions (HEIs) and beyond. The concept recognizes the importance of shifting heartsets and mindsets, instilling hope, and activating the potential of individuals towards entrepreneurial endeavors. SHAPE emphasizes the need to create an multi-disciplinary enabling environment that encourages and supports entrepreneurial feeling, thinking, learning, and

---

[5] Dhliwayo (2008), Van der Westhuizen (2016).
[6] Hannon et al. (2013).
[7] Van der Westhuizen (2017).

action. Through targeted interventions, such as curriculum development, experiential learning opportunities, mentorship programs, action research and access to resources, SHAPE aims to equip students with the necessary confidence, skills and knowledge to embark on entrepreneurial ventures. By incorporating SHAPE into HEIs, South Africa can harness the transformative power of entrepreneurship, driving economic growth, job creation, and societal development.

SHAPE YES Network

The SHAPE YES Network is an academic concept that fosters an entrepreneurial ecosystem for young entrepreneurs. It spans various domains, including the youth's internal traits, and interacts with external entities. The network includes Higher Education Institutes as project hosts, with government agencies providing support units and mentorship programs. Private sector agencies offer platforms and guidance, while communities provide crucial encouragement. Collaboration with entrepreneurs and small businesses is also emphasized. Internships and on-the-job learning opportunities are offered by corporations. By integrating the SHAPE YES Network, South Africa can cultivate a thriving environment for young entrepreneurs, promoting entrepreneurship, economic growth, and innovation.

Social Technology

Social technology can be defined as a 'process of innovation, conducted collectively and participative by actors interested in building that desirable scenario'. Social technology is a way of using human, intellectual and digital resources to influence social processes.

Student Entrepreneurs

A student entrepreneur is "an individual who participates in an experiential learning programme about entrepreneurship while having an infrastructure of intermediaries to support the learning process".[8] The student entrepreneurs, who are the subject of this book, were studying at the University of Kwazulu-Natal, intending to become successful small business owners or managers engaged in entrepreneurship activities. All the student entrepreneurs participated in the SHAPE social technology described previously.

Systemic Action Learning and Action Research (SALAR)

SALAR is an extension of action learning and action research and can be defined as: 'interactive processes' between local stakeholders and the researcher that enable individuals involved to bring diverse knowledge to a dialogical process and to a problem or challenge that allows the researcher to observe and act upon dynamics at the systemic level.[9]

In this study, 'systemic action learning and action research' applies specifically to the 2014–2015 SHAPE project where research and action-based study focused on understanding systems in relation to their complex parts.

Systemic Approach

The term 'systemic intermediaries' applies to the investigation of linked systems and their joint effects on youth entrepreneurship.[10] An 'approach' can be described as the process of going towards something. For this research, a systemic approach implies attention to the

---

[8] Dhliwayo (2008).
[9] Schweikert et al. (2013).
[10] Jackson (2003).

whole support structure for youth entrepreneurs as set out by scholars specialising in this doctrine.[11]

Systemic Levels

The four systemic levels that apply to this study are the mundo-, macro-, meso- and microlevels. The 'mundo-system' refers to global governance, the 'macrosystem' refers to national governance, the 'mesosystem' refers to organisations and culture, and the 'microsystem' refers to individuals.[12] Different systemic levels may have an integrative effect on entrepreneurship.[13]

Systems Thinking

In this study, systems thinking is applied in the reviewing of information from a holistic perspective. It attempts to solve problems by encouraging people to view a problem from different perspectives to understand the parts that constitute a whole; it is an approach for solving complex problems in the interests of change, and it becomes a key element in decision-making.[14]

Triple H of Entrepreneurship

The Triple H of Entrepreneurship refers to the interconnectedness of our entrepreneurial Heartset, Mindset, and Handset in fostering the psychological development of entrepreneurial behavior. The term "entrepreneurial heartset" pertains to the neurological processes that shape our mindset, while "entrepreneurial mindset" represents the

---

[11] Dhliwayo (2008), Van der Westhuizen (2016).
[12] Scharmer (2009).
[13] Scharmer and Kaüfer (2013).
[14] Briscoe (2016).

resulting framework of our thoughts. Lastly, "entrepreneurial handset" signifies the behavioral actions we take towards entrepreneurship. Essentially, it encompasses the dynamic tapestry of intertwining entrepreneurial heart, head, and hand (Triple H).

Youth Entrepreneurs

In the South African National Youth Policy for 2015–2020, youths are defined as 'all people between the ages of 14 and 35 years', while the legal age in South Africa for children to enter the labour market is 15.[15] In this study, 'youths' is accordingly defined as people between the ages of 15 and 35, and 'youth entrepreneurs' are persons in that age group who are attempting to become entrepreneurs.

Youth Entrepreneurship

Youth entrepreneurship refers to the practical elements of personality involved in enterprising activities, such as initiative, innovation, creativity, and risk-taking in the working environment (either in self-employment or in employment in small start-up firms) and using skills necessary for success in that environment.[16] For this research, youth entrepreneurship implies entrepreneurial activities being undertaken by youths between the ages of 15 and 35 who are in the process of applying entrepreneurial qualities, including the individual entrepreneurial orientation (IEO) factors of taking a risk and being innovative and proactive.

In addition, entrepreneurship signifies the process of creating and launching a new business.[17] For this study, the term 'youth entrepreneurship' refers to youths seeking to commence a new business.

---

[15] Republic of South Africa (2015).
[16] Chigunta (2002).
[17] Roland (2016).

Youth Entrepreneurship Programmes

Youth entrepreneurship programmes are initiatives to encourage and support youths in being more entrepreneurial. In this study, the term applies to both structured and unstructured events aiming to promote business-mindedness among youths.

References

Briscoe, P. (2016). Global systems Thinking in education to end poverty: Systems leaders with a concerted push. *International Studies in Educational Administration, 43*(3), 5–19.

Chigunta, F. (2002). *Youth entrepreneurship: Meeting the key policy challenges.* Education Development Centre, Wolfson College.

Dhliwayo, S. (2008). Experiential learning in entrepreneurship education: A prospective model for South African tertiary institutions. *Education and Training, 50*(4), 329–340.

Hannon, V., Gillinson, S., & Shanks, L. (2013). *Learning a living: Radical innovation in education for work.* Bloomsbury.

Jackson, M. (2003). *Systems thinking: Creative holism for managers.* Wiley.

Krasniqi, B. A. (2007). Barriers to entrepreneurship and SME growth in transition: The case of Kosova. *Journal of Developmental Entrepreneurship, 12*(1), 71–94.

Leonard, A. (2010). *The story of stuff: How our obsession with stuff is trashing the planet, our communities, and our health—and a vision for change.* Simon & Schuster.

Republic of South Africa. (2015). *National Youth Policy 2015–2020.* The Presidency Republic of South Africa. https://www.gov.za/sites/default/files/gcis_document/201610/nationalyouthpolicy.pdf

Roland, P. (2016). *Comments by South African business owner.* Personal communication to Wade Krieger.

Scharmer, C. O., & Käufer, K. (2013). *Leading from the emerging future: From ego-system to eco-system economies.* Berrett-Koehler Publishers.

Scharmer, C. O. (2009). *Theory U: Learning from the future as it emerges.* Berrett-Koehler Publishers.

Schweikert, S., Meissen, J. O., & Wolf, P. (2013). Applying Theory U: The case of the creative living lab. In O. Gunnlaugson, C. Baron, & M. Cayer (Eds.), *Perspectives on Theory U: Insights from the field.* IGI Global.

Van der Westhuizen, T. (2016). *Developing individual entrepreneurial orientation: A systemic approach through the lens of Theory U* [PhD thesis]. UKZN.

Van der Westhuizen, T. (2017). Theory U and individual entrepreneurial orientation in developing youth entrepreneurship in South Africa. *Journal of Contemporary Management, 14*, 531–553.

Contents

Part I Connecting Systems

1 Introduction to Youth Entrepreneurship   3
   1.1 Introduction   3
   1.2 Systems and Ecosystems   4
        1.2.1 Systems in Crisis   7
   1.3 Youth Entrepreneurship   8
   1.4 Shifting Hope Activating Potential Youth Entrepreneurship SHAPE   12
   1.5 SHAPE Ecosystem Strategy for Youth Entrepreneurs   14
   1.6 Typologies of Youth Entrepreneurs in South Africa   16
   1.7 Entrepreneurship Frameworks and Models   18
   1.8 Youth Entrepreneurship: Enablers and Barriers   19
   1.9 Conclusion   23
   References   24

2 Internal Domains Entrepreneurial Heartset, Mindset, and Handset — 31
- 2.1 Introduction — 31
- 2.2 The Entrepreneurial Heartset and Mindset — 33
- 2.3 Entrepreneurial Self-Efficacy (ESE) — 37
- 2.4 Individual Entrepreneurial Orientation (IEO) — 40
  - 2.4.1 Individual Risk-Taking — 41
  - 2.4.2 Individual Innovation — 42
  - 2.4.3 Individual Proactiveness — 44
  - 2.4.4 The Illusion of External Opportunity Identification as an Act of Individual Proactivity — 46
- 2.5 Entrepreneurial Intention (EI) — 48
- 2.6 Entrepreneurial Action (EA) — 49
- 2.7 Conclusion — 52
- References — 53

3 Youth Entrepreneur Ecosystem — 57
- 3.1 Introduction — 57
  - 3.1.1 Context — 58
- 3.2 The SHAPE Ecosystem Strategy for Youth Entrepreneurship — 62
  - 3.2.1 Co-initiating — 66
  - 3.2.2 Co-sensing — 66
  - 3.2.3 Co-inspiring — 68
  - 3.2.4 Co-creating — 68
  - 3.2.5 Co-evolving — 68
- 3.3 Educational Institutions — 68
  - 3.3.1 The Entrepreneurial University — 71
  - 3.3.2 Academic Entrepreneurship — 73
  - 3.3.3 Studentpreneurship — 78
- 3.4 Government Agencies — 79
  - 3.4.1 Entrepreneurship Development in Higher Education — 81
  - 3.4.2 Other Government Agencies — 83

3.5	Private-Sector Agencies	86
3.6	Communities	89
3.7	Small-and-Medium-Sized Enterprises (SMEs)	92
3.8	Corporations and Large Businesses	96
3.9	Internationalisation	102
3.10	Synthesis	104
3.11	Conclusion	104
References		107

Part II The SHAPE Lab: Tools for Enabling Youth Entrepreneurship

4 Toolkit—Tools to Shift Hope and Activate Potential Entrepreneurship — 117

4.1	Introduction	117
4.2	Our dream	117
4.3	Co-initiating: Uncovering our Intent	119
4.4	Finding a Life Purpose and Passion	121
4.5	Competencies and Abilities for Entrepreneurs	123
4.6	Introspection: Thinking About Hopes and Dreams	125
	4.6.1 The SHAPE process of discovering our business idea	127
4.7	Supporting our Entrepreneurial Dream—The Five People Around Us	131
4.8	Entrepreneurship is a Career	131
4.9	Conclusion	133
References		134

5 Toolkit—Enabling Tools for Entrepreneurship in South Africa — 137

5.1	Introduction	137
5.2	Inspired Action	138
5.3	Opportunities	138
	5.3.1 Economic Sectors in South Africa	138
	5.3.2 South Africa Needs Entrepreneurs	140
	5.3.3 We Can Succeed as Well	142
	5.3.4 Addressing a Niche	142

		5.3.5	What About Exporting?	144
		5.3.6	What Are We Importing?	144
	5.4	Financial Returns for Entrepreneurs Versus Employees		147
	5.5	A Youth Entrepreneur Development Tool		148
	5.6	Conclusion		150
	References			150
6	Toolkit—Tools to Assist in Making the Move into Entrepreneurship			153
	6.1	Introduction		153
	6.2	Strategy		153
	6.3	Innovation		154
	6.4	Developing a Business Model		156
	6.5	The SHAPE Four-Quadrant Business Model Canvas		156
	6.6	Where to Start with the SHAPE Four-Quadrant BMC		158
	6.7	Conclusion		158
	Reference			159
7	Toolkit—New Customers and Product Development			161
	7.1	Introduction		161
	7.2	The 'New' for Our New Business		162
	7.3	Cost of Finding Customers		163
	7.4	Building a Reputation		164
	7.5	Expressing Our Uniqueness		164
	7.6	Doing Market Research		164
	7.7	What Does Our Business Sell?		166
	7.8	Sales and Marketing: Two Sides of the Same Coin		166
	7.9	Marketing to Get People Interested		169
	7.10	What to Do with a Qualified Lead?		169
	7.11	Marketing Funnel		169
	7.12	The Buyer 'Persona'		171
	7.13	Sales Activity		172
	7.14	Brochures and Prototypes		173
	7.15	Sales are About Getting People to Buy		174
		7.15.1	The Sales Process	175

		7.15.2 After-Sales Revenue	175
	7.16	B2C Versus B2B Trade	176
	7.17	Starting a Business with No Products: Drop-Shipping	177
		7.17.1 Tools to Make Drop-Shipping Work for Start-Ups	177
		7.17.2 Pros and Cons of Drop-Shipping	178
	7.18	Tools to Starting a Business with No Money	180
		7.18.1 Businesses That Can Be Started with Little or No Capital	181
		7.18.2 Businesses Requiring a Low Initial Investment	182
	7.19	Tools in Applying the Transaction Model: How Are We Going to Get Money from the Customer?	183
	7.20	Conclusion	184
	References		184
8	**Toolkit—Tools to Develop Core Business, Growth, and Sustainability**		**187**
	8.1	Introduction	187
	8.2	Work on Our Business	188
	8.3	When It's Not Working: Tools to Pivot or Persevere	189
	8.4	Tools to Apply the SHAPE Start-Up Strategies for Funding	190
		8.4.1 Bootstrap from Sales	190
		8.4.2 Fund from Savings	193
		8.4.3 Pitch Our Needs to Friends and Family	193
		8.4.4 Access Small Business Funding	193
		8.4.5 Crowdfunding	193
		8.4.6 Angel Investors	194
		8.4.7 Venture Capital Investors	194
		8.4.8 Start-Up Incubator or Accelerator	194
		8.4.9 Pre-contracting	194
		8.4.10 Bartering	195
		8.4.11 Bank Loans or Lines of Credit	195
	8.5	People as Resources: Start Building Our Team	195
	8.6	Understanding Our Value Chain	197

	8.7	Experimenting to Improve	199
		8.7.1 There Is an App for That—Use for Free Until We Need to Pay	199
		8.7.2 Free Accounting Services	200
		8.7.3 Free Prototyping	201
		8.7.4 Free Online Supply Chain	201
	8.8	Start Getting Some Sales	202
	8.9	Experimentation and Expanding the Product Range	203
	8.10	Conclusion	203
	References		204

Part III Journaling of the Author on Working as a Youth Entrepreneur: Self-Reflections Pre-, During & Post-SHAPE

9	**En Route: A Self-Reflective Lens as a Case Study**		**209**
	9.1	Introduction	209
		9.1.1 My Journey Leading to the SHAPE Project	209
		9.1.2 Pre-SHAPE	213
		9.1.3 During SHAPE	214
		9.1.4 Post-SHAPE	216

Index 219

About the Author

Thea van der Westhuizen (Ph.D./CPRP): primary investigator and project leader of SHAPE, University of KwaZulu-Natal, School of Management, Information Technology and Governance: Discipline of Management and Entrepreneurship (Academic Leader); Chairperson: Entrepreneurship Development in Higher Education (EDHE) Community of Practice for Learning and Teaching.

Abbreviations and Acronyms

ADB	African Development Bank (also AfDB)
B-BBEE	Broad-Based Black Economic Empowerment
BEP	Breakeven Point
BRICS	Brazil, Russia, India, China, South Africa (economic grouping)
CBT	Community-Based Tourism
CSI	Corporate Social Investment
DHET	Department of Higher Education and Training
DSBD	Department of Small Business Development
DTI	Department of Trade and Industry
EA	Entrepreneurial Action(s)
EDHE	Entrepreneurship Development in Higher Education
EI	Entrepreneurial Intent/Intentions
ESE	Entrepreneurial Self-Efficacy
EU	European Union
GDP	Gross Domestic Product
ICT	Information (and) Communication Technology
IEO	Individual Entrepreneurial Orientation
NAFCOC	National African Chamber of Commerce
NGO	Non-Governmental Organisation

SALAR	Systemic Action Learning and Action Research
Seda	Small Enterprise Development Agency
SHAPE	Shifting Hope, Activating Potential Entrepreneurship
SME	Small-and-Medium-Sized Enterprise
TIA	Technology Innovation Agency
UKZN	University of KwaZulu-Natal
USD	United States (of America) dollars
VIF	Variance Inflation Factor
YE	Youth Entrepreneur/Ship
YES Network	Youth Entrepreneur Support Network

List of Figures

Fig. 1.1	The Triple H of entrepreneurship	10
Fig. 1.2	The Youth entrepreneur development process (*Source* Van der Westhuizen, 2022)	11
Fig. 1.3	The SHAPE YES network for youth entrepreneurs (expanded)	15
Fig. 1.4	Entrepreneurship frameworks and key theories (*Source* Van der Westhuizen, 2022)	19
Fig. 1.5	Models of entrepreneurship (*Source* Steenberg, 2022)	20
Fig. 1.6	Top 10 barriers and enablers in the youth entrepreneurial ecosystem (*Source* Van der Westhuizen, 2022)	22
Fig. 2.1	Internal domains of youth entrepreneurs (*Source* Van der Westhuizen, 2022)	33
Fig. 2.2	The Triple H of entrepreneurship: heart, head, and hand (*Source* Van der Westhuizen, 2022)	34
Fig. 2.3	Elements of entrepreneurial heartset and mindset that lead to entrepreneurial action (handset) (*Source* Van der Westhuizen, 2022)	36
Fig. 2.4	Elements of the entrepreneurial heartset, mindset, and handset (*Source* Van der Westhuizen, 2022)	37

Fig. 2.5	Relationship of self-efficacy to tasks and roles in the entrepreneurial life cycle (*Source* Cox et al., 2002)	38
Fig. 2.6	Youth entrepreneurial intentions (EI) (*Source* Van der Westhuizen, 2022)	49
Fig. 3.1	The SHAPE YES Network for youth entrepreneurs—Personality traits (*Source* Van der Westhuizen, 2022)	64
Fig. 3.2	The SHAPE YES Network for youth entrepreneurs—Educational institutions	69
Fig. 3.3	Overview of entrepreneurial education (*Source* Lackéus, 2015)	76
Fig. 3.4	The SHAPE YES Network for youth entrepreneurs—Government agencies	80
Fig. 3.5	The EDHE CoP landscape (2021–2023) (*Source* EDHE, 2021)	84
Fig. 3.6	Model of university structures conducive to entrepreneurship and economic activation (*Source* EDHE, 2021)	84
Fig. 3.7	The SHAPE YES Network for youth entrepreneurs—Private sector agencies	87
Fig. 3.8	The SHAPE YES Network for youth entrepreneurs—Communities	90
Fig. 3.9	The SHAPE YES Network for youth entrepreneurs—The entrepreneur & S/M business	93
Fig. 3.10	The SHAPE YES Network for youth entrepreneurs—Corporations and large businesses	97
Fig. 3.11	The SHAPE YES Network for youth entrepreneurs—Internationalisation	103
Fig. 4.1	Entrepreneurial dream	118
Fig. 4.2	The SHAPE major entrepreneurial discovery processes (a Theory U approach) (*Source* Van der Westhuizen and Steenberg, 2022)	120
Fig. 4.3	Basic SHAPE entrepreneurial ability model (*Source* Van der Westhuizen, 2022)	120
Fig. 4.4	Life, purpose, and passion	121
Fig. 4.5	The SHAPE model for entrepreneurial competencies (*Source* Steenberg and van der Westhuizen, 2022)	124

Fig. 4.6	Entrepreneurial hopes and dreams	125
Fig. 4.7	The SHAPE start-up 'Entrevolution' process (*Source* Steenberg & van der Westhuizen, 2022)	128
Fig. 4.8	SHAPE intention influence factors (*Source* Steenberg & van der Westhuizen, 2022)	129
Fig. 4.9	Five people around you (*Source* Steenberg & van der Westhuizen, 2022)	132
Fig. 5.1	Economic development sectors in the South African economy (Adapted for South African indexing from the North American Industry Classification System)	139
Fig. 5.2	Digital ecosystem for 'laptop-preneurs' (*Source* Van der Westhuizen, 2022)	143
Fig. 5.3	Example (*Source* Authors)	148
Fig. 5.4	A toolbox for enabling ecosystemic interpersonal actions (*Source* Adapted from Harrington (2016, 2017); Scharmer & Käufer, 2013)	149
Fig. 6.1	What happens in an internet minute (*Source* Lori Lewis via AllAccess)	155
Fig. 6.2	The SHAPE Four-Quadrant Business Model Canvas (*Source* Van der Westhuizen, 2022)	157
Fig. 7.1	The SHAPE lean model (*Source* Steenberg, 2017)	162
Fig. 7.2	Five key questions for innovative thinking	163
Fig. 7.3	Key questions for personal differentiation	164
Fig. 7.4	Market research questions	165
Fig. 7.5	The SHAPE lean product development cycle (*Source* Steenberg, 2017)	167
Fig. 7.6	Validating leads	168
Fig. 7.7	The SHAPE marketing and sales funnel (*Source* Steenberg, 2017)	170
Fig. 7.8	End-user characteristics	172
Fig. 7.9	Five-step sales process	175
Fig. 7.10	Drop-shipping four steps (*Source* Van der Westhuizen, 2022)	178
Fig. 7.11	Advantages of drop-shipping	179
Fig. 7.12	Disadvantages of drop-shipping	180
Fig. 7.13	Businesses that can be started with little or no capital	181
Fig. 7.14	Businesses requiring a low initial investment	182
Fig. 7.15	Applying the transactional model	183

List of Figures

Fig. 8.1	Business owner objectives	188
Fig. 8.2	Forming our team	196
Fig. 8.3	The SHAPE value chain model (*Source* Steenberg, 2017)	198
Fig. 8.4	Start getting some sales	202

List of Tables

Table 1.1	The SHAPE typology of entrepreneurs	18
Table 3.1	Basic taxonomy of a youth entrepreneurial ecosystem	67
Table 3.2	Example of local government support for youth entrepreneurship	82
Table 3.3	Summary of the SHAPE youth entrepreneurship ecosystem	105
Table 4.1	Topics for reflection before starting out	126
Table 4.2	SHAPE Self-assessment tool on entrepreneurial attitudes	130
Table 5.1	Business turnover (income) by industry sector (2019) (*Source* Statistics SA [2020])	141
Table 5.2	Total South African exports to all foreign markets (2019) (*Source* Wits, 2019)	145
Table 5.3	Total South African imports from all foreign markets (2019) (*Source* Wits, 2019)	146
Table 7.1	Example of a persona map	173
Table 8.1	Pivoting strategies (*Source* Van der Westhuizen, 2022)	191

Part I

Connecting Systems

1

Introduction to Youth Entrepreneurship

1.1 Introduction

South Africa is facing its biggest crisis ever in relation to youth unemployment. Under the expanded definition of total national unemployment, which includes discouraged job seekers, the rate rose to a record of 43.2% in the first quarter of 2021 from 42.6% in the previous quarter. Underscoring the gravity of the situation, the youth's jobless rate based on the expanded definition now stands at 74.7%, which means that only one in four school leavers who are 24 or younger have a job in South Africa. This should urgently be addressed as a matter of national priority and is a national crisis.[1] A link between youth unemployment and low economic development is evident in South Africa, and the low economic growth influences the total labour market. It is important to examine the effects that unemployment has on youth development because unemployed youths are unable to gain valuable entrepreneurial skills.

Entrepreneurship is often seen as a strategy to improve youth unemployment, but by no means can it be seen as a save-it-all

---

[1] Stoddard (2021).

© University of Kwazulu-Natal 2024
T. van der Westhuizen, *Practical Tools for Youth Entrepreneurs*,
https://doi.org/10.1007/978-3-031-44362-6_1

strategy for national social-economic development. Attempting to investigate possible support strategies for youth entrepreneurs, the SHAPE ecosystem for youth entrepreneurs was first theoretically created and then practically applied over time. The key barriers and enablers to youth entrepreneurship were identified as perceived by youths in relation to the ecosystem and results are presented in part two of the book. Youth unemployment and mitigating barriers to youth entrepreneurship are everybody's business, and all systems are held responsible for overcoming this crisis collectively. Failure to do so will result in a national socio-economic collapse.

1.2 Systems and Ecosystems

The world around us consists of integrated and interrelated systems, and these systems are facing severe challenges in all aspects.[2] The decay in systems in the different environments around us is the cause of collective deconstructive actions of people, and only a transformation of collective consciousness towards sustainable and responsible systemic development practices will bring forward possible solutions to turn around the decay within our systems.[3] The need for not only change but the deep systemic transformation has come to a boiling point where global governing practices such as the United Nations are reviewing sustainability approaches. Systemic transformation needs enablers of transformation which brings forward the desired change.[4] A system can be described as a complex whole whose functioning depends on its parts and the interactions between those parts,[5] where systemic elements affecting the whole, rather than just parts of it, refers to the interrelatedness and integrativeness of systems.[6]

---

[2] Van der Westhuizen (2016).
[3] Gunnlaugson et al. (2013).
[4] Fitch and O'Fallon (2013).
[5] Jackson (2003).
[6] Leonard (2010).

Systems are distinguished on four different levels: mundo-level, macrolevel, meso-level, and micro-level systems.[7] The *mundo-system* refers to global governance, the *macrosystem* refers to national governance or institutionalising, the *mesosystem* refers to organisations and culture, and the *microsystem* refers to individuals and their thinking.[8] From a multi-level systemic perspective, the global society in relation to the global economy is described as the mundo-system, society at large as the macrosystem, organisational structure, culture and climate as the mesosystem, and the personal characteristics and traits of an individual as the microsystem.[9]

Characteristics of systems and their components and determinants include[10]:

- A system has processes and certain outputs since a system is something.
- When components are added or removed from a system, these actions change the system.
- When any component is added to a system, it is affected by being included in the system.
- When components are added to a system, it is perceived that related hierarchical structures are formed.
- The survival of a system requires certain forms of control and communication that support system survival.
- Some of the system's properties are emergent and not easy to predict.
- The system has a boundary.
- The external environment to the boundary of the system affects the system.

Systems can further be distinguished between physical or natural structures as hard systems and people, organisations, and their culture as soft systems.[11] Hard systems operate in a process that goes from extraction to

---

[7] Scharmer (2009).
[8] Townsend and MacBeath (2011).
[9] Mark Edward's as cited in Thompson and Bevan (2013).
[10] Waring (1996).
[11] Jackson (2003).

production, distribution, consumption, and ultimately disposal—otherwise referred to as the materials economy.[12] The materials economy system is in crisis because it is confined to a linear sequence of hard systems which minimally incorporate soft-system approaches.[13] On this topic, twenty-first-century scholars concur that systems at all levels are in a crisis.[14] It is important to highlight the need for collective change within systems because the impact of irresponsible and unsustainable leadership practices results in the decay of all systemic environments, whether it is a political, economic, or ecological environment. These systemic challenges are evident in both developed and developing countries.

Soft-system development scholars propose an anthropomorphic descriptive terminology of the system. They suggest, for example, that integrative systems cannot 'breathe' without one another or that systems are 'living', 'dying', and being 'reborn'.[15] Viewing systems as anthropomorphic ties in with the term 'ecosystem'. An ecosystem, derived from the Greek *oikos* (house or habitation) and *systema* (organised whole) is derived from biology, denoting the complexity of the relationship of living things to their environment. An ecosystem describes how various organisms live closely together, their mode of interaction with each other, and how they depend on each other for existence and survival. Ecosystems are complex, supporting elements that are both biotic (living) and abiotic (non-living). The biotic are divided based on their type of nutrition: some of them are producers, and others are consumers.[16]

Similarly, youth entrepreneurs function in an ecosystem and they need a systemic support network to exist—and vice versa—because of the co-dependency of systems.

---

[12] Leonard (2010).
[13] Leonard (2010).
[14] Scharmer (2009), Goleman and Senge (2014).
[15] Checkland (1999), Jackson (2003), Senge, Scharmer et al. (2008a), Senge, Smith et al. (2008b), Scharmer (2009), Scharmer and Kaüfer (2013).
[16] Moore (1996).

1.2.1 Systems in Crisis

Globally, social systems are in a crisis and dying. In the same process, something else is being reborn. Death and rebirth of systems, specifically ecosystems, are associated with disruption and change, which can be a painful process for individuals. Hard systems on the planet that are dying include its ecology and the functioning of the materials economy as we know it, and on a soft systemic level traditional leadership and policy approaches are changing beyond recognition. In reflecting on systems and their disconnect, there are three basic feelings shared by many people in the world[17]:

- We live in a world in which we hit the wall with larger systems. Our civilisation is in the process of dying. And that is happening right now, visible among other things in the disruptions around us and between us.
- I want to be part of another story of the future that I want to help create through my life and work; and
- I do not know.

In the rebirth of socio-economic development, the microsystem takes priority, with the values, heartset and mindset of the individual shaping the integrative actions of the system as a whole. The 'spinners' of systemic development going forward are individual values, vision, and levels of self-confidence.[18] These aspects are essential for the sustainability of national wealth creation of the flow of goods and services. Wealth creation is complex and abstract and not synonymous with the accumulation of vast amounts of money.[19]

---

[17] Scharmer (2009).
[18] Senge, Scharmer et al. (2008a), Senge, Smith et al. (2008b), Song et al. (2010), Hermans (2012), Hannon et al. (2013), Hoy (2013).
[19] Remenyi (2021).

1.3 Youth Entrepreneurship

A world without entrepreneurs would be a world without newness and uncertainty.[20] The youth entrepreneur then evolves as someone searching for profit and initiating new combinations and innovating products, processes, sources of supply, selling markets, and organisational forms.

Youth entrepreneurship refers to practical elements of personality in enterprising activity such as taking the initiative, innovation, creativity, and risk-taking in the working environment (either in self-employment or employment in small start-up firms) and using skills necessary for success in that environment.[21] Entrepreneurship is a social function whose ultimate objective is value creation through the recognition of enabling factors. This involves four processes: innovation and creativity, enabling creation, creating a market, and creating an identity formation.[22] Youth entrepreneurship is not an isolated concept. It takes place within a nondual social-economic environment comprised of people who are entrepreneurs, employees, and customers of businesses. For this book, youth entrepreneurship is taken as those entrepreneurial activities being undertaken by youths in the process of applying enterprising qualities, including the individual entrepreneurial orientation (IEO) factors of taking risks and being innovative and proactive. In addition, youth entrepreneurship signifies the process of creating and launching a new business.[23]

The entrepreneurial journey's premise is said to be that of 'new' value creation in which new identities, new ideas, new products and services, new companies, and new entrepreneurs are collectively co-created by the entrepreneur and their interaction with society.[24] Youth entrepreneurship education is an initiative to encourage and support youths in becoming more entrepreneurial and facilitate interactions with society. These initiatives can be academic or non-academic with a common

---

[20] Stefanović and Stošić (2012).
[21] Chigunta (2002).
[22] Goss (2005).
[23] Roland (2016).
[24] Bruyat and Julien (2000), Henry et al. (2005).

denominator to enrich the entrepreneurial experiences of youths with the aim to potentially facilitate entrepreneurial action (EA). The term applies to both structured and unstructured events aimed at promoting business-mindedness among the youth.

The activity of youth entrepreneurship in the informal economy is difficult to determine. However, the *Quarterly Labour Force Survey* released by Statistics South Africa shows that approximately 2.9 million people were actively involved in the informal economy in the first quarter of 2020.[25] With youth unemployment peaking in formal economic activities, it is essential for policymakers and academics—in particular—to review the current relevance of entrepreneurship strategies to enable sustainable and effective youth entrepreneurship. Equally important for youths is to recognise available national strategies and enabling initiatives that can support them in co-initiating an entrepreneurial ecosystem. Key success factors for an effective youth entrepreneur ecosystem strategy include recognising and bridging systemic disconnect, emphasising microsystemic transformation, innovation strategy formulation for economic development, and social growth in an environment of sharply competitive globalisation.[26]

The popularity of youth entrepreneurship has been attributed to its positive influence on wealth and job creation,[27] with particular importance of entrepreneurship as a self-employment option for present-day graduates who can no longer count on the security of wage employment after completing their studies.[28] In a similar vein, youth entrepreneurship can be seen as a tool that minimises unemployment levels and is a source of sustainable economic development.[29] However, there are key barriers within the youth entrepreneur ecosystem that need to be addressed to increase efficiency, success rates, and, most importantly, sustainability.

The demographic significance of youth entrepreneurship in South Africa needs to be considered. Highly successful and efficient youth entrepreneurship is related to value creation in a location-specific

---

[25] Statistics South Africa (2020).
[26] Béchard and Toulouse (1998), Matlay and Westhead (2005), Schaper and Volery (2004).
[27] Gürol and Atsan (2006), Kantis et al. (2002).
[28] Brown (1996), Kamau-Maina (2006).
[29] Awogbenle and Iwuamadi (2010).

context. In addition, youth entrepreneurship in South Africa is impaired by factors such as bureaucratic obstacles to accessing finance, a shortage of specialised skills, and a general lack of innovation.[30] Young South Africans are nonetheless positively disposed towards entrepreneurship.[31] The driver for young people venturing into business is increasingly considered as being a wish to pursue perceived opportunities rather than merely from basic necessity (Fig. 1.1).[32]

To acquire entrepreneurial self-efficacy (ESE) in meeting business challenges and succeed in business communication and interpersonal negotiations: youths will need to develop a sense of self-responsibility over their own lives and a resilient desire and capacity to influence the world around them; consciously helping to shape a new world and participate in it; actively making a difference to improve the crisis

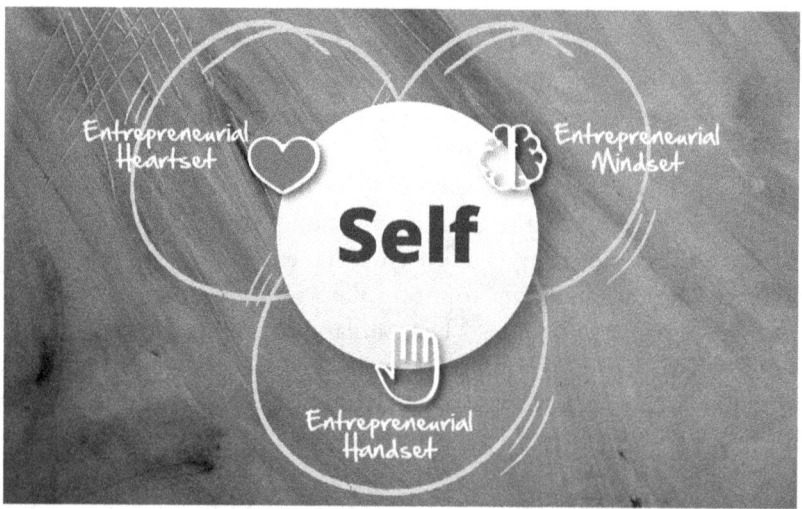

Fig. 1.1 The Triple H of entrepreneurship

---

[30] Steenekamp et al. (2011).
[31] Maas and Herrington (2007).
[32] Mpafa (2008).

various systems are in.[33] Another factor consistently identified as important in youth entrepreneurship promotion in South Africa is the level of education and grades achieved at school.[34] Entrepreneurship education is fundamental to youth entrepreneurial development. Figure 1.2 shows the youth entrepreneur development process.

As the diagram shows, youth entrepreneurship is the total of psychological, social, commercial, and economic interactions. The entrepreneurial process can be decomposed into three major phases: self-innovation, self-management, and self-leadership.[35] It is evident that self-development for youth entrepreneurs is embedded in actions of co-inspiring and feedback from their ecosystem: Thus, connecting a support system with each other and engaging with feedback through dyadic conversations where discussions and feedback-looping are essential.

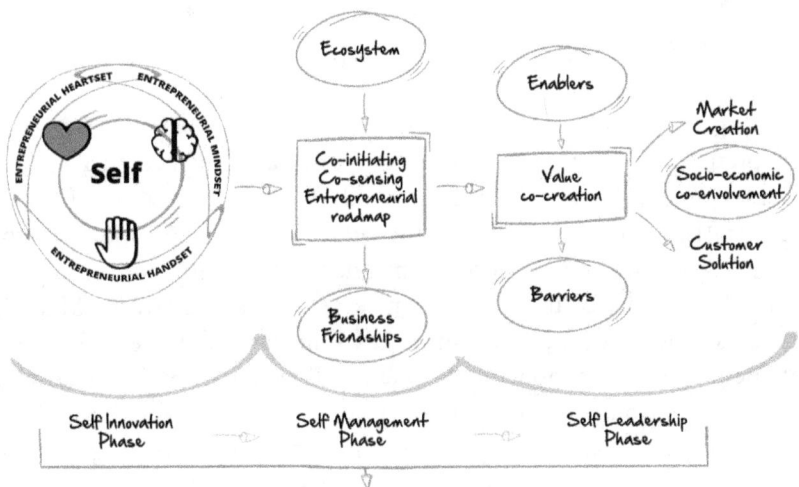

Fig. 1.2 The Youth entrepreneur development process (*Source* Van der Westhuizen, 2022)

---

[33] Hannon et al. (2013), Scharmer (2009).
[34] Maas and Herrington (2007).
[35] Shambare et al. (2020).

The entrepreneurial heartset, mindset, and handset of youths is fundamental to their entrepreneurial journey and is described in more detail in Chapter 2. In the self-innovation phase, youths will need to break down their old mental models and start looking at the world with fresh eyes—growing in developmental maturity and transforming the 'Self'. In the self-management phase, youths are taking EA and co-initiating, co-sensing and co-inspiring with role players in their ecosystem to establish business friendships and explore how value creation can occur through collaborative efforts. In the self-leadership phase, youths take an instrumental role in bringing change to their socio-economic environment, contributing to market-creation and inspiring customer solutions for collective socio- economic development.

1.4 Shifting Hope Activating Potential Youth Entrepreneurship SHAPE

SHAPE, an acronym for Shifting Hope Activating Potential Entrepreneurship, is an academic concept designed to foster entrepreneurship within South African Higher Education Institutions (HEIs) and beyond. The concept recognises the importance of shifting heartsets and mindsets, instilling hope, and activating the potential of individuals towards entrepreneurial endeavors. SHAPE emphasises the need to create a multi-disciplinary enabling environment that encourages and supports entrepreneurial feeling, thinking, learning, and action. Through targeted interventions, such as curriculum development, experiential learning opportunities, mentorship programmes, action research, and access to resources, SHAPE aims to equip students with the necessary confidence, skills, and knowledge to embark on entrepreneurial ventures. By incorporating SHAPE into HEIs, South Africa can harness the transformative power of entrepreneurship, driving economic growth, job creation, and societal development.

SHAPE was created initially as a theoretical framework and then validated by creating the proposed youth entrepreneurial ecosystem. The practical application of the strategy's sustainability was further validated through a series of assessments. The 'SHAPE' strategy refers to processes on the journey to developing the entrepreneurial heartset, mindset, and handset of an individual. This process occurs through moving from reactive response fields to generative response fields, where ideation of entrepreneurial possibilities can be brought into action.

The proposed strategy aims to assist youths in transforming (growing in developmental maturity) personality traits by focusing on ESE, IEO, entrepreneurial intent (EI), and EA. Self-development occurs within a support network, also referred to as the youth entrepreneurial ecosystem. Facilitation of the youth entrepreneurial ecosystem is initially co-initiated by educational institutes, where functions shift as the youth entrepreneurial system develops towards self-sustainability.

As SALAR, the SHAPE strategy consists of three cycles, executed through eleven phases to bring about the desired entrepreneurial change and empirically measure development over time. As a theoretical framework, SHAPE can assist in boosting youth entrepreneurship through starting, inspiring and developing the entrepreneurial heartset, mindset, and handset of youth entrepreneurs. SHAPE is designed to connect youths with a support network and leadership (ecosystemic connection) to inspire them to become successful entrepreneurs.[36] These successful youth entrepreneurs are described as individuals who are consistently motivated to achieve financial sustainability and feel confident in overcoming challenges by being proactive. The continuum of high youth unemployment in South Africa forces many youths to find a way to survive, therefore becoming grassroots entrepreneurs. Youths are limited by their perceptual framework, value system, culture, and work experiences.[37] Thus, youths' culture, family, role models, education, and work experience affect their growth and survival.[38] Youths pursue entrepreneurship because they perceive it to offer flexibility in an improved work-life balance, but they often do not understand what it takes to become a successful entrepreneur. Connecting to a

---

[36] Van der Westhuizen (2016).
[37] Meyer et al. (2016).
[38] Geldhof et al. (2014).

support network in the youth entrepreneur ecosystem might assist the youth entrepreneurs to take EA and, more importantly, to sustain their entrepreneurial efforts.

1.5 SHAPE Ecosystem Strategy for Youth Entrepreneurs

The SHAPE ecosystem strategy for youth entrepreneurs identifies internal and external domains for youth entrepreneur support. These domains consist of seven categories that form a support network—ecosystem—needed by youths. The youth entrepreneurial ecosystem may help youths propel their nascent business idea into a reality through a journey *en route* to EA. The young entrepreneur's ecosystem is therefore the same as their youth entrepreneur support network.

The SHAPE YES Network, an acronym for the SHAPE Youth Entrepreneurship Support Network, is an academic concept that represents an entrepreneurial ecosystem tailored for young entrepreneurs. This network holds immense potential for implementation in South African Higher Education Institutes (HEIs) and beyond. It encompasses multiple domains, starting with the youth's internal domain, which encompasses their personality traits and characteristics. This internal domain interacts with several external domains to create a comprehensive support network for youth entrepreneurs.

The external domains of the SHAPE YES Network include the Higher Education Institute (HEI), which serves as the project host and provides leadership, facilitation, administrative support, and monitoring for the support network. Government agencies play a crucial role by offering a business support unit, integrating entrepreneurial strategies at the municipal level, and providing mentorship and support programmes for youth entrepreneurs. Private sector agencies, such as local chambers of commerce and other organisations, contribute by offering platforms and mentorship opportunities to young entrepreneurs.

Communities, including local communities, families, and friends, form an essential part of the support network, providing encouragement and support to youth entrepreneurs. Additionally, the SHAPE

YES Network incorporates collaboration with entrepreneurs and small to medium-sized businesses, establishing an ecosystem of support and knowledge exchange. Lastly, corporations and large businesses offer internships and on-the-job learning opportunities, creating platforms for practical experience and skill development.

By integrating the SHAPE YES Network into HEIs and beyond, South Africa can cultivate a robust environment for young entrepreneurs. This comprehensive ecosystem enables youth, leverages external support systems, and facilitates collaboration across various domains, fostering entrepreneurship, economic growth, and innovation. Figure 1.3 illustrates these eight aspects, which are discussed throughout the book.

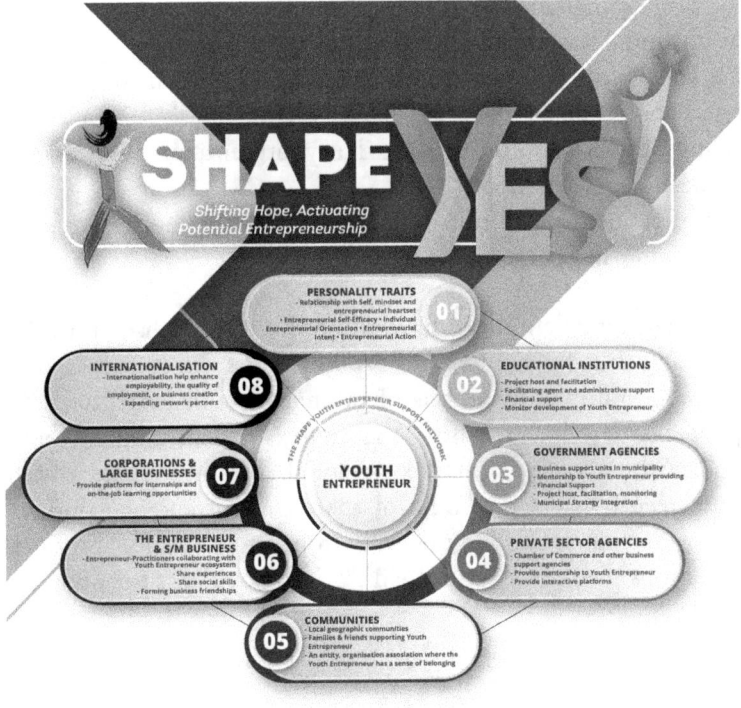

Van der Westhuizen, T. 2023. Effective Youth Entrepreneurship. Sunbonani Scholar. South Africa. 447 pages.

Fig. 1.3 The SHAPE YES network for youth entrepreneurs (expanded)

1.6 Typologies of Youth Entrepreneurs in South Africa

There are at least seven types of definitions of 'youth entrepreneurs' and 'youth entrepreneurship' that have been found in literature[39]:

1. Who the youth entrepreneur is (focusing on the entrepreneur as a particular type of person or the entrepreneur as the product of a particular type of environment).
2. What the youth entrepreneur does (focusing on the entrepreneur as performing a particular role in society).
3. The youth entrepreneur is a type of business owner.
4. The process that the youth entrepreneur experiences, entrepreneurial events, and entrepreneurial input into the economy.
5. The youth entrepreneur as an innovator, an actor in the creation of future goods and services.[40]
6. Definitions focusing on the fact that youth entrepreneurs own small businesses.
7. Archetypal definitions classify different types of youth entrepreneurs into broad categories.

It seems that these definitions have all been operationalised for different purposes and thus serve different purposes in the literature.

There are multiple definitions of the term 'youth entrepreneur', and an applicable description within the context of this book is that they are rogues who actualise a market potential. This is consistent with the early nineteenth-century coining of the term 'entrepreneurship' as the process of shifting economic resources from an area of low productivity into situations that have higher yields.[41] Also popular is the definition of

---

[39] Steenberg (2017).
[40] Sarasvathy and Venkataraman (2011).
[41] Say (1851).

radical 1980s scholars, which is that youth entrepreneurs take advantage of opportunities without regard for the resources they currently control.[42]

The traditional nomenclature of youth entrepreneurial activities revolves around two forms of youth entrepreneurship: necessity (survivalist) and opportunity-driven youth entrepreneurship. These are generally distinguished as follows: Youths who are initially unemployed before starting businesses are defined as 'necessity' youth entrepreneurs and youths who are not unemployed (e.g., wage/salary workers, enrolled in school or college, or are not actively seeking a job) before starting businesses as 'opportunity' youth entrepreneurs.[43]

While the foregoing is taken in the literature as a widely accepted practice, this book adopts a different and more comprehensive approach to classifying entrepreneurial activities. In considering the development of youth entrepreneurs: it is often assumed that entrepreneurship is competence and that when entrepreneurs start, they are incompetent. Literature has failed to answer why some people are better at starting businesses than others, as the construct for the definition of entrepreneurship has not been focused on a market-based view of entrepreneurial activity.

The definition above describes the entrepreneur as an essential mechanism for translating the demand of customers into supply.[44] It also differentiates the entrepreneur from the business owner, as an entrepreneur develops a sustainable business.

More work needs to be done to create a complete ontology of entrepreneurs.[45] Table 1.1 combines the work of various authors in an attempt at a description of various types of entrepreneurs as observed in the literature. There are many different descriptions of what we call entrepreneurs today.[46]

---

[42] Gartner et al. (2017).
[43] Fairlie and Fossen (2018).
[44] Steenberg (2017).
[45] Ucbasaran et al. (2008).
[46] Rogoff and Lee (1996).

Table 1.1 The SHAPE typology of entrepreneurs[47]

1.7 Entrepreneurship Frameworks and Models

There is a myriad of approaches to entrepreneurship in general. Broadly attempting to understand youth entrepreneurship better, the figure below illustrates general entrepreneurship frameworks and key theories (Fig. 1.4):

---

[47] Steenberg (2017).

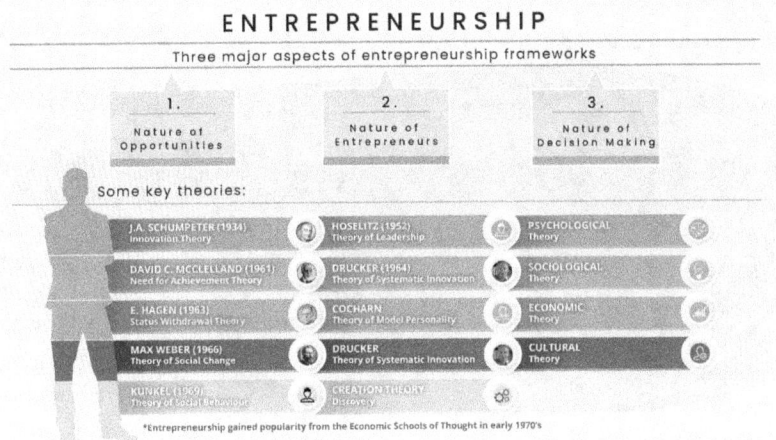

Fig. 1.4 Entrepreneurship frameworks and key theories (*Source* Van der Westhuizen, 2022)

Entrepreneurship is also broadly classified as process-based, events-based, strengths-based, market-based, and functional skills-based models, as shown in Fig. 1.5.

At a broad level, entrepreneurship scholarship is a process undertaken by many authors, and it shows potential in terms of finding a valid approach to entrepreneurship education.[48]

1.8 Youth Entrepreneurship: Enablers and Barriers

Enablers can be defined as a person, thing, or phenomenon that makes, or helps make, something possible. Barriers are obstacles that block the processes of youths' EA. Earlier research on youth entrepreneurship education tends to argue that it is increasingly difficult to become a successful youth entrepreneur. Data from the *2019 to 2020 Global*

---

[48] Steenberg (2017).

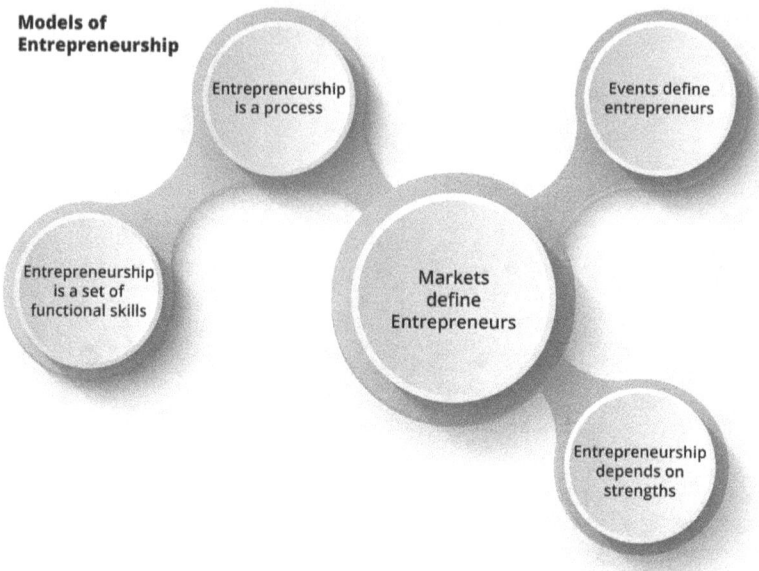

Fig. 1.5 Models of entrepreneurship (*Source* Steenberg, 2022)

Entrepreneurship Monitor[49] show that worldwide youth entrepreneurial activity is low and shows no signs of improvement occurring currently.[50] The low level of youth entrepreneurial activity is exacerbated by inadequate support from government projects and policies, private-sector agencies, communities, and educational institutions.[51]

As a consequence of these barriers, a multitude of 'daily management challenges' are experienced by youth entrepreneurs. Finding ways to overcome some of the identified barriers could help to alleviate the crisis of youth unemployment.[52] A revised approach to teaching entrepreneurship is required.[53] The revised approach used in SHAPE focuses on action-based learning and encourages youth entrepreneurs

---

[49] GERA (2020).
[50] Herrington and Kew (2016).
[51] Van der Westhuizen (2016).
[52] Meyer et al. (2016).
[53] Dhliwayo (2008).

to practise experiential learning, problem-solving, and creativity. This provides practical experience representative of real-world scenarios. It occurs from a nondual perspective where the youth entrepreneurship ecosystem is created to effectively enabling a support network for youth entrepreneurs.[54]

Youth entrepreneurs face both internal and external barriers. Internal barriers affect the entrepreneurial heartset, mindset, and handset, which is a specific state of Being that orientates human conduct towards entrepreneurial activities and outcomes. Youths with an entrepreneurial mindset are often drawn to opportunities, innovation and new value creation.[55] Elements of the entrepreneurial heartset, mindset, and handset specifically noted are ESE, IEO, EI, and EA.[56]

Systemic external barriers, which youths who are in the process of becoming youth entrepreneurs encounter in generating momentum for their nascent business ideas, can be identified. These external barriers affect the entrepreneurial mindset and often give rise to further internal barriers within the entrepreneurial mind.[57]

The study upon which this book is based investigates enablers and barriers that youth entrepreneurs face in South Africa in relation to the theoretical youth entrepreneurial ecosystem, as illustrated in Fig. 1.3.[58]

The youth's perceived enablers and barriers are summarised and illustrated below (Fig. 1.6):

The theoretical model of the youth entrepreneur ecosystem, known as the SHAPE YES Network, highlights the significance of a robust support network for young entrepreneurs. This network encompasses educational institutions, government agencies, private-sector entities, communities, SMEs, and large businesses and corporations. These stakeholders collectively contribute to providing the necessary resources, mentorship, and opportunities to empower and enable youth in their entrepreneurial endeavours. By recognising the pivotal role of these interconnected

---

[54] Van der Westhuizen (2016).
[55] Fayolle (2013).
[56] Cox et al. (2002), Kickul and D'Intino (2005), Ramkissor (2013).
[57] Kickul and D'Intino (2005).
[58] Van der Westhuizen (2016).

Fig. 1.6 Top 10 barriers and enablers in the youth entrepreneurial ecosystem (*Source* Van der Westhuizen, 2022)

entities, the SHAPE YES Network emphasises the importance of collaboration and integration across various sectors to create a conducive environment that facilitates the growth and success of young entrepreneurs through facilitating an increased enabling environment and overcoming perceived barriers.

1.9 Conclusion

Youth entrepreneur development has been identified as fundamental to any country's long-term socio-economic development, but not a save-it-all solution to the deep socio-economic crisis global systems face. Developing the entrepreneurial heartset, mindset, and handset can lead to EA and potential value creation. To create value, youth entrepreneurs need to co-initiate and co-sense an entrepreneurial roadmap within their ecosystem and form crucial business friendships. During these processes, they will encounter barriers and enablers, but an anchored sense of Self can help youth entrepreneurs conquer barriers and optimise enabling factors. Processes of self-innovation, self-management, and self-leadership will strengthen positive personality traits to conquer the barriers encountered, especially if these barriers relate to psychological health aspects.

This chapter introduced SHAPE social technology, which was used as a strategy for the empirical research described in this book. The SHAPE support network, which illustrates a youth entrepreneur ecosystem, is used as the key model for the empirical premise of the book.

This chapter builds on the SHAPE project-supported research supported in part by the National Research Foundation of South Africa (Grant Number: 122002-Shape). These works include: Adelakun and Van der Westhuizen (2021), Awotunde and Van der Westhuizen (2021a), Awotunde and Van der Westhuizen (2021b), IGI Global (2020), Nhleko and van der Westhuizen (2022), Ruba et al. (2021), Van der Westhuizen (2017a), Van der Westhuizen (2017b), Van der Westhuizen (2018a), Van der Westhuizen (2018b), Van der Westhuizen (2019), Van der Westhuizen (2021).

References

Adelakun, Y., & Van der Westhuizen, T. (2021). Delineating government policies and individual entrepreneurial orientation. *Journal of Sociology and Social Anthropology, 12*(3–4), 106–117. https://doi.org/10.31901/24566764.2021/12.3-4.371

Awogbenle, A. C., & Iwuamadi, K. C. (2010). Youth unemployment: Entrepreneurship development programme as an intervention mechanism. *African Journal of Business Management, 4*(6), 831–835.

Awotunde, O. M., & Van der Westhuizen, T. (2021a). Entrepreneurial self-efficacy development: An effective intervention for sustainable student entrepreneurial intentions. *International Journal of Innovation and Sustainable Development, 15*(4), 475–495.

Awotunde, O.M., & Van der Westhuizen, T. (2021b). Entrepreneurial self-efficacy and the SHAPE ideation model for university students. In *ECIE 2021 16th European conference on innovation and entrepreneurship* (Vol. 1, p. 37).

Béchard, J. P., & Toulouse, J. M. (1998). Validation of a didactic model for the analysis of training objectives in entrepreneurship. *Journal of Business Venturing, 13*(4), 317–332.

Brown, S. P. (1996). A meta-analysis and review of organizational research on job involvement. *Psychological Bulletin, 120*(2):235–255. [Retrieved 29 May 2020].

Bruyat, C., & Julien, P. A. (2000). Defining the field of research in entrepreneurship. *Journal of Business Venturing, 16*(2), 165–180.

Checkland, P. (1999). *Systems thinking, systems practice: Includes a 30-year retrospective.* Wiley.

Chigunta, F. (2002). *Youth entrepreneurship: Meeting the key policy challenges.* Education Development Centre, Wolfson College.

Cox, L. W., Mueller, S. L., & Moss, S. E. (2002). The impact of entrepreneurship education on entrepreneurial self-efficacy. *International Journal of Entrepreneurship Education, 1*(2), 229–245.

Dhliwayo, S. (2008). Experiential learning in entrepreneurship education: A prospective model for South African tertiary institutions. *Education and Training, 50*(4), 329–340.

Fairlie, R. W., & Fossen, F. M. (2018). Opportunity versus necessity entrepreneurship: Two components of business creation. *IZA Discussion Paper No. 11258*. Bonn, North Rhine-Westphalia, Germany: Forschungsinstitut zur Zukunft der Arbeit [Research Institute on the Future of Work], University of Bonn.

Fayolle, A. (2013). Personal views on the future of entrepreneurship education. *Entrepreneurship and Regional Development, 25*(7–8), 692–701.

Fitch, G., & O'Fallon, T. (2013). Theory U applied in transformation development. In O. Gunnlaugson, C. Baron, & M. Cayer (Eds.), *Perspectives on theory U: Insights from the field*. IGI Global.

Gartner, W. B., Teague, B. T., Baker, T., & Wadhwani, R. D. (2017). A brief history of the idea of opportunity. In C. Leger-Jarniou & S. Tegtmeier (Eds.), *Research handbook on entrepreneurial opportunities* (pp. 47–65). Edward Elgar.

Geldhof, G. J., Porter, T., Weiner, M. B., Malin, H., Bronk, K. C., Agans, J. P., Mueller, M., Damon, W., & Lerner, R. M. (2014). Fostering youth entrepreneurship: Preliminary findings from the Young Entrepreneurs Study. *Journal of Research on Adolescence, 24*(3), 431–446.

GERA (Global Entrepreneurship Research Association). (2020). *Global entrepreneurship monitor: 2019/2020 global report*. GERA, London Business School.

Goleman, D., & Senge, P. (2014). Seeking the big picture: Systems thinking for schools. *Education Week, 34*(2), 22–23.

Goss, D. (2005). Schumpeter's legacy? Interactions and emotions in the society of entrepreneurship. *Entrepreneurship Theory and Practice, 29*(2), 205–218.

Gunnlaugson, O., Baron, C., & Cayer, M. (Eds.). (2013). *Perspectives on Theory U: Insights from the field*. IGI Global.

Gürol, Y., & Atsan, N. (2006). Entrepreneurial characteristics amongst university students. *Education and Training, 48*(1), 25–38.

Hannon, V., Gillinson, S., & Shanks, L. (2013). *Learning a living: Radical innovation in education for work*. Bloomsbury.

Henry, C., Hill, F., & Leitch, C. (2005). Entrepreneurship education and training: Can entrepreneurship be taught? Part 1. *Education and Training, 47*(2), 98–111.

Hermans, C. A. M. (2012). Towards a 'U-turn' by the churches: How (not) to possibilise the future. *Religion & Theology, 19*(3/4), 237–264.

Herrington, M., & Kew, P. (2016). Is SA heading for an economic meltdown? *Global Entrepreneur Monitor: South African Report 2015/2016.* Retrieved January 15, 2018, from www.gemconsortium.org/report/49537.

Hoy, F. (2013). Handbook of research on innovation and entrepreneurship. In D. B. Audretsch, O. Falck, S. Heblich, & A. Lederer (Eds.), *Science & public policy (SPP), 40*(2), 274–275.

IGI Global. (2020). *What is social technology?* Retrieved May 12, 2020, from www.igi-global.com/dictionary/social-technology/37941.

Jackson, M. (2003). *Systems thinking: Creative holism for managers.* Wiley.

Kamau-Maina, R. (2006, June 2). *Structured qualitative methods, stimulating youth entrepreneurship in Kenya* (pp. 1–38). EDMP 638. Concept Paper. Weatherhead School of Management.

Kantis, H., Ishida, M., & Komori, M. (2002). *Entrepreneurship in emerging economies: The creation and development of new firms in Latin America and East Asia.* Inter-American Development Bank.

Kickul, J., & D'Intino, R. S. (2005). Measure for measure: Modeling entrepreneurial self-efficacy onto instrumental tasks within the new venture creation process. *New England Journal of Entrepreneurship, 8*(2), 6.

Leonard, A. (2010). *The story of stuff: How our obsession with stuff is trashing the planet, our communities, and our health—and a vision for change.* Simon & Schuster.

Maas, G., & Herrington, M. (2007). *Global entrepreneurship monitor: South African report 2007.* Graduate School of Business, University of Cape Town.

Matlay, H., & Westhead, P. (2005). Virtual teams and the rise of e-entrepreneurship in Europe. *International Small Business Journal: Researching Entrepreneurship, 23*(3), 279–302. [Retrieved 10 May 2020].

Meyer, N., Meyer, D. F., & Molefe, K. N. (2016). Bariery rozwoju malych nieformalnych przedsiebiorstw i przedsiebiorczosci: Przypadek regionu emfuleni [Barriers to the development of small informal enterprises and entrepreneurship: The case of the Emfuleni region]. *Polish Journal of Management Studies, 13*(1), 121–133.

Moore, J. F. (1996). *The death of competition: Leadership & strategy in the age of business ecosystems.* HarperBusiness. ISBN 0-88730-850-3.

Mpafa, D. (2008). *Youth positive about being entrepreneurs*. Retrieved February 15, 2012, from http://www.gem.consortium.org/document.aspx?id=778.

Nhleko, Y., & van der Westhuizen, T. (2022). The role of higher education institutions in introducing entrepreneurship education to meet the demands of industry 4. 0. *Academy of Entrepreneurship Journal, 28*(1), 1–23

Ramkissor, M. S. (2013). *The entrepreneurial orientation and intention of UKZN MBA students* [MCom thesis]. University of KwaZulu-Natal (UKZN).

Remenyi, D. (2021). *7th e-learning excellence awards 2021: An anthology of case histories*. University of Applied Sciences.

Rogoff, E. G., & Lee, M.-S. (1996). Does firm origin matter? An empirical examination of types of small business owners and entrepreneurs. *Academy of Entrepreneurship Journal, 1*(2), 1–17.

Roland, P. (2016). Comments by South African business owner. Personal communication to Wade Krieger.

Ruba, R. M., Van der Westhuizen, T., & Chiloane-Tsoka, G. E. (2021). Influence of entrepreneurial orientation on organisational performance: Evidence from Congolese Higher Education Institutions. *Journal of Contemporary Management, 18*(1), 243–269.

Sarasvathy, S. D., & Venkataraman, S. (2011). Entrepreneurship as method: Open questions for an entrepreneurial future. *Entrepreneurship Theory and Practice, 35*(1), 113–135.

Say, J.-B. (1851). *A treatise on political economy; or the production, distribution, and consumption of wealth* (Translated from the 4th Ed. of the French. C. B. Clement [Ed] & C. B. Prinsep [Trans.]). Lippincott, Grambo & Co.

Schaper, M., & Volery, T. (2004). *Entrepreneurship and small business: A Pacific Rim perspective*. John Wiley & Sons.

Scharmer, C. O., & Käufer, K. (2013). *Leading from the emerging future: From ego-system to eco-system economies*. Berrett-Koehler Publishers.

Scharmer, C. O. (2009). *Theory U: Learning from the future as it emerges*. Berrett-Koehler Publishers.

Senge, P., Scharmer, C. O., Jaworski, J., & Flowers, B. S. (2008a). *Presence: Human purpose and the field of the future*. Doubleday.

Senge, P., Smith, B., Kruschwitz, N., Laur, J., & Schley, S. (2008b). Anatomy of inspiration. *T & D, 62*(8), 52–55.

Shambare, R., Chakuzira, W., & Shambare, J. (2020). Revisiting entrepreneurship marketing research: Towards and framework for SMEs in developing countries. In S. Nwankwo & A. Gbadamosi (Eds.), *Entrepreneurship marketing: Principles and practice of SME marketing*. Routledge.

Song, L. Z., Song, M., & Parry, M. E. (2010). Perspective: Economic conditions, entrepreneurship, first-product development, and new venture success. *Journal of Product Innovation Management, 27*(1), 130–135.

Statistics South Africa. (2020). *Quarterly labour force survey: Q1 2020.* Retrieved May 12, 2020, from https://www.statssa.gov.za/publications/P0211/P02111stQuarter2020.pdf

Steenberg, R. (2017b). *The entrepreneurial spirit—Towards an education model for entrepreneurial success in South African entrepreneurs* [PhD thesis]. Texila American University in association with the University of Central Nicaragua.

Steenberg, (2022). *The Entrepreneurial Spirit. In Van der Westhuizen, T. (Ed.), Effective youth entrepreneurship.* Sunbonani. https://omp.sunbonani.co.za/index.php/sunbonani/catalog/book/6

Steenekamp, A. G., Van der Merwe, S. P., & Athayde, R. (2011). An investigation into youth entrepreneurship in selected South African secondary schools: An exploratory study. *South African Business Review, 15*(3), 46–75.

Stefanović, S., & Stošić, D. (2012). Specifics and challenges of female entrepreneurship. *Economic Themes, 50*(3), 327–343.

Stoddard, E. (2021, June 1). First-quarter unemployment rate hits record high of 43.2%, youth jobless rate 74.7%. *Business Maverick.* https://www.dailymaverick.co.za/article/2021-06-01-first-quarter-unemployment-rate-hits-record-high-of-43-2-youth-jobless-rate-74-7/

Tamošiūnaitė, R. (2018). *Socialinių technologijų taikymo galimybės gyventojų dalyvavimui viešojo valdymo sprendimų priėmimo procesuose [Possibilities of social technologies application for population participation in public management decision-making processes].* Mykolas Romeris University.

Thompson, M. J. B. D., & Bevan, D. (2013). *Wise management and organisational culture.* Palgrave MacMillan.

Townsend, D., & MacBeath, J. (2011). *International handbook of leadership for learning.* Springer.

Ucbasaran, D., Alsos, G. A., Westhead, P., & Wright, M. (2008). *Habitual entrepreneurs.* Now Publishers.

Van der Westhuizen, T. (2016). *Developing individual entrepreneurial orientation: A systemic approach through the lens of Theory U* [PhD thesis]. UKZN.

Van der Westhuizen, T. (2017a). The use of theory U and individual entrepreneurial orientation to increase low youth entrepreneurship in South Africa. *Journal of Contemporary Management, 14*, 531–553.

Van der Westhuizen, T. (2017b). A systemic approach towards responsible and sustainable economic development: Entrepreneurship, systems theory and socio-economic momentum. In Z. Fields (Ed.), *Collective creativity for responsible and sustainable business practice*. IGI Global.

Van der Westhuizen, T. (2018a). The SHAPE project: Shifting hope, activating potential entrepreneurship. In D. Remenyi & D. A. Grant (Eds.), *Incubators for young entrepreneurs—20 case histories*. ACPIL.

Van der Westhuizen, T. (2018b). *Open heart, open mind and open will in transformative individual entrepreneurial orientation pedagogies* (pp. 443–448). Academic Conferences and Publishing International Limited.

Van der Westhuizen, T. (2019). *Action! Methods to develop entrepreneurship* (pp. 331–337). 18th European conference on research methodology for business and management studies.

Van der Westhuizen, T. (2021). Applying Theory U through SHAPE to develop student's individual entrepreneurial orientation in a university eco-system. In O. Gunnlaugson & W. Brendel (Eds.), *Advances in presensing volume III: Collective approaches, in Theory U* (pp. 395–435). Trifoss Business Press.

Van der Westhuizen, T. (2022). *Effective youth entrepreneurship*. Sunbonani. Available at https://omp.sunbonani.co.za/index.php/sunbonani/catalog/book/6

Waring, A. (1996). *Practical systems thinking*. International Thomson Business Press.

Open Access This chapter is licensed under the terms of the Creative Commons Attribution 4.0 International License (http://creativecommons.org/licenses/by/4.0/), which permits use, sharing, adaptation, distribution and reproduction in any medium or format, as long as you give appropriate credit to the original author(s) and the source, provide a link to the Creative Commons license and indicate if changes were made.

The images or other third party material in this chapter are included in the chapter's Creative Commons license, unless indicated otherwise in a credit line to the material. If material is not included in the chapter's Creative Commons license and your intended use is not permitted by statutory regulation or exceeds the permitted use, you will need to obtain permission directly from the copyright holder.

2

Internal Domains Entrepreneurial Heartset, Mindset, and Handset

2.1 Introduction

On the assumption that raising levels of self-confidence and value expectations for individuals, as definers of the microsystem, constitutes a fundamental starting point for extended development at higher systemic levels; value-centred development of individuals will, in turn, require from them deeper levels of knowledge both about themselves and about the larger system, with the ability to relate on a multi-dimensional level with everything around them. Therefore, a change in an individual's attitude towards transforming different systemic levels might lead to bridging the decay within systemic development. No matter if these individuals are from developed or developing countries, collective transformation is needed.[1]

The SHAPE ecosystem strategy for youth entrepreneurs introduces youths' internal domains as the cornerstone and starting point of creating an entrepreneurial ecosystem, referred to as the SHAPE YES Network (youth entrepreneur support network). It starts by maturing a relationship with oneself through fostering an entrepreneurial heartset, mindset

---

[1] Weinberg (2014).

© University of Kwazulu-Natal 2024
T. van der Westhuizen, *Practical Tools for Youth Entrepreneurs*,
https://doi.org/10.1007/978-3-031-44362-6_2

and handset. In other words, the entrepreneurial heart, head, and hand—the Triple H of Entrepreneurship.

A youth entrepreneur's personality traits are both enablers and personal barriers for themselves. It can also enable or obstruct crucial relationships with other role-players in the ecosystem. Core personality traits needed by youth entrepreneurs to execute entrepreneurial tasks effectively can be listed as vision, resilience, teamwork, innovation, passion, leadership, integrity, customer focus, and flexibility. These personality traits can also be seen as being a nonconformist at the same time as being a team player; being motivated, driven, focused, and persistent; being 'an architect of one's personal view'; being able to build an ecosystem or community of people able to achieve an outcome; being able to find opportunities and niches in the market, and living following one's belief system, therefore aligning values.[2] An internal locus of control is positively linked with youth entrepreneurship through a desire to solve problems and a willingness to seek out niches in the market. It also assists youth entrepreneurs because of the social benefits derived through networking within the ecosystem (Fig. 2.1).[3]

The way forward to transform (change) global systems and steer collective creativity for responsible and sustainable business practice starts with individual human beings. Unless people change their attitudes or perspectives towards collective transformation, the desired change will not kick in. A change in people's levels of self-confidence (self-efficacy), as well as their individual entrepreneurial orientation (IEO), might lead to a transformation in their attitudes and perspective towards systemic change, therefore, increasing entrepreneurial intent (EI) and action (EA).

---

[2] Ernst & Young (2017).
[3] Hsiao et al. (2016).

2 Internal Domains Entrepreneurial Heartset, Mindset …

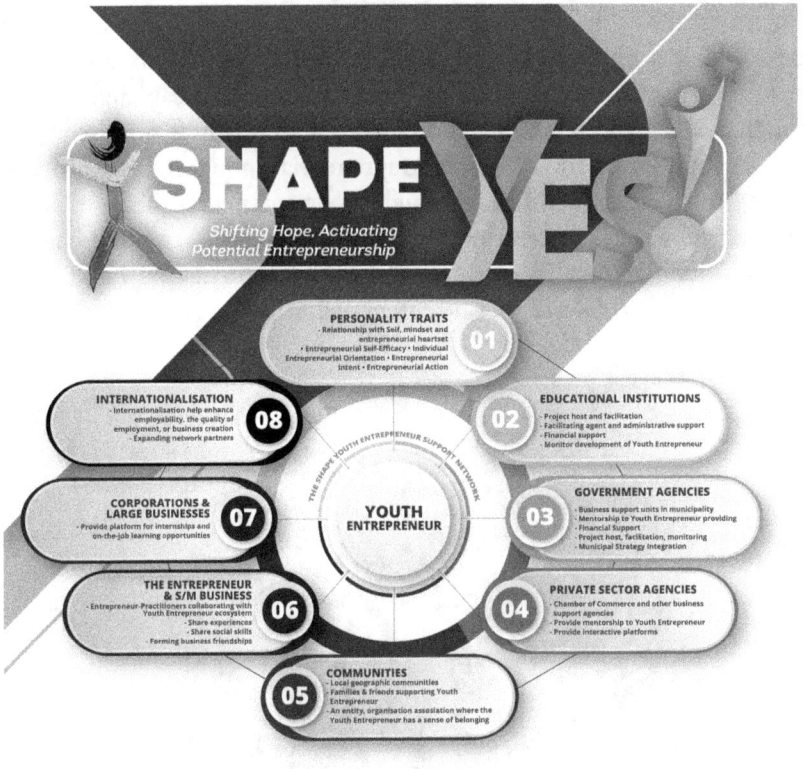

Fig. 2.1 Internal domains of youth entrepreneurs (*Source* Van der Westhuizen, 2022)

2.2 The Entrepreneurial Heartset and Mindset

The mind is the biggest part of a human being and includes thinking, feeling, and choosing. The mind is not the brain; it is produced by the brain. The mind and brain are separate. Brain activity rather reflects mind activity. The mind uses the brain when thinking, feeling, and choosing in response to life experiences. This pushes energy through the brain, and the brain responds to the energy electromagnetically, chemically, and genetically and builds the mind-energy into physical protein thought-trees within the brain. Thoughts are the end product of the mind which is thinking, feeling, and choosing. Thoughts also propel us into action. Therefore, looking at behaviours, one can deduce one's thoughts, and by looking into thoughts, one can deduce mindset.[4]

This study uses the terms 'entrepreneurial mindset' as a concept relating to the end product of thought, 'entrepreneurial heartset' as the neurological process of creating a mindset, and 'entrepreneurial handset' as behavioural action. In other words, the entrepreneurial heart, head, and hand—the *Triple H* of Entrepreneurship (Fig. 2.2).

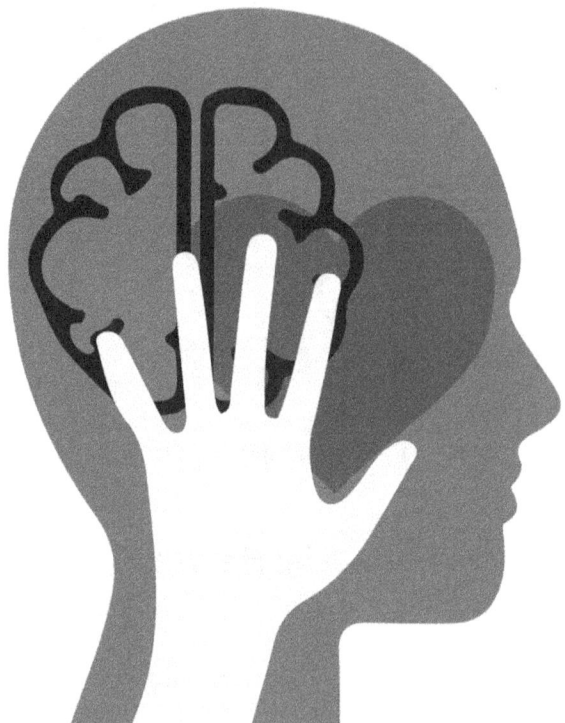

Fig. 2.2 The Triple H of entrepreneurship: heart, head, and hand (*Source* Van der Westhuizen, 2022)

---

[4] Leaf (2013).

Various definitions have been proposed for 'entrepreneurial mindset' and what it encompasses, especially from a psychological perspective. However, for the purpose of this discussion, the following definition will be adopted:

> The entrepreneurial mindset refers to a specific state of mind which orientates human conduct towards entrepreneurial activities and outcomes. Individuals with entrepreneurial mindsets are often drawn to opportunities, innovation, and new value creation.[5]

The SHAPE ecosystem strategy focuses on developing youths' personality traits through concepts empirically associated with an entrepreneurial heartset, mindset, and handset. These concepts comprise entrepreneurial self-efficacy (ESE), IEO, EI and entrepreneurial actions (EA) (Fig. 2.3).[6]

The entrepreneurial heartset, mindset, and handset and their relationship to the entire ecosystem needs to be interpreted as nondual. The notion of nonduality is a philosophical perspective of non-separation, which implies that impulses of the entrepreneurial heartset, mindset, and handset, as noted above, emerge from the overall being of the individual as a whole, rather than as linear or fragmented sequential processes. Nonduality can be defined as 'not two' or 'non-separation'.[7] It is the sense that all things are interconnected and not separate, while at the same time, all things retain their individuality. An awareness of nonduality gives individuals a bigger perspective on life, a greater sense of freedom, and brings them more stable happiness.[8] Building on the philosophy of nondualism, the environment external to the individual cannot be divorced from the internal state of an individual.[9] How the entrepreneurial heartset, mindset, and handset develop, thus is a combination of an internal orientation in relation to the external whole, forming an individual's perceived reality.

---

[5] Fayolle (2015).
[6] Cox et al. (2002), Kickul and D'Intino (2005).
[7] Pillay (2014).
[8] Katz (1997).
[9] Pillay (2014).

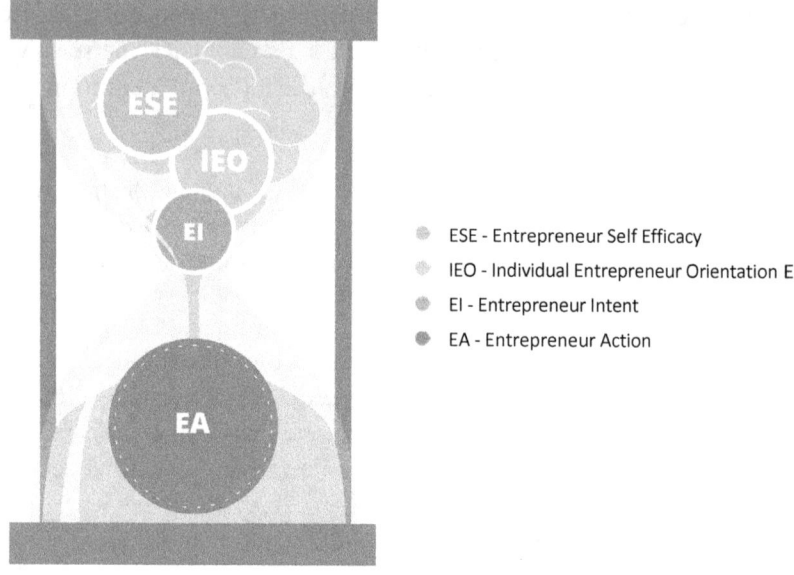

Fig. 2.3 Elements of entrepreneurial heartset and mindset that lead to entrepreneurial action (handset) (*Source* Van der Westhuizen, 2022)

[The] world is not just a system of interconnected objects and processes – a concept that has been pioneered by systems thinking for more than six decades – but that there is no separate, solid, physical world existing independently of consciousness.[10]

Therefore, the entrepreneurial heartset, mindset, and handset (heart, head, and hand apply to both individuals and collectives: thinking and acting entrepreneurially (having an entrepreneurial mindset) is as significant for managers or employees in an established company as it is for the individual entrepreneur.[11]

Illustrating how processes within the entrepreneurial internal domains should be seen from a nondual perspective, Fig. 2.4 sets out the interrelationship between these various aspects in the context of this research.

---

[10] Pillay (2015).
[11] Covin and Slevin (2002).

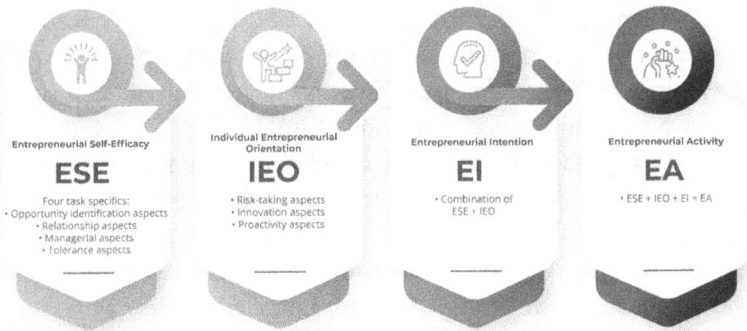

Fig. 2.4 Elements of the entrepreneurial heartset, mindset, and handset (*Source* Van der Westhuizen, 2022)

2.3 Entrepreneurial Self-Efficacy (ESE)

ESE is described as a construct that measures a person's belief in their ability to successfully launch an entrepreneurial venture. Belief in oneself is necessary for the development of entrepreneurship. Individuals with a higher degree of self-confidence are more likely to become successful entrepreneurs and sustain EA.

ESE includes levels of self-confidence for achieving success and meeting difficult objectives in business start-ups and can be broken down into four task-specific types:

- Self-efficacy in identifying opportunities and developing new market offerings
- Relationship self-efficacy: being able to build investor relationships
- Managerial self-efficacy: perception of economics and financial management capabilities; and
- Tolerance self-efficacy: perception of the ability to cope with stress and change.

These self-efficacy dimensions reinforce the importance of personality traits and the ability to interact with the forces at play within the environment.

Existing validated empirical research on ESE proposes a comprehensive theoretical framework of ESE factors determining the success of an entrepreneur, which extends to ten task-specific entrepreneurial skills in four venture creation phases, as illustrated in Fig. 2.5.

ESE and its associates' skills sets, in relation to the venture creation process, was tested and validated to have a significant and positive relationship to IEO, EI and EA. ESE is an important factor in shaping youths' reactions to the environment, and low ESE will reduce youths' intention to start a business and youths' confidence in embracing opportunities. ESE is therefore positively correlated with youths' intention to start a business in the belief that it can be achieved. Youths' level of ESE in relation to a given task can affect their willingness to undertake the task.

A possible way to raise ESE towards skill sets is to enhance the individual in question through training or coaching. The SHAPE ecosystem

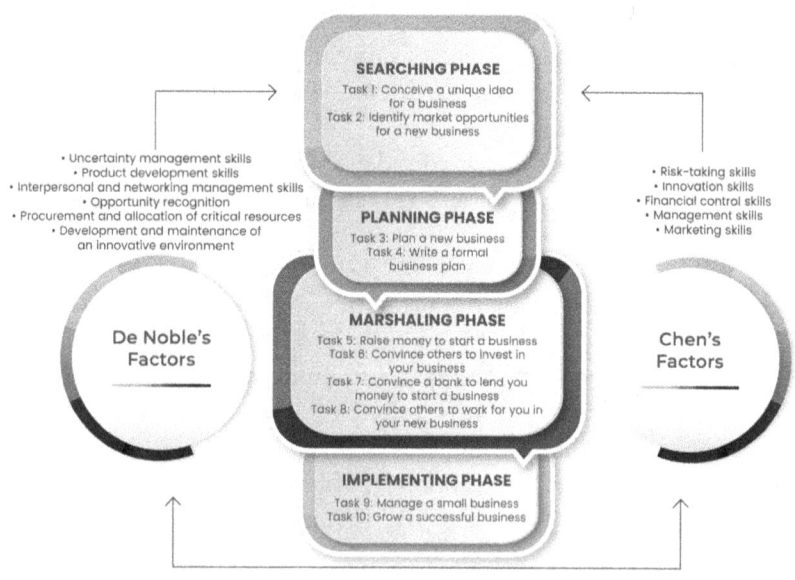

Fig. 2.5 Relationship of self-efficacy to tasks and roles in the entrepreneurial life cycle (*Source* Cox et al., 2002)

strategy proposes that an ecosystem is necessary to support youth entrepreneurs' ESE development and strengthen crucial relationships with networks. Therefore, the development of ESE levels can take place as intrapersonal development processes where the individual enhances his or her own ESE through exposure to a variety of external processes and support networks.

A possible technique that pivots ESE development, either as an inter-personal or intra-persona process, is called co-inspiring. In the psychological and neurological literature on the entrepreneurial heartset, mindset, and handset, the term 'co-inspiring' is proposed as a technique to enable innovative thought to occur as an internal pre-cognitive process within the individual. This technique was proved to transform (grow developmental maturity) an individual's ability to innovate by moving from reacting to cognitions to generative new innovative cognitions. Co-inspiring signifies the birth of a creative and novel idea that can lead to innovation or an 'aha moment'. The part of the brain identified as reflecting the 'aha moment' is the anterior portion of the superior temporal gyrus of the non-dominant hemisphere and is associated with a short burst of Gamma EEG activity of 40 Hz. The profoundness of the innovation might relate to an individual's psychoneuroendocrinological (PNE) engagement with their source of inspiration and will. PNE is terminology from neurological sciences, which implies that mind, body, and soul are an interactive whole with no separation between these functions. Therefore, the integrativeness and interrelations of the entrepreneurial heartset, mindset, and handset. PNE relates directly to the paradigm of nondualism which was introduced at the beginning of this chapter. As a result, low or high levels of ESE directly influence low or high levels of IEO when co-initiating and taking risks in the entrepreneurship process.

ESE development towards the new venture creation process and perceptions of own skills cannot be measured in a quantitative manner because this approach leaves no scope for incorporating individuals' PNE levels, feelings and emotions. Therefore, a qualitative or mixed-method approach is a better fit to measure ESE and its relation to entrepreneurial skills.

Entrepreneurship education often and commonly focus on entrepreneurial management and planning skills but often without addressing the deep fundamental underpinnings of ESE. More specifically, youth entrepreneurship development courses in entrepreneurship tend to teach technical skills with little or no focus in their planning of cognitive or belief systems on the part of the youths, which might underpin entrepreneurial attitudes and perceptions. Another way for youths to develop ESE, IEO and EI might be to observe youth entrepreneurs and actual settings where entrepreneurship takes place. Therefore, creating the SHAPE ecosystem for youth entrepreneurship development has value in enabling shared learning experiences within a wide-reaching support network—learning from each other's experiences and co-inspiring one another.

2.4 Individual Entrepreneurial Orientation (IEO)

IEO signifies the processes, practices, and decision-making activities of an individual that lead to entrepreneurship. The entrepreneurial decision-making process is influenced by external and internal domains. Internal domains include factors of risk-taking, proactivity, and innovation, and external domains include aspects of the economy, society, technology, competition, and politics. IEO is considered to have a direct impact on the entrepreneurial performance and EA of youths.

A country's socio-economic development relates directly to individuals who make up the microsystemic attitudes, activities, and aspirations. For socio-economic development to occur through acts of entrepreneurialism (and intrapreneurialism), it is necessary to develop individuals' ability to take risks, proactivity, and degree of innovativeness. These propensities of development will require individuals to connect with a much deeper level of knowledge.

Deep action learning, especially to spark innovative thought in the field of entrepreneurship and intrapreneurship, might be necessary for successful socio-economic development. A possible strategy is SHAPE, of which the theoretical model and its application are introduced in this book.

2.4.1 Individual Risk-Taking

The risk-taking propensity is described as the perceived probability of receiving the rewards associated with the success of a proposed situation, which is required by an individual before subjecting to the consequences associated with failure. The alternative situation provides less reward as well as less severe consequences than the proposed situation. Important predictors in risk-taking are how the risk problem is framed, the results of past risk-taking, and the ability to perform under risky conditions.

Risk-taking propensity is a behavioural dimension of IEO that helps to trigger the pursuit of an opportunity. It involves major decisions individuals need to take, which might bring high rewards. The process includes an element of uncertainty and self-management of ESE task-related skills necessary to enable individual risk-taking qualities and reduce the fear associated with possible future barriers. This can also be regarded as a cognitive orientation directed towards EA since, from an IEO perspective, the youth entrepreneur acts in an individual capacity. Youth entrepreneurs, therefore, bear the personal risk intrinsic to the occupational choice being made.

Two different aspects of entrepreneurial risk are distinguished: the general risk-taking propensity of a potential entrepreneur and the perceived probability of failure. General risk-taking propensity is described as accessibility to research across role-players within the entrepreneurial ecosystem due to differences in individual venture probabilities for success and failure. By choosing to take EA, the youth entrepreneur becomes a risk-bearer and is liable for personal choices associated with taking business risks.

Youth entrepreneurs operate within their entrepreneurial ecosystem. Therefore, economic failure and barriers do not solely fall on the youth entrepreneur; it is the responsibility of the ecosystemic role-players to help bear risk factors and mitigate barriers in the process of enabling socio-economic development from a bigger-picture systems perspective.

2.4.2 Individual Innovation

Innovation, as in the creation and development of new products and processes, lies at the heart of youth entrepreneurship and entrepreneurship in general. The generation of new business ideas and innovation is positively linked to the success of effective youth entrepreneur business development. Entrepreneurial innovation is described as the willingness to support creativity and experimentation in introducing new products/services, novelty, technological leadership, and research and development in developing new processes. As an IEO propensity, innovation is an important means of pursuing opportunities.

Individual innovation is exemplified as the youth entrepreneur who most strictly confines him or herself to the characteristic entrepreneurial function: carrying out new combinations. It is also interpreted as the purest type of entrepreneur genus. Individual innovation is a process of creative destruction by which wealth is created when existing market structures are disrupted by the introduction of new goods or services. Innovation by youth entrepreneurs is linked to learned behaviours reflected in the pursuit of entrepreneurial opportunities.

In society, emphasis is placed by SMEs and large corporations on research and development that might lead to the innovation of new products and services. This occurs on a business, enterprise, or organisational level. On the contrary, there is a disconnect and gap in the entrepreneurial ecosystem to provide all-round support to youth entrepreneurs, including the provision of transformative entrepreneurial education (growth in developmental maturity to produce generative thought). The importance for youth entrepreneurs and their ecosystem to apply co-inspiring strategies to reach individual innovation is crucial for effective youth entrepreneurship development and sustainability.

For national socio-economic development, especially in developing countries, more is needed than just improving entrepreneurial ability and reducing the pressure for necessity entrepreneurship. It also implies that governments must focus on a deeper and more people-centred level to enhance individual youth entrepreneurs' innovative abilities and their levels of education and skills. Given the important role that entrepreneurial attitude, aspirations, and actions play in socio-economic development, it is recommended that: governments should have an innovation policy in place for the promotion of youth entrepreneurship; youth entrepreneurs in developing countries such as South Africa have a considerable propensity for innovation, and these personality traits are not given sufficient recognition in literature or by policymakers.

In South Africa, as a developing country, stimulation of innovation has not on the whole been a key focus area for youth entrepreneurial ecosystem role-players such as development agencies, private-sector development programmes, or national programmes in support of entrepreneurship. In governmental youth entrepreneurship support programmes, the main concern needs to be people-centred approaches to advance innovation which could engender the kind of dynamic efficiency that would drive job creation, transformation (growth in developmental maturity) and entrepreneurial ecosystemic growth.

Where innovation policy is apparent in government programmes, it often has a dualistic character, combining structuralist approaches with laissez-faire, non-interventionist approaches derived from the neo-liberal school of thought. A possible reason why structuralist approaches are used might be that the leaders who facilitate these types of government programmes see policy-making for innovation from the stereotypical perspective of the national economy as a set of separate structures and processes rather than as an integrative whole—a nondual paradigm. Both approaches see innovation policy as an infrastructural development factor in government strategies for hard and soft-system development. However, innovation policy alone most certainly cannot inspire youths' EA towards innovation. Therefore, the emphasis on moving towards individual innovation by youth entrepreneurs is placed on connecting the entrepreneurial ecosystem. Within the youth entrepreneurship ecosystem, enabling mechanising is created in a process to co-initiate, co-sense, co-inspire, co-create, and co-evolve. The process of 'co' is proven to facilitate entrepreneurial heartset, mindset, and handset to lever from reactive to generative responses, therefore, birthing individual innovation.

Adopting a national government approach towards including policies to enable individual innovation and facilitate innovative entrepreneurial ecosystems are fairly new on all systemic levels. Measuring instruments for government innovation policy to enable individual innovation for entrepreneurial ecosystems is difficult to create because of the fast and continuous pace of youth entrepreneurship development initiatives.

Successful innovative socio-economic development requires governments to increase the development impact of entrepreneurship by readjusting their policy frameworks and focus. The key for governments in addressing the developmental impact of socio-economic challenges might be to focus on creating deeper level youth entrepreneurial ecosystems where the emphasis is on entrepreneurial heartset, mindset, and handset. Without a deep transformation and innovation of individual introspective processes of total ecosystems, a broader level of national socio-economic development will remain in a crisis as youth unemployment and sustainability issues continue to soar.

In summary, individual innovation's 'aha moment' is linked to increased levels of ESE and IEO. Individual Innovation is further liked to transformation (growth in development maturity). Youth entrepreneurs, especially in developing countries, reach an 'aha moment' with great difficulty because they are entrapped within barriers of disconnected entrepreneurial ecosystems. It might be helpful if there are innovation policies from the national government. However, commitment from all role-players is needed for efficient implementation and sustainability, which is vastly and all-round complex.

2.4.3 Individual Proactiveness

Individual proactiveness is related to initiative and first-mover advantages through the pursuit of new opportunities and acting in anticipation of future problems. The importance of proactiveness is its 'forward-looking perspective' for entrepreneurial activity and innovation. Proactiveness is a behavioural trait where youth entrepreneurs and role-players in the entrepreneurial ecosystem are constantly seeking opportunities and having a forward-looking perspective. Young entrepreneurs or individuals entering the market for the first time need to be proactive in looking for new opportunities since they do not have a high profile in the market. These opportunities might include access to finance, partnerships, or skills development. Proactivity also links to the ESE skill set of management (Fig. 2.3) since proactive individuals adopt an active management style.

Although youths displaying proactive propensities are more likely to display leadership traits, being proactive and having leadership qualities does not guarantee that they will have a competitive pioneer advantage or be able to sustain EA; likewise, increased earnings might not necessarily be predictably associated with higher levels of proactiveness. This would depend on the specific context and dimension of IEO.

Proactiveness stands at one end of a continuum with passiveness as its opposite end. Proactiveness can therefore be seen as a form of reactiveness or a reactive response. The IEO proactivity propensity is closely associated with the ESE skill set of opportunity identification. High levels of IEO support opportunity recognition and opportunity creation. While individuals may change their goals and aspirations to match the requirements of changing environments around them because they see new opportunities to raise their level of performance, these proactive steps may not necessarily be efficient or bring increased earnings unless the individual reconfigures his or her own resources and adapts to the changing environment in a renewed manner.

Proactiveness may thus lead youths to perform differently, but not necessarily more effectively, should the efficiency of the individual not be improved. Proactiveness will not contribute to increased performance or successful attainment of personal goals and aspirations. Not all contexts will necessarily offer the opportunity for the individual to increase efficiency through proactive behaviour.

If proactiveness is associated with seizing the initiative and acting opportunistically in order to shape the environment and increase demand, then the intent of proactiveness is growing willingness. Willingness can be described as a measure of the degree to which the intention to increase demand exists, and growth willingness is therefore taken to represent a measure of proactiveness. In addition, education is likely to have a strong influence on growth willingness, both in encouraging an entrepreneur to aim higher and in boosting overall ESE.

2.4.4 The Illusion of External Opportunity Identification as an Act of Individual Proactivity

In cognitive sciences, the concepts of individual proactivity and opportunity identification are often seen as synonymous. Within this context, the entrepreneurial opportunity is central to the scholarship of entrepreneurship since entrepreneurs are individuals who pursue entrepreneurial opportunities, therefore, acting proactively. Conceptually speaking, without entrepreneurial opportunities, there could be no entrepreneurship. It could, however, be argued that the idea of 'entrepreneurial opportunity' is a misconception. Could it then be described that those entrepreneurial opportunities are external factors existing in the entrepreneurship ecosystem or nexus, independent from an individual's personality traits and the core of our being (an individual's entrepreneurial heartset and mindset)?

Entrepreneurial opportunities can be regarded as situations where products and services can be sold at a price greater than the cost of production. From this, it can be argued that to make a profit, action needs to be taken by the youth entrepreneur pursuing an entrepreneurial opportunity. Business situations—situations that are profit-driven—do exist, and there are many businesses making money and exploiting niche markets or gaps in the market.

However, a dichotomy lies within the concept of entrepreneurial opportunity. It is a future-orientated action: How does one know that a profitable opportunity did exist before the youth entrepreneur tried it out? The dichotomy is this: Before youth entrepreneurs pilot the opportunity and try to sell the products or services, they do not have a confirmation or a certainty that selling these products or services will be profitable. If the youth entrepreneurs make money, then an entrepreneurial opportunity must have existed because the EA resulted in a profit. But, if a loss was made, or the venture failed in some other way, was it because not enough market research was put into ideating or prototyping the product or service, or was the opportunity not even there in the first place?

If people are not able to establish beforehand whether an entrepreneurial opportunity exists, then the concept of risk-taking towards an entrepreneurial opportunity advises youth entrepreneurs to act in post facto risk calculation.

A future opportunity can be said to exist as an abstract phenomenon; it becomes tangible only when combined with the personality traits and actions of the entrepreneur. It can, therefore, be said that the entrepreneurial heartset + the entrepreneurial mindset + EA = pursuit of entrepreneurial opportunity. This can further be deconstructed into 'opportunities for someone' and 'opportunities for me'. A potential business opportunity in the entrepreneurial ecosystem may be a real opportunity for 'me' only if 'I' possess the right qualities to make a profit in pursuing it. A further dichotomy is created within this argument because, without involving clinical experts, it is difficult to determine what qualities are needed to pursue a specific entrepreneurial opportunity and whether the youth entrepreneur does have such traits. Even if the youth entrepreneur knows that he or she has the right qualities in relation to a specific opportunity, they will still need to act to determine—after the event—the success, or otherwise, of the action they have taken.

Another lens on the concept of opportunity identification is to shift focus from 'opportunity discovery' to 'opportunity creation'. This philosophy is aligned with several schools of thought supporting youth entrepreneurs moving from reactive thought to generative thought, which will bring forth innovation in thought and potential prototypes of business models, products, and services. Youth entrepreneurs can discover niches in markets and opportunities that already exist. However, this viewpoint of opportunity creation leads to a tautology inherent in the concept of 'entrepreneurial opportunity': What if the youth entrepreneur tries to create an opportunity and fails? Were they not entrepreneurial because an opportunity was created, and because they failed? Using a practical example: Before Instagram, there was PhotoMe; Instagram founders are billionaires; PhotoMe founders are not. The 'opportunity creation' school suffers from the same tautology as the 'opportunity discovery' school because of its focus on the opportunity: all it does (from an entrepreneurship-scholarly lens) is to spark entrepreneurial momentum for youth entrepreneurs to take calculated risks.

Therefore, if the concept of an entrepreneurial opportunity is dichotomic and its schools of thought are tautological, how should youth entrepreneurs move forward to gain entrepreneurial momentum? Is taking a calculated risk, after performing various paper-based activities such as writing a business plan, budgeting, and market research, only a projection of something that could potentially result in an opportunity? The results of a written business plan are often very different from those envisaged (and often discarded) once the youth entrepreneur's venture meets the realities and barriers in the ecosystem or nexus.

In summary, the IEO concept with its associated propensities relates to stimuli within an individual as well as external domains. The internal and external domains interact with one another in a nondual manner. Only through diminishing systemic disconnect, socio-economic will gain momentum.

2.5 Entrepreneurial Intention (EI)

EI is linked to ESE, IEO, and its effects on entrepreneurial personality traits, perception, and actions. EI is related to the likelihood or desirability of becoming an entrepreneur. Further, EI is a determinant for youth entrepreneurs to engage with EA and the sustainability of the actions. Figure 2.2 gives a schematic representation of the way aspects of ESE and IEO contribute to levels of EI. Without relationships to ESE and IEO, EI cannot exist as a single entity.

The outflow of EI leads to taking EA, where the action does not necessarily equate to a start-up. EI involves process building up to a possible business start-up. When youth entrepreneurs are developing EI, the entrepreneurial heartset and mindset actively combine to further develop the entrepreneurial handset (EA). Therefore, an action-orientated and enabling process occurs.

Participation of individuals in a facilitated entrepreneurial ecosystemic intervention might potentially enhance youths' EI, as well as the role-players in their direct support network. Personal entrepreneurial

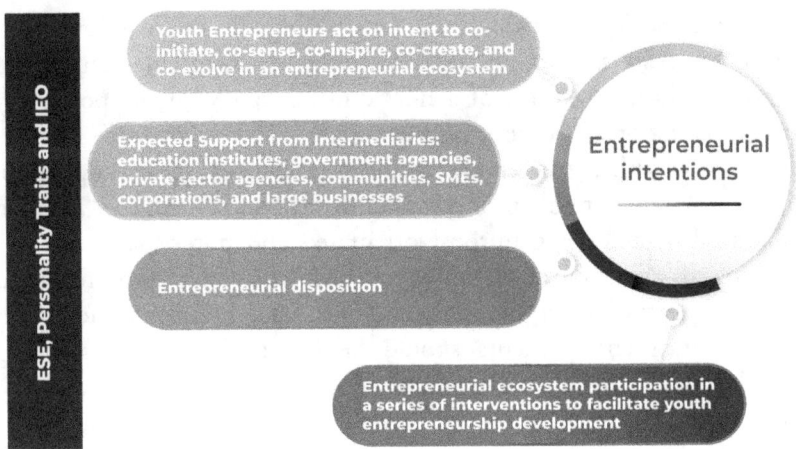

Fig. 2.6 Youth entrepreneurial intentions (EI) (*Source* Van der Westhuizen, 2022)

exposure and support expected for a variety of intermediaries and entrepreneurial disposition all influence the levels of EI that individuals might form through participating in a facilitated intervention or strategy, for example, the SHAPE ecosystem strategy for youth entrepreneurs (Fig. 2.6).

2.6 Entrepreneurial Action (EA)

Following the schematic indication set out in Fig. 2.2 of EA as a process that results from ESE, IEO and EI. Therefore, EA is conceived as emanating from an inner place of an individual's being.[12] This inner place from which an individual's intentions and actions arise are associated with an individual's being, described as an individual's values, aspirations, and dreams—the purpose behind entrepreneurial passion.[13] These elements of heartset and mindset are propelled by various processes that result in an individual's actions. The combination of the inner

---

[12] Scharmer and Käufer (2013).
[13] Hayes in Gunnlaugson et al. (2013).

sources from which individuals act and the processes that follow eventuate in the results of individual behaviour, which might include EA, not necessarily in the form of a new venture, but with the possibility that youths' actions become entrepreneurial.

For some youth entrepreneurs, without guidance and developmental support, EA might result in a continuum process of being *en route* to 'X' because of not being purpose-orientated and purpose-driven. It is impossible to apply linear planning to a nondual youth entrepreneurial ecosystem. Instead of trying to pin down what might be merely an illusion, youth entrepreneurs should be experimenting: prototyping and piloting taking EA. The emphasis is on producing generative response fields—innovation—and executing entrepreneurial activities through fresh, innovative lenses. Co-initiating, co-sensing, co-inspiring, co-creating, and co-evolving between youth entrepreneurs and the ecosystem start to occur and propels as new ideas are created as a result of collective interactions. If a prototype does not work, then pivot—change direction. The initial deep development of ESE, IEO and EI will boost youth entrepreneurs who engage with EA to sustain self-confidence and vision when an initial prototype does not work. The combination of enhanced internal and external domains helps youth entrepreneurs to start with an idea and continue to ideate and not give up entrepreneurial hopes and dreams.

Further emphasis is on the continuum of cyclical processes for youth entrepreneurs to take action and then collaborate with the ecosystem and potential customers to co-create and co-evolve a value-based outcome for all concerned. Therefore, creating entrepreneurial momentum towards socio-economic development.

Youth entrepreneurs should put less emphasis on long-term and potentially outdated business planning and (within reasonable limits) put more emphasis on action. Youth entrepreneurs need to focus on their entrepreneurial heartset and mindset because, ultimately, these will determine the success of their EA (handset). Their internal qualities are thus not barriers anymore, but rather the vehicle sparking entrepreneurial momentum. Instead of chasing 'opportunities' in an abstract 'market', it is essential for the youth entrepreneur (as a microsystem) to integrate with other systemic role-players, therefore, taking responsibility for co-creating and co-evolving a potential sustainable support structure. Ideally, those with whom the youth entrepreneurs choose to collaborate are individuals with like-minded, like-hearted and like-willed qualities.

One can argue that 'entrepreneurial barriers' can only be experienced by youth entrepreneurs once they have taken 'entrepreneurial action'. Therefore, acting on a possible opportunity and proactively taking a potential risk without having a guarantee that the opportunity will result in wealth creation. The premise of youth entrepreneurs' ability to experience barriers in the external environment in relation to their EA implies that they demonstrated initial signs of positive qualities associated with being entrepreneurs. Therefore, they demonstrate qualities of ESE, IEO and EI.

As life continuously moves on for youth entrepreneurs, the future scenario becomes the current one. The current problem-solving situations that EA youth entrepreneurs face are necessary to fulfil their entrepreneurial aspirations. Therefore, they grow to think and act upon new experiences in the process of developing their entrepreneurial heartset, mindset, and handset en route to potential EA. Therefore, their journey through transforming (growing in developmental maturity) might have moved youth entrepreneurs to crystallise their ideas (envisioning the new), prototype them (enacting the new), and perform them (the new in praxis).[14] This implies that they are developing new knowledge—generative thought[15]—through embodying new experiences.

Might this imply that the lived-through experiences of youth entrepreneurs might self-teach them to overcome barriers and exposure to entrepreneurial realities within the ecosystem is necessary to sustain EA?

---

[14] Cox (2013).
[15] Scharmer (2009).

2.7 Conclusion

In the SHAPE ecosystem strategy for youth entrepreneurs, enabling the development of youths' personality traits, ESE, IEO, EI, and EA occur through educational institutes playing the facilitating role to co-initiate. Entrepreneurship education, inter and cross-curricula, in both formal academic programmes and informal youth development initiatives is an essential starting point. From a nondual perspective, youth entrepreneurs and role-players in the entrepreneurial ecosystem need to share the vision and purpose for EA. This can be facilitated through education institutes, especially in higher education universities. The role of entrepreneurial orientated universities to facilitate the creation of an entrepreneurial ecosystem for youths and sustain crucial relationships might help bridge the systemic disconnect and unite people through an inspiring vision for wealth creation through socio-economic development.

In summary, transformative academic entrepreneurship education can facilitate ESE, EIO, EI, and EA through learning, teaching and research. It was actioned by youths, education institutes, government agencies, private-sector agencies, communities, SMEs, and corporations/ large businesses. Within the SHAPE youth entrepreneurial ecosystem strategy, an educational institute such as a university can be the facilitating agent to co-initiate the ecosystem creation for youths. However, the SHAPE strategy is flexible to allow movement, generalisation and adaptation of role-players, and location-specific aspects will influence the unique co-creating of a youth entrepreneurial ecosystem to add value in a location-specific context and a broader sense. This is further investigated in the next chapter.

This chapter builds on the SHAPE project-supported research supported in part by the National Research Foundation of South Africa (Grant Number: 122002-Shape). These works include: Adelakun and Van der Westhuizen (2021), Awotunde and Van der Westhuizen (2021a), Awotunde and Van der Westhuizen (2021b), Nhleko and van der Westhuizen (2022), Ruba et al. (2021), Van der Westhuizen (2017a), Van der Westhuizen (2017b), Van der Westhuizen (2018a), Van der Westhuizen (2018b), Van der Westhuizen (2019), Van der Westhuizen, (2021).

References

Adelakun, Y., & Van der Westhuizen, T. (2021). Delineating government policies and individual entrepreneurial orientation. *Journal of Sociology and Social Anthropology, 12*(3–4), 106–117. https://doi.org/10.31901/24566764.2021/12.3-4.371

Awotunde, O. M., & Van der Westhuizen, T. (2021a). Entrepreneurial self-efficacy development: An effective intervention for sustainable student entrepreneurial intentions. *International Journal of Innovation and Sustainable Development, 15*(4), 475–495.

Awotunde, O. M., & Van der Westhuizen, T. (2021b). Entrepreneurial self-efficacy and the SHAPE ideation model for university students. In *ECIE 2021 16th European Conference on Innovation and Entrepreneurship* (Vol. 1, p. 37).

Covin, J. G., & Slevin, D. P. (2002). The entrepreneurial imperatives of strategic leadership. In M. Hitt, R. D. Ireland, S. M. Camp, & D. Sexton (Eds.), *Strategic entrepreneurship: Creating a new mindset*. Blackwell.

Cox, L. D. (2013). Presencing our absencing: A collective reflective practice using Scharmer's 'U' model. In O. Gunnlaugson, C. Baron, & M. Cayer (Eds.), *Perspectives on Theory U: Insights from the field*. IGI Global.

Cox, L. W., Mueller, S. L., & Moss, S. E. (2002). The impact of entrepreneurship education on entrepreneurial self-efficacy. *International Journal of Entrepreneurship Education, 1*(2), 229–245.

Ernst & Young. (2017). *Entrepreneurs share core traits: Decoding the DNA of the entrepreneur*. www.ey.com/gl/en/services/strategic-growth-markets/ey-nature-or-nurture-5-entrepreneurs-share-core-traits. Retrieved 15 September 2017.

Fayolle, A. (2015). Entrepreneurial mindset. *Financial Times*. Lexicon. http://lexicon.ft.com/Term?term=entrepreneurial-mindset. Retrieved 21 August 2015.

Gunnlaugson, O., Baron, C., & Cayer, M. (Eds.). (2013). *Perspectives on Theory U: Insights from the field*. IGI Global.

Hsiao, C., Lee, Y.-H., & Chen, H.-H. (2016). The effects of internal locus of control on entrepreneurship: The mediating mechanisms of social capital and human capital. *The International Journal of Human Resource Management, 27*(11), 1158–1172.

Katz, J. (1997). *Nonduality.com—An introduction*. http://www.nonduality.com/lrn.htm. Accessed 15 September 2015.

Kickul, J., & D'Intino, R. S. (2005). Measure for measure: Modeling entrepreneurial self-efficacy onto instrumental tasks within the new venture creation process. *New England Journal of Entrepreneurship, 8*(2), 6.

Leaf, C. (2013). *Switch on your brain: The key to peak happiness, thinking, and health*. Baker Books.

Nhleko, Y., & van der Westhuizen, T. (2022). The role of higher education institutions in introducing entrepreneurship education to meet the demands of industry 4.0. *Academy of Entrepreneurship Journal, 28*(1), 1–23.

Pillay, K. (2014). Learning, the whole and Theory U: Reflections on creating a space for deep learning. *Problems and Perspectives in Management, 12*(4), 340–346.

Pillay, K. (2015, July 6). Learning and the illusion of solid and separate things: Troublesome knowledge and the curriculum. In *Edge Hill University Centre for Learning and Teaching University Learning and Teaching Day Conference*.

Ruba, R. M., Van der Westhuizen, T., & Chiloane-Tsoka, G. E. (2021). Influence of entrepreneurial orientation on organisational performance: Evidence from Congolese Higher Education Institutions. *Journal of Contemporary Management, 18*(1), 243–269.

Scharmer, C. O. (2009). *Theory U: Learning from the future as it emerges*. Berrett-Koehler Publishers.

Scharmer, C. O., & Käufer, K. (2013). *Leading from the emerging future: From ego-system to eco-system economies*. Berrett-Koehler Publishers.

Van der Westhuizen, T. (2017a). The use of Theory U and individual entrepreneurial orientation to increase low youth entrepreneurship in South Africa. *Journal of Contemporary Management, 14*, 531–553.

Van der Westhuizen, T. (2017b). A systemic approach towards responsible and sustainable economic development: Entrepreneurship, systems theory and socio-economic momentum. In Z. Fields (Ed.), *Collective creativity for responsible and sustainable business practice*. IGI Global.

Van der Westhuizen, T. (2018a). The SHAPE project: Shifting hope, activating potential entrepreneurship. In D. Remenyi & D. A. Grant (Eds.), *Incubators for young entrepreneurs—20 case histories*. ACPIL.

Van der Westhuizen, T. (2018b). Open heart, open mind and open will in transformative individual entrepreneurial orientation pedagogies. In *Academic conferences and publishing international limited* (pp. 443–448).

Van der Westhuizen, T. (2019). Action! Methods to develop entrepreneurship. In *18th European conference on research methodology for business and management studies* (pp. 331–337).

Van der Westhuizen, T. (2021). Applying theory U through SHAPE to develop student's individual entrepreneurial orientation in a university eco-system. In O. Gunnlaugson & W. Brendel (Eds.), *Advances in pre-sensing volume III: Collective approaches, in theory U* (pp. 395–435). Trifoss Business Press.

Van der Westhuizen, T. (2022). *Effective youth entrepreneurship*. Sunbonani. Available at: https://omp.sunbonani.co.za/index.php/sunbonani/catalog/book/6

Weinberg, I. (2014). *The complete triangles model: Exploring the foundations of neuromodulation*. http://www.pninet.com/articles/Memory.pdf. Retrieved 1 September 2017.

Open Access This chapter is licensed under the terms of the Creative Commons Attribution 4.0 International License (http://creativecommons.org/licenses/by/4.0/), which permits use, sharing, adaptation, distribution and reproduction in any medium or format, as long as you give appropriate credit to the original author(s) and the source, provide a link to the Creative Commons license and indicate if changes were made.

The images or other third party material in this chapter are included in the chapter's Creative Commons license, unless indicated otherwise in a credit line to the material. If material is not included in the chapter's Creative Commons license and your intended use is not permitted by statutory regulation or exceeds the permitted use, you will need to obtain permission directly from the copyright holder.

3

Youth Entrepreneur Ecosystem

3.1 Introduction

The previous chapter established that the mind uses various brain processes when thinking, feeling, and choosing responses to life experiences. Youth entrepreneurs gain said life experiences through being and interacting within ecosystems. This chapter, therefore, proposes the establishment of an ecosystem to promote youth entrepreneurship. This proposed theoretical ecosystem model has been practically created and applied to youth entrepreneurs as a means to test their entrepreneurial mindset and discover the enablers and barriers that youth entrepreneurs come into contact with in relation to their ecosystems. The application and findings related to this model are discussed further in Part II of this book.

3.1.1 Context

The SHAPE ecosystem, which has been created to promote youth entrepreneurship strategies, fundamentally starts with education, training, skills development, and mentorship within the microsystem. Since youths are central to this ecosystem, they form both the recipients of stimuli and, in return, offer shared experiences and insights to the various role-players operating within their ecosystem. The process of this model is, thus, dynamic, interactive, and reflective, with the facilitating agent of this ecosystem being the education institute that drives the system's creation and evolution.

In order for higher education institutions in South Africa to effectively provide the necessary skills and learning for entrepreneurial development in our emerging economy, a radical change in intellectual and educational priorities is needed.[1] Higher-order thinking or a deeper dimension to and towards entrepreneurship learning is especially necessary to address the current socio-economic crisis and rising youth unemployment rates.[2] Similar to other living-theory approaches (e.g., Theory U, systemic action learning and action research [SALAR]), SHAPE-activated learning experiences are proposed to have the potential to enable a paradigm shift amongst youth entrepreneurs and their intermediaries that can help to advance socio-economic development in pursuit of macro- and mundo-system visions.[3]

With pedagogy in the field of entrepreneurship shifting the emphasis from classroom teaching to action learning, 'static' or 'content-orientated' teaching, which has been common practice for more than two decades, is now frequently criticised as it is no longer appropriate in or for South Africa's complex and change-driven society.[4] Such traditional educational methods, focusing on theory and information, are now regarded as inappropriate for content and pedagogy.[5] Rather, entrepreneurship curriculum pedagogies based on discovery and creation

---

[1] Chia (2014).
[2] Scharmer and Käufer (2013).
[3] Chia (1996, 2014), Harrison et al. (2007), Nonaka et al. (2014), Paton et al. (2014).
[4] Sahay and Nirjar (2012).
[5] Garavan and O'Cinneide (1994), Oyugi (2014).

theories now provide a basis for shifting from static classroom approaches to an action learning methodology.

Most current undergraduate curricula in South African higher education have adopted principles from discovery theory, where the emphasis is on creativity, scanning, shaping ideas, and developing business plans.[6] Developing and presenting an entrepreneurship programme needs a suitable programme process to help aspirant entrepreneurs assimilate entrepreneurial practice. This process should be action-orientated and include appealing themes that promote student-centredness and encourage reflective thinking.[7]

While the discovery approach is prominent in the complex and continually evolving South African context, there are also cases for adopting pedagogic approaches that draw on principles from creation theory. In such an approach, the emphasis is on overall programme processes and how ideas transform over time. Programme participants, in this instance, have the opportunity to practice entrepreneurship skills by adapting initial ideas in response to new knowledge and information.

One key benefit of the creative entrepreneurship programme approach is how it can help students to problem-solve through the creation of a challenging environment where students have to face relevant challenges and learn to overcome these through taking action (learning-by-doing). This approach is, thus, also referred to as experiential learning or action learning. By promoting action, such a programme helps to promote self-direction and adaptability in its participants, which, in turn, makes it easier to assess the overall impact of an entrepreneurship endeavour. By comparison, more traditional programme participants would merely be allocated a 'pass' or 'fail' with little to no consideration of the broader implications. The cyclical approach of the experiential or action learning process thus shapes students into lifelong learners.[8]

Despite this move towards less traditional teaching and learning approaches, entrepreneurship programmes in South Africa currently still face a number of challenges, including:

---

[6] Sahay and Nirjar (2006), Rahimi et al. (2015).
[7] Chia (2014), McIntyre-Mills et al. (2014), Yeo and Marquardt (2015).
[8] Rahimi et al. (2015).

- Making students aware of (the need for) socio-economic change. Otto Scharmer and Peter Senge believe that society has a 'blind spot' in respect to deeper dimensions of systemic change. This blind spot can be related to the systems thinking paradigm, where systems are seen only as interconnected and interrelated and, as such, might imply fragmentation of systems.[9] Our current era, however, calls for new levels of cognition processes that adopt a nondual perspective.[10] This more holistic and unified understanding could potentially allow youths to create a future filled with greater opportunities.[11]
- Enhancing levels of self-efficacy, individual entrepreneurial orientation (IEO), and entrepreneurial intent (EI) among programme participants. Young people often lack commitment, work ethic, and motivation, and South Africa has the third-lowest level of youth entrepreneurship globally.[12]
- Developing problem-solving thought processes and generating new ideas to solve existing problems. Strategy-making processes in both public and private sector organisations can provide a basis for entrepreneurial initiatives and create opportunities for young people to be involved in decisions and actions.[13]
- Developing a support network for youth entrepreneurs. In South Africa, it is difficult for youth entrepreneurs to engage with an entrepreneurial ecosystem, as not enough private sector organisations or small-and-medium-sized enterprise (SME) owners are willing to form 'business friendships' with youth entrepreneurs to harness their entrepreneurial drive and help them develop sustainable entrepreneurial skills.[14]

These common challenges facing entrepreneurship programmes call for the reframing of their focus on enhancing programme participants' levels

---

[9] Pillay (2015b).

[10] This is where systems are perceived as a whole and stemming from a single source; Pillay (2015a), Scharmer (2009).

[11] Scharmer (2009).

[12] Xavier et al. (2013).

[13] Bolton and Lane (2012).

[14] DTI (2017).

of self-confidence and motivation. Thus, entrepreneurship programmes presented at higher education institutes should embrace active learning that includes practices aimed at teaching both *for* entrepreneurship (e.g., by offering case studies, guest speakers, group projects, business plans, student oral presentations, survey-participation) and *about* entrepreneurship (e.g., lecturers, set tests, individual assignments and written exams).[15] These programmes should also aim to develop students' entrepreneurial self-efficacy (ESE) and individual entrepreneurial orientation (IEO) so that they make the pursuit of entrepreneurship a primary goal.

A further consideration is that youths require comprehensive facilitation and mentorship in order to develop a deeper cognitive perception of the challenges and issues faced both by young entrepreneurs and the broader socio-economic context. Such understanding could help students to develop their own internal domains.

The challenge is to develop an innovative action model—a kind of 'living theory'—that truly inspires youths on a much deeper level and brings about the needed attitude change at an ontological level.

Shepherd Dhliwayo, who wrote this book's preface, previously indicated that 'to ensure effective sustainability of youth entrepreneurial endeavours', it is necessary to link youth entrepreneurs' gained life experiences to an interrelated ecosystem (a support structure). Several support structures[16] aimed at developing and aiding youth entrepreneurs already exist. However, youth entrepreneurs frequently experience barriers caused by these very intermediaries who, at times, may obstruct rather than promote entrepreneurial growth.

---

[15] Oyugi (2014).
[16] Also referred to as 'intermediaries' or 'nexus'.

3.2 The SHAPE Ecosystem Strategy for Youth Entrepreneurship

The concept of youth entrepreneur ecosystems is relatively new to the body of knowledge on youth entrepreneurship but has begun gaining in popularity over the past few years. Entrepreneurial systems, on the other hand, have been discussed in the literature for more than 30 years.[17] In terms of the newer youth entrepreneur ecosystem literature, special attention is currently paid to policy circles, as the Government seeks ways to address the crisis of high national youth unemployment in South Africa. There are still several empirical shortcomings within the literature surrounding youth entrepreneur ecosystems:

1. There remains a need for a clear analytical framework to explicitly demonstrate what causes and effects such ecosystems currently lack. Due to the varied locations and culture-specific nature of youth entrepreneurial ecosystems, it might not be possible to create a 'one-solution-fits-all' framework; multiple frameworks are necessary to effectively address the complex adaptive nature of these systems.
2. Although it is a systemic concept, the (youth) entrepreneur ecosystem still needs to incorporate insights from network theory to further exploit the co-initiation of the ecosystem. The interconnectivity and integrativeness of relationships between various internal and external domains are not currently clear.
3. Institutions or agents' impact and special scale on the structure and performance of youth entrepreneur ecosystems remains unclear.
4. Studies have often focused on the (youth) entrepreneur ecosystem in a single region or cluster. Thus, the literature lacks a comparative and collective perspective.
5. The literature on (youth) entrepreneur ecosystems tends to provide a static framework that does not consider these systems' evolution over time.[18]

---

[17] Alvedalen and Boschma (2017, 887–903).
[18] Ibid.

As a longitudinal intervention, the SHAPE ecosystem model has been created to support youth entrepreneurs' thinking, feelings, and decisions surrounding entrepreneurial behaviours and actions. The model aims to facilitate entrepreneurial 'heartset' by promoting an entrepreneurial mindset and 'handset'. The facilitating agents of this model have built on Shepherd Dhliwayo's model for experiential learning in entrepreneurship education, which proposes a prospective model for South African tertiary institutions. SHAPE is also grounded within Theory U's premise that a process of shifting from reactive to generative thought is necessary for deep transformative socio-economic development. In Theory U, the pinnacle of an 'aha moment' is referred to as 'presencing' (synonymous with 'co-inspiring' or 'innovative thought'). The presencing process occurs through youth entrepreneurs and role-players who, as Theory U states, co-initiate, co-sense, co-inspire, co-create, and co-evolve.

The occurrence of Shifting Hope, Activating Potential Entrepreneurship is seen as essential to addressing the deep-rooted socio-economic crisis faced by various systems in this country (Chapter 1). Therefore, theSHAPE YES (Youth Entrepreneur Support) Network (Fig. 3.1) was put into practice, and the related ecosystem was created, applied, and facilitated for the purposes of this research. The SHAPE ecosystem model was also validated through a series of assessments over seven years.

In a biological ecosystem (see Chapter 1), the heterogeneous concept of 'home' interrelates and interacts in an interdependent and complex relationship (non-dually). The youth entrepreneur ecosystem is similarly positioned within systemic levels, as described in Chapter 1 (micro-, meso-, macro-, and mundo-systems). Therefore, from a non-dualistic perspective, the youth entrepreneur ecosystem and its systemic levels cannot be separated due to the interrelatedness common to the source of origin (see Chapter 5).[19] Powerful centripetal forces, thus, bring youth entrepreneurs' internal and external domains together into a single ecosystem.[20]

One starting point in creating the youth entrepreneur ecosystem may be to look into the entomological origin of the word 'home'; and how

---

[19] Ibid.
[20] Brown and Mason (2017, 11–30).

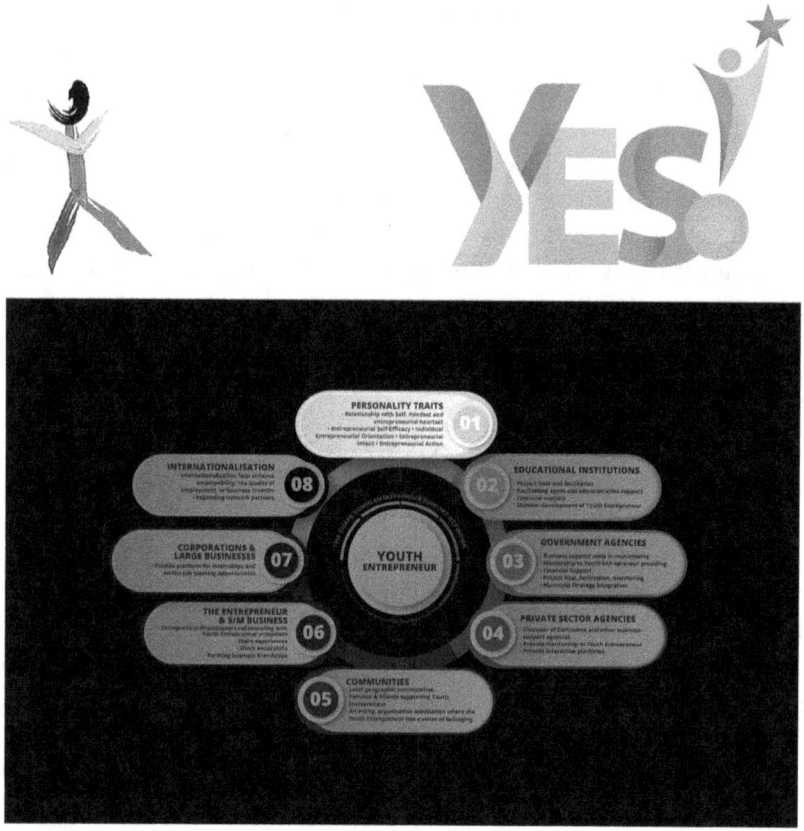

Fig. 3.1 The SHAPE YES Network for youth entrepreneurs—Personality traits[21] (*Source* Van der Westhuizen, 2022)

it relates to connecting components forming the youth entrepreneur environment. The facilitating agent from a given education institute, who is responsible for co-initiating the architecture of the proposed model, could start by bringing together a support network from within the same geographical location. These parties would, and should, be mutually dependent on one another for their own existence, as these

---

[21] *The Shape Youth Entrepreneur Support (YES) Network. First submitted for publication consideration to the International Journal of Entrepreneurial Behavior and Research.

location-specific characteristics make up a youth entrepreneur ecosystem (a 'home').

Since this support network and the youth entrepreneurs in the area share a common location, it is assumed that they can easily reach out to one another and draw support from one another. Of further note is that while technology could further broaden the scope and reach of the network role-players, a deeper understanding is still needed with respect to the physical location of 'home'. There is a need to better understand the location-specific problems and opportunities that youth entrepreneurs encounter in order to find the best niche market for value creation. There is also the understanding that, due to the location-specific nature of the microsystem, the architecture of bringing together different role-players will be different for each location.

Besides location-specific aspects, the youth entrepreneur ecosystem can also be industry-specific, depending on the youths' needs and available value creation opportunities. The youth entrepreneurial ecosystem can, therefore, be a highly variegated, multi-actor, and multi-scalar phenomenon that requires bespoke policy interventions.[22] The SHAPE strategy could allow for better adaptation and movement across different geographical locations as well as within the understanding of the nature of 'home'.

One common denominator within the youth entrepreneurial ecosystem is the commitment to sustainable socio-economic development. This means that the contribution(s) from each actor must add value to systemic development. All parties must also share a vision to address multiple systemic crises (see Chapter 1).

The centripetal forces in the youth entrepreneurial ecosystem's complex environment demand competitive advantage and innovation for existence, survival, and growth. The competition around resources within this ecosystem is, however, extremely high, as the same actors within the same ecosystem require access to the same resources. Despite this competitive nature, there still exists co-creation and co-evolvement amongst actors, which enables a conducive environment. According to Theory U, it is necessary for like-minded, like-hearted, and like-willed

---

[22] Ibid.

individuals to engage in the process of social emergence ('economies of creation'), as, without cooperation, a continuation of systemic disconnect and social pathology ('economies of destruction') will occur.[23]

Since the nature and scope of the youth entrepreneur ecosystem, along with its centripetal forces linked to location and industry, differ, Table 3.1 provides only a basic taxonomy of youth entrepreneurial ecosystems.

Theory U implies that for socio-economic development to occur—as in the development of (youth) entrepreneurship—on different systemic levels, the co-growth of all role-players is necessary. Five stages are proposed in this regard.[24]

3.2.1 Co-initiating

Co-initiating entails working with others from the outset, as there exists a strong connection between people who share common ground. In the case of entrepreneurs, having similar connections helps to build long-lasting relationships with like-minded individuals. When there is a shared vision for a country, there is also greater synergy because people have similar goals. The SHAPE social technology focuses on building common intent through macrosystemic initiatives similar to those set out in South Africa's *National Development Plan (NDP) 2030*.

3.2.2 Co-sensing

Co-sensing, in the South African context, connects entrepreneurs and key stakeholders through an in-depth understanding of all relevant interconnected systems. Understanding the dynamics can provide entrepreneurs and key stakeholders greater clarity and increase the likelihood of achieving mutual benefits. This is not necessarily a simple matter, and all parties need to understand clearly the challenges involved.

---

[23] Scharmer (2011).
[24] Scharmer and Käufer (2013), Van der Westhuizen (2016).

Table 3.1 Basic taxonomy of a youth entrepreneurial ecosystem

Basic Taxonomy of a Youth Entrepreneurial Ecosystem

Youth Ecosystem Dynamics	Embryonic Youth Ecosystem	Scale-up Youth Ecosystem
Dominant actors	Limited numbers of start-ups; Established incumbent enterprises are the bedrock of the local economy and often drive youth ecosystem momentum	High numbers of growth-orientated start-ups; Consists of rapidly growing, ambitious enterprises and enables more spin-off start-ups
Nature of ecosystem interactions	Limited interactions within the youth entrepreneurial ecosystem with other start-ups; weak vertical interactions between youth entrepreneurs, their support network, and sources of growth capital	Strong levels of interaction between start-ups; rapidly growing enterprises that scale up; heavily configured ecosystem architecture; strong vertical inter-actor networks
Levels of entrepreneurial orientation	Low start-ups focussed on early and/or premature endeavours	High, strong growth focus on generating new 'blockbuster' firms (e.g., IPOs)
Nature of funding escalator and availability of funding	Funding driven by the needs of start-ups; good sources of seed and early-stage funding; often publicly funded through co-investment schemes	Full range of funding sources across the entire funding escalator; nearly all privately funded
Importance and role of dealmakers	Limited numbers of dealmakers who tend to dominate most key deals focussed on single sectors	Large numbers of dealmakers with strong inter-regional and cross-sectoral connectivity
Fluidity and diversity of ecosystem actors	Predominantly locally domiciled entrepreneurs; low levels of 'transnational entrepreneurs'	Large numbers of entrepreneurs are non-native; high immigration of 'transnational entrepreneurs'
Level of 'blockbuster' entrepreneurship	Limited but occasional 'blockbuster' entrepreneurial 'events'	Frequent 'blockbusters' that lead to a cumulative process that generates a virtuous cycle of blockbuster 'events'
Nature of entrepreneurial recycling	A small number of major endeavours; low levels of entrepreneurial recycling limited to small projects; a limited number of angels – mostly syndicated and co-investment with Government sources of venture capital	Large numbers of 'blockbusters' exits; substantial levels of recycling and experimental learning for serial entrepreneurs; a large number of high-net-worth individuals who become angels
Spatial dynamics	Mostly locally focussed, with some connection to other national interactions for funding, human capital, and innovation	Strong local, national, and global interactions; resources drawn from a myriad of different sources and actors
Importance and focus of public policy	A strong role for policy; typically focussed on increasing resources (especially funding) to new technology-based firms	Limited role for policy; many initiatives are industry-led and focus on building vertical network connectivity across the ecosystem

Source Brown and Mason (2017)[25]

---

[25] Brown and Mason (2017, 11–30).

3.2.3 Co-inspiring

Co-inspiring (also referred to as 'presencing') is the ability to focus on new thought processes while removing inhibiting ideologies and pre-existing theories. This practice relates to developing the ability to react appropriately in new, unexperienced situations. Developing this ability gives entrepreneurs a competitive edge in unpredictable and difficult scenarios, as well as greater confidence in tackling difficult problems and making difficult decisions.

3.2.4 Co-creating

Co-creating relates to 'exploring the future by doing' and focusing on the needs of entrepreneurs' projected businesses in order to remove obstacles that prevent them from achieving their objectives.

3.2.5 Co-evolving

Finally, co-evolving occurs after the formulation of a prototype solution. In this stage, the focus is on the impact of the given solution on the entire system. Co-evolving can also pertain to creating initiatives based on the interacting meso- and macro-fields involved.

3.3 Educational Institutions

An educational institute is, in essence, a business. The SHAPE youth entrepreneurial ecosystem strategy positions higher education institutes (universities) as key centripetal forces and facilitators for co-initiating, co-sensing, co-inspiring, co-creating, and co-evolving the support network for, and of, youth entrepreneurs. Indeed, entrepreneurial-orientated institutions can provide would-be entrepreneurs with the necessary foundation to start a business through providing necessary formal and/or informal training and skills development that increase entrepreneurial self-confidence (Fig. 3.2).

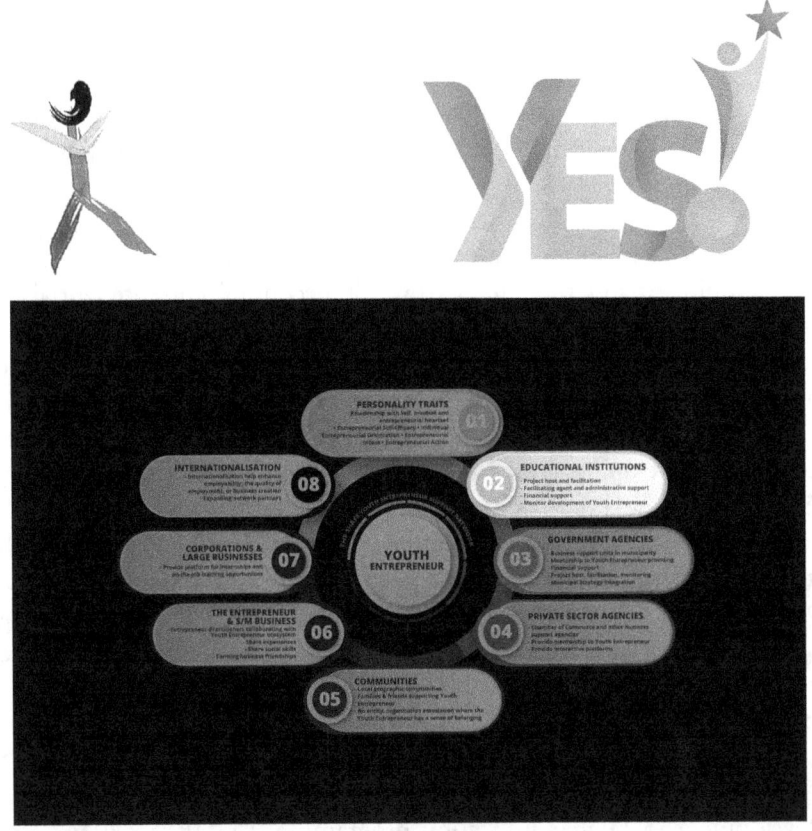

Fig. 3.2 The SHAPE YES Network for youth entrepreneurs—Educational institutions

In *The University of the Future*, edited by Dan Remenyi, Kenneth A. Grant, and Shawren Singh, there is an emphasis on how educational institutes, especially universities, are under considerable pressure to change towards producing work-ready graduates. Specifically, the work argues:

Universities reflect society and thus they are always a work-in-progress, continually in need of reinventing themselves.[26]

They have been criticised for their intense focus on research which has sometimes been said to have been at the cost [of] their mandate to educate.[27]

There are also ongoing debates between scholars as to whether universities should expand their focus towards becoming entrepreneurial in nature and, thereby, facilitate the entrepreneurship of students. Scholars from developing countries, which are generally faced with high graduate unemployment rates, tend to be more eager to support the new direction of universities becoming entrepreneurial, as this could provide greater scope for developing individuals' internal entrepreneurial domains. Developing these inner domains towards entrepreneurial inclinations should occur both inter-disciplinarily and cross-disciplinarily, where all programmes and modules incorporate elements of entrepreneurship. Developing the initial entrepreneurial heart- and mindset before tackling the entrepreneurial skillset could also take place both in formal academic programmes as well as through support or supplementary programmes and initiatives.[28]

The South African Department of Higher Education and Training's (DHET) university education branch established the Entrepreneurship Development in Higher Education programme (EDHE) in 2016. The vision was for universities to enable (a) every student and graduate to be fully equipped to participate in the economy, aside from traditional employment; and (b) teaching, research, innovation, entrepreneurship, and commercialisation pipelines that are supported within universities.[29] The EDHE focuses on developing entrepreneurial universities, entrepreneurship in academia, and student entrepreneurship. The role of the EDHE is discussed in more detail in the next section.

---

[26] Remenyi et al. (2019).
[27] Ibid.
[28] Preedy et al. (2020).
[29] EDHE (2021).

It should be noted at this point, however, that the creation of the EDHE aligns with global trends towards increasingly recognising entrepreneurship as a vital part of a university's role.[30] Development of entrepreneurship should, thus, be executed by academics in the form of academic entrepreneurship, by students in the form of student or graduate entrepreneurship, and by leadership in the form of creating entrepreneurial universities.[31]

3.3.1 The Entrepreneurial University

The concept of an entrepreneurial education institute gained popularity towards the end of the twentieth century due to the socio-economic need for universities, and educational institutes in general, to relook at their business model and sources of income. The entrepreneurial university creates, facilitates, and maintains an ecosystem for the youth, which impacts systemic development on micro-, meso-, macro-, and mundo-systemic levels.

Both education and research, as an industry, hold scope for entrepreneurial behaviour and approaches like providing services and products to clients. The concept of an entrepreneurial university, thus, adopts both a linear and a reverse linear model, thereby enabling entrepreneurship *in* universities. The linear model relates to teaching and research, knowledge, skills, and technology transfer. The reverse linear model occurs as these aspects are adapted from the place of research into active use. This transfer is aided by interface capabilities, such as activation and transfer officers. The university's incubator or accelerator facilitators and mentors to youths, whose responsibilities would be to manage and market knowledge as a product and as protected intellectual property, can also aid in this process.

Based on this joint model, it is understood that the entrepreneurial university's primary characteristics include:

---

[30] Davey et al. (2016).
[31] Ibid.

1. the university itself, which, as an organisation, becomes entrepreneurial
2. the members of the university who turn themselves into entrepreneurs; and
3. the interaction of the university with the environment.[32]

Key factors influencing the effective practice of an entrepreneurial university relate to entrepreneurial-orientated inner domains-based leadership, which can enable an entrepreneurial and value-adding environment. The entrepreneurial-orientated staff, as well as learning and teaching, exist in this environment. The entrepreneurial university's success is, furthermore, associated with the presence of leadership with a vision towards addressing various systemic crises and inspiring both staff and youths to generate problem-solving ideas and possible inventions that support spin-off creation.[33]

At many education institutes, working towards such a vision might not be possible through the academic programme alone. In this sense, institutions may require support programmes, initiatives, or units to collate these universities' total entrepreneurial actions (EA). Such collation may take the form of an economic activation unit, which functions as a central institutional point.

Currently, many universities do have incubation, acceleration, and technology transfer offices in place that hold the potential to co-initiate the broader sense of the youth entrepreneurial ecosystem. Since students eventually graduate from these education institutes, hopefully with an entrepreneurial concept in place to enable initial career steps, it is the responsibility of the entrepreneurial university to educate and train role-players in students' external support networks to provide effective mentorship and support after graduation. Through support from Government agencies, private sector agencies, communities, corporates and large businesses, and SME owners in their direct environment, graduates may be better able to further develop themselves as youth entrepreneurs. These alumni, in return, become part of the future

---

[32] Röpke (1998).
[33] Dominici and Gagnidze (2021, 13–30).

youth entrepreneurial ecosystem through continuous cycles of providing support and mentorship, passing on knowledge and skills, and introducing new role-players to the network. Through this cycle, students graduating from entrepreneurial universities begin to contribute to future interconnected local systems where co-beneficial support structures occur and co-develop.

3.3.2 Academic Entrepreneurship

Value creation is widely recognised as the common core of both academic entrepreneurship and how different stakeholders in society create value for each other. It can, therefore, be reasoned that value co-creation is essential for an effective youth entrepreneur ecosystem. The development of entrepreneurship, as part of a university's role, should, thus, be executed by academics in the form of 'academic' entrepreneurship. University academics, generally through research conducted at universities, are a significant source of entrepreneurial activity, and their role in stimulating economic activity has become more pronounced over the past 30 years.

Initially, academic entrepreneurship was described as involving academics who attempt to generate funds from external agencies as a means of pursuing research at a university. This developing entrepreneurial activity has since manifested in increasing numbers of patents, licencing income, numbers of academic spinouts and start-ups, and applied research conducted with partners and consultancy engagements.[34] Through such developments, more extended research-led community engagements now take place, and the entrepreneurial ecosystem of the university has become a natural outflow of co-engagement, co-creation, and co-evolvement processes with the larger external community of the university.

The South African national agenda, through the EDHE goal on academic entrepreneurship, is to

---

[34] Davey et al. (2016).

> [...] support (university) academics in instilling an entrepreneurial mindset within all students and graduates through the offering of relevant knowledge, transferral of practical skills and the application of business principles, not only to a specific discipline, but across disciplines.[35]

The idea of infusing elements of entrepreneurship into education has gained great traction in many educational institutes around the world as a response to addressing socio-economic problems and facilitating graduate employment. However, putting this idea into practice poses significant challenges. The initial co-initiating, co-sensing, co-inspiring, co-creating, and (eventually) co-evolving of the youth entrepreneur ecosystem is complex and time-consuming for individuals at these education institutes who facilitate the process. Despite these challenges, the positive long-term effects (systemic transformation and value creation) make it necessary to expand this ecosystem as much as possible in a responsible and sustainable manner.

The main problem that educational institutes might initially encounter when establishing a youth entrepreneurship environment is related to the capacity and ability to change. This issue includes, but is not limited to, a lack of time and various resources; academic staff's trepidation towards commercialism; educational structures that are currently not able to promote entrepreneurialism; and a lack of clarity,[36] as locations, institutional architecture, programme offerings, and staff abilities differ both within and across institutions.[37]

A further issue is that *what* is meant by 'entrepreneurship *in* education' (or entrepreneurship education) differs significantly across existing literature reviews. Some perspectives view the concept as a process involving various academic and non-academic programmes to encourage students to start up their own enterprises. Other perspectives include that this concept is, instead, about making students more creative, opportunities-orientated, proactive, and/or innovative towards problem-solving. Furthermore, regarding promoting entrepreneurship education in developing countries with high unemployment: the emphasis and

---

[35] EDHE (2021).
[36] No 'ten-step plan' of 'how to' infuse entrepreneurship into education.
[37] Lackéus (2015).

common denominator tend to fall on value creation (training students to create value for other people). Indeed, value creation is at the core of systemic development and a key factor in and for addressing different socio-economic crises on and across various systemic levels (see Chapter 1). As such, value creation is a key competency required by all staff and students, no matter what career is being pursued or whether activities take place internally or externally from an educational institute. Creating new and innovative enterprises could, thus, be viewed as one of many different means for creating value.[38]

In addition, while *why* entrepreneurship education is relevant is mostly viewed from a socio-economic development perspective, it can by no means be seen as a 'save-all' solution for high youth unemployment. This is because as much as entrepreneurship education can work as a formal academic programme, with elective courses or components of entrepreneurship being incorporated into general modules or course learning outcomes within higher education, it can still be problematic when infused into the primary or secondary levels of education. At these lower levels, it can, however, still be impactful to trigger students' entrepreneurial heartsets and mindsets, which could result in deeper learning over time.[39]

Effective youth entrepreneurship is, furthermore, linked to students' resilience within their inner domains. Through resilience, students can become motivated to engage in creating value in their environment based on the knowledge they acquire through entrepreneurial education. Thus, both academic and non-academic entrepreneurship education programmes have certain implications for planning, executing, assessing, and co-initiating the youth entrepreneur ecosystem within their respective programme or module offerings.

In comparison to *what* and *why*, *when* to infuse entrepreneurship into education tends to be clearer in its theory (Fig. 3.3). Yet, its practical application is often difficult and will vary between educational institutes, locations, and students. The theory ambitiously proposes that entrepreneurship education should be embedded into curricula that are

---

[38] Ibid.
[39] Ibid.

relevant to all students, preferably as early as pre-primary and primary school. Some countries (e.g., in the Middle East) have managed to do so. These countries' success in this endeavour may be related to how their education systems are relatively new and specifically created in response to the need to add value to extreme national problems (e.g., to address the over-extraction of oil and gas and its related potential to reduce income gained from this resource).

At a later stage in the educational system, both academic and non-academic programmes can be complemented by offering youths voluntary enabling opportunities for entrepreneurship practice. Currently, on both the secondary and tertiary levels, most initiatives, besides curricula offerings, focus on business start-ups. This focus is problematic, as it often lacks embeddedness in other teaching subjects. A possible way to better infuse theory and practice could be through the adoption of SALAR. However, effective implementation requires academic staff, support staff, and mentors from institutes' external environments to collaborate. Furthermore, an action takes time to co-initiate and sustain,

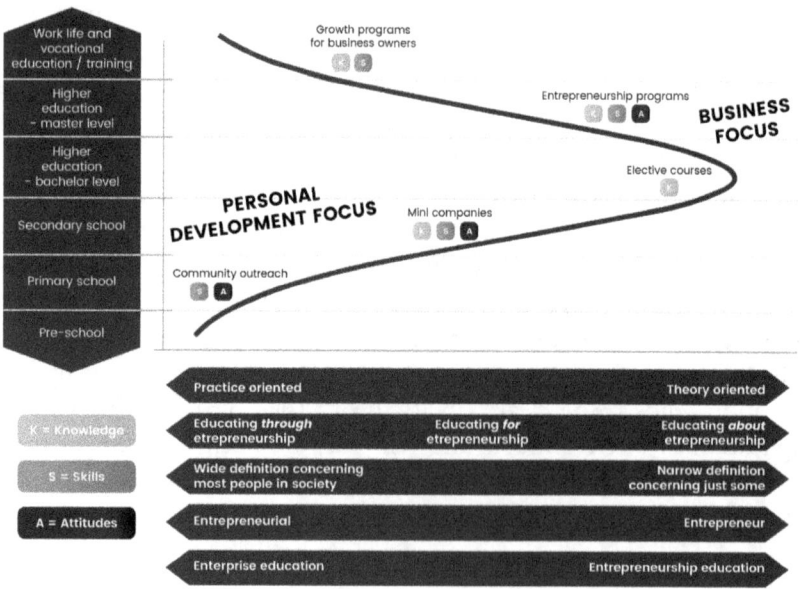

Fig. 3.3 Overview of entrepreneurial education (*Source* Lackéus, 2015)

as maintaining relationships is complex, and coordinating the various role-players can be time-consuming for facilitators. In vocational education and training, youths' EA is also generally associated with the actualisation of learning outcomes and value creation; however, gaps still exist in connecting youths to tools, methods, and processes for sustaining actions and the value creation process.

It is necessary, therefore, to determine *how* to develop staff and students with enhanced entrepreneurial heartsets and mindsets in order to address complex situations. While determining this 'how' may be a difficult endeavour, it is still vital, as successfully answering this question could translate into significant reductions in the currently high levels of graduate and youth unemployment.

One popular approach to developing youth entrepreneurial abilities is 'learning-by-doing'. Indeed, there is increasing consensus in the body of knowledge that students working in interdisciplinary teams and interacting with people outside the educational institute can be a particularly powerful way to develop entrepreneurial competencies. However, in order to effectively adopt this approach, the *what* (what needs to be learnt by doing?) needs to be properly answered.

If experiential and action learning, similar to learning-by-doing, is based on EA as an outcome, then it could be argued that value creation should occur within the extended youth entrepreneurial ecosystem. By employing such an approach, it may be that role-players outside of educational institutes could significantly benefit from the youths' value creation, both indirectly and directly. While this value creation might not be immediately visible or tangible, there is a vision that the ecosystem could coherently move towards a common 'big picture' vision. For this to occur, however, the facilitating agent within the educational institute needs to draw from other institutional resources to support the scope of activities serving as a node by bringing together total youth EA. Traditionally, acting as a node was not associated with the role, function, and/or mandate of education institute staff.[40]

The Organisation for Economic Co-operation and Development (OECD) created a model to provide an overview of different concepts

---

[40] Ibid.

within entrepreneurship education (Fig. 3.3). The model illustrates youth entrepreneurial progression in the education system and could be a starting point for facilitators when planning to co-initiate the youth entrepreneurial ecosystem.[41] It details the development of the entrepreneurial heartset and mindset from pre-youth years through to higher education conclusion.

According to the model, four approaches[42] can be considered:

1. teaching about entrepreneurship, which pays attention to theoretical concepts[43];
2. education related to entrepreneurial competencies, behaviours, and hard and soft skills;
3. education for entrepreneurship, which creates a platform for training or practice sessions and may demand a form of informal course structure; and
4. education in entrepreneurship for youths or staff who have existing enterprise concepts and demonstrate existing EA.

Entrepreneurship education can offer a way for societies to progress based on problem-solving competencies, innovation, and innovative and creative thinking.

3.3.3 Studentpreneurship

Studentpreneurship is a term used to describe youths with an open heart, open will, and open mind to connect to their entrepreneurial ecosystem en route to EA. The term refers to youths who are learning to be entrepreneurial or who have, in some cases, initiated a start-up. Studentpreneurs develop their heartset, handset, and mindsets with support from an educational institute or participate in development or mentorship initiatives from other agents. These studentpreneurs have a responsibility

---

[41] Ibid.
[42] Maas (2015).
[43] Davey et al. (2016), Parsons (1951).

to co-initiate, co-sense, co-inspire, co-create, and co-evolve with other people in their youth entrepreneurial ecosystem and to maintain positive interpersonal relationships so as to hopefully gain sustained EA and create value.

Some educational institutes, especially in higher education, enable an environment of entrepreneurial support and allow studentpreneurs to engage in business activities on and off-campus, with or without the support of the educational institute. These institutions do so by offering their students incubation, acceleration, shop-space, patenting, and licencing opportunities. Such activities often take place extra-curricularly and are not linked to academic assessment. Oftentimes, educational institutes provide formal studentpreneur policies or agreements that stipulate rules for doing business with, or to the external environment of, the educational institute with support of the educational institute itself.

The EDHE programme of DHET envisions South African universities mobilising national student and graduate resources to create successful enterprises that will eventually lead to both wealth and job creation. Graduates, under this vision, would continue to add value to the ecosystem and, in return, offer support to the new generation of youth entrepreneurs moving into the education system cycle. In this context, wealth refers more to national value creation than the accumulation of money.

3.4 Government Agencies

The SHAPE strategy for developing an effective youth entrepreneurial ecosystem underlines the need for robust links between governmental agencies, educational institutes, and the full range of entrepreneurial factors in the ecosystem. In terms of (youth) entrepreneurial development, Government plays two important roles. The first is regulatory, which is related to creating and providing conducive policies and responsibly and ethically ensuring justice. The second is developmental, which aligns to initiating various programmes and offering financial and other forms of assistance (e.g., policy creation that enables entrepreneurial ventures and safeguards its interest, including conflict resolution mechanisms, patent policies, taxation laws, and other business-related regulations)[44] (Fig. 3.4).

In South Africa, Sector Education Training Authorities (SETAs) are responsible for initiating and sponsoring internships or learnership programmes. In 2005, 22 different economic sector-related organisations were re-established by the South African Minister of Labour. They had

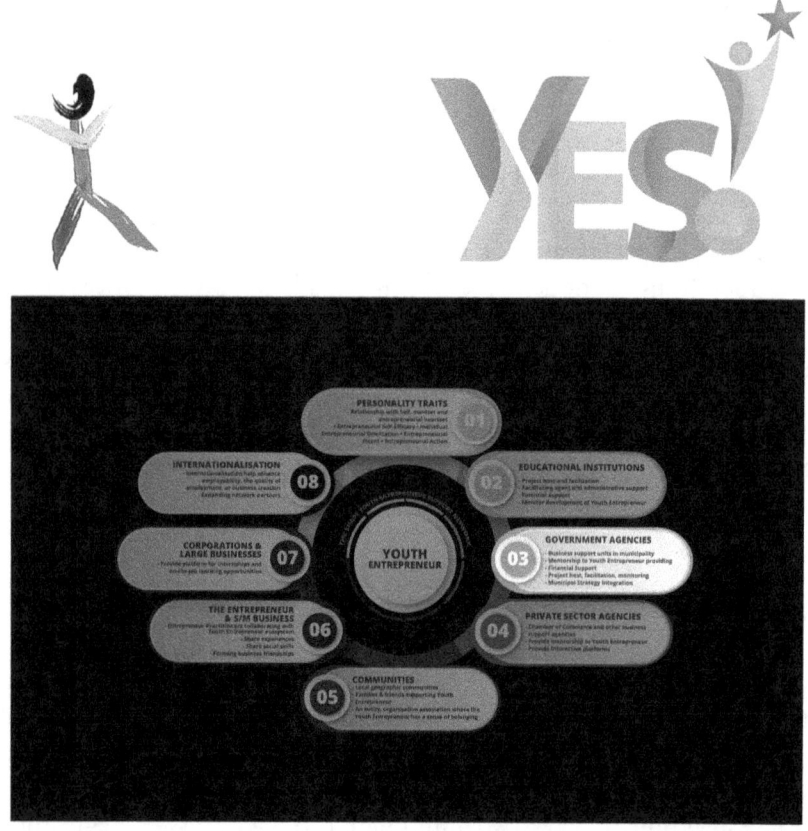

Fig. 3.4 The SHAPE YES Network for youth entrepreneurs—Government agencies

---

[44] Mujahid et al. (2019).

since been allocated responsibility for educating and training individuals to develop skills in relation to each specific economic sector (e.g., one for the banking sector, one for information technology, etc.) as a means to implement the global National Skills Development Strategy.[45] A sector is made up of economic activities that are linked and related to macrosystemic socio-economic development. These SETAs provide experiential learning to individuals, with 60% of the training taking place outside the classroom (in a workplace-related milieu). There are currently, however, no SETAs specifically allocated to youth entrepreneurship, nor is there any track record of sustainable job creation for youths who undergo SETA-based programmes.[46]

Government bodies, such as local municipalities, also provide business support to youth entrepreneurs and have programmes to boost entrepreneurship. One example of a local municipality in South Africa that has implemented such initiatives is the eThekwini Municipality (in which central Durban is located). In this municipality, 15 types of business support offerings and programmes exist to support individuals and enhance entrepreneurship (Table 3.2).[47]

One problem with these kinds of municipality-based business support programmes is a lack of reliable data on their successes or sustainability in the long term. The focus of these programmes also tends to be on the most basic level, with no core focus on innovation, creativity, or sustainable mentorship post-completion of such a programme.

3.4.1 Entrepreneurship Development in Higher Education

The EDHE, as a government agency, offers a platform primarily aimed at addressing the issues of graduate unemployment and the need for universities to become more entrepreneurial. It was created in 2016 within the South African DHET and is part of the University Capacity Development Programme (UCDP). The EDHE intends to co-initiate, co-sense,

---

[45] Seta's South Africa (2021).
[46] Records are available on pass and failure rates.
[47] eThekwini Municipality (2017).

Table 3.2 Example of local government support for youth entrepreneurship

co-inspire, co-create, and co-evolve with South African public universities to create a national impact. This intended impact is to (a) equip every student for economic participation through economic activity, with an emphasis on student women; (b) support academics and professionals to develop entrepreneurship through learning, teaching, and research across all disciplines; and (c) support universities as entrepreneurial and innovative ecosystems, which include relevant policy development.

This government agency further describes its approach as propelling the economic participation of students and graduates by leveraging strong and existing networks in and through its community of practice (CoPs—detailed a bit later in this section). The EDHE also champions relationships by utilising existing university structures and resources to capacitate each South African university in a lean, scalable way.

It should be noted, however, that the mandate of this agency does not include entrepreneurship in basic education or general entrepreneurship in the community but rather has a specific focus on universities. The vision, thus, needs to mobilise resources across the nation and different universities to promote the desired facilitation of entrepreneurship programmes aimed at improving the systemic crises faced at the macrosystems level. A primary strategy to mobilise these noted resources is to create different CoPs by bringing together university staff and students from various public universities into a central node. Such national CoPs currently include the following:

- EDHE CoP for Student Entrepreneurship (CoP for SE)
- EDHE CoP for Entrepreneurship Learning and Teaching (CoP for ELT)
- EDHE CoP for Entrepreneurship Research (CoP for ER)
- EDHE CoP for Entrepreneurial Universities (CoP for EU)
- EDHE Studentpreneurs (CoP for SPs); and
- Upcoming in 2022, EDHE CoP for Entrepreneurial Alumni (CoP for EA).

The national entrepreneurship/entrepreneurial CoP structure enables the youth entrepreneurial ecosystem to develop between educational institutes, governmental agencies, and private sectors (Fig. 3.5).

3.4.1.1 The EDHE CoP Landscape

The EDHE further envisions replicating the national CoP structure of general government agencies within South African universities. This, in turn, could boost the concept of entrepreneurial universities where universities actively collaborate with governmental agencies through establishing an economic activation office as a central internal node (e.g., an existing incubator or accelerator), which would be responsible for facilitating the internal co-creation of the CoP structure. This node would also leverage existing university support structures (Fig. 3.6).

3.4.2 Other Government Agencies

Aside from the EDHE, there are a number of other government agencies responsible for promoting (youth) entrepreneurship. For example, the

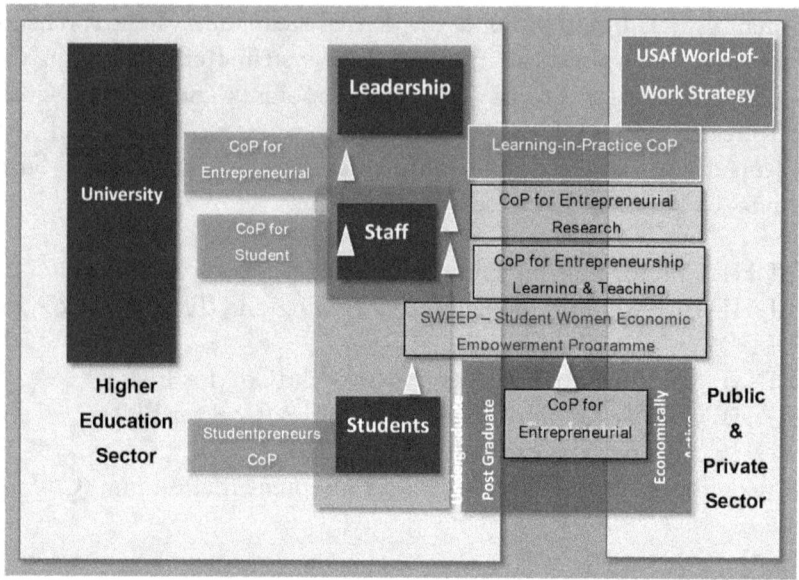

Fig. 3.5 The EDHE CoP landscape (2021–2023) (*Source* EDHE, 2021)

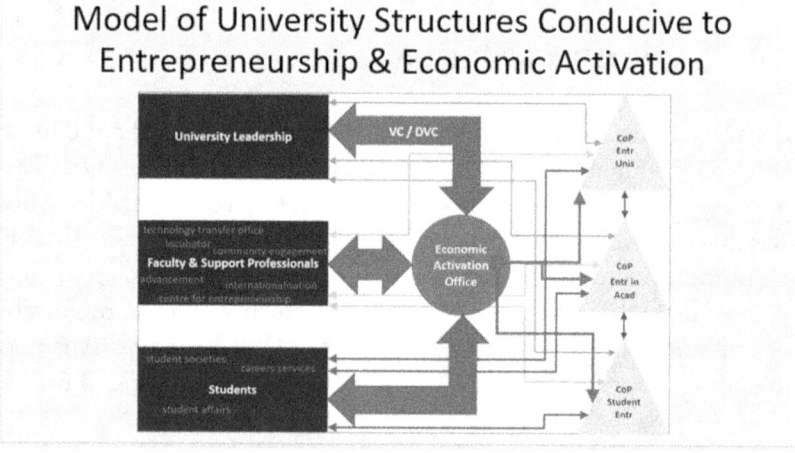

Fig. 3.6 Model of university structures conducive to entrepreneurship and economic activation (*Source* EDHE, 2021)

Industrial Development Corporation (IDC) is a national development finance institute mandated to promote economic growth and industrial development and improve domestic industrial capacity.[48] This agency is capacitated to develop opportunities for youth entrepreneurs in alignment with development policies and develop programmes and functions in collaboration with educational institutes.

The IDC also promotes entrepreneurial development through its subsidiary, namely the Small Enterprise Finance Agency (SEFA). SEFA is responsible for supporting the establishment and developing and growing SMEs with the aim of reducing poverty and creating jobs.[49] When youth entrepreneurs receive funds from this agency for the establishment of their businesses, such ventures can employ other youths. SEFA also partners with financial intermediaries to foster the support of entrepreneurs and creates an avenue for monitoring allocated funds.

Of further note is the South African Institute for Entrepreneurship (SAIE), which is aimed at impacting South Africa's entrepreneurial culture to foster job creation and promote entrepreneurial behaviour, which should result in reducing the currently high levels of unemployment, poverty, and inequality.[50] With a focus primarily on agriculture, education, information technology, and enterprise development sectors, SAIE is enabled to develop relevant initiative programmes and methodologies.

Similarly, the National Youth Development Agency (NYDA) was established by an act of parliament (Act 54 of 2008) to address matters relating to youth development at the national, provincial, and local government levels.[51] NYDA ensures that stakeholders, such as Government, the private sector, and civil society, give attention to the development of youths by offering programmes to solve challenges and improve their lives. At the micro-level, NYDA provides training, mentorship, and entrepreneurial support to youths, while at the macro-level, it facilitates

---

[48] SEFA (2021).
[49] SA Institute for Entrepreneurship (2021).
[50] NYDA (2021).
[51] CHIETA (2021).

the contribution of the youth to policy development, partnership, and research.

The Chemical Industries Education and Training Authority (CHIETA) was established by the Skills Development Act in 1998[52] and is responsible for the identification of skills needed to be developed to promote growth in the chemical industries sector. Such growth is achieved through training and development initiatives.

Furthermore, the Umbsombuvu Youth Fund[53] has been equipped to attract investment partnerships to fund youth entrepreneurs. This Fund helps youth entrepreneurs to grow their ventures by teaching them the required skills and offering programmes, such as franchises, fund-a-loan, and the voucher financing system. The Fund also supports entrepreneurship education and training, co-operative training, graduate development training, and business consulting service vouchers.

As a macrosystem role-player, governmental agencies set out to support youth entrepreneurship through various programmes and initiatives. These initiatives can be presented on a national, provincial, or local municipal level. The support provided by these agencies can also be through various avenues, including mentorship, resource exchange, leverage, and/or possible financial support.

3.5 Private-Sector Agencies

Private-sector agencies are community, regional, national, or international-based agents operating for the collective promotion of private sector organisations. These agencies have the potential to support youth entrepreneurs by enabling networking opportunities with other entrepreneurs and business friends. The agencies also assist with forming further business friendships, possible collaboration opportunities in the value chain, possible financing schemes, and other support platforms to enable youth entrepreneurs over time (Fig. 3.7).

---

[52] SACCI (2021).
[53] Danns and Danns (2019).

Fig. 3.7 The SHAPE YES Network for youth entrepreneurs—Private sector agencies

Networks within private-sector agencies are necessary because youth entrepreneurs access intangible resources (e.g., access to new markets, information, trust, and knowledge) and tangible resources (e.g., facilities and finances) through these avenues. In the SHAPE ecosystem, specifically, the collaboration between educational institutes and private sector agencies is necessary to facilitate[54] the sharing of resources such as capital, knowledge, expertise, and technologies. Private-sector agencies can also

---

[54] Hernández-Chea et al. (2021).

serve as incubators by providing business support and physical spaces for youth entrepreneurs through or within their physical proximity or online platforms. Furthermore, many private-sector agencies operate on a membership system, where members benefit from various organised services offered by respective private sector agencies.[55] The following paragraphs offer more details regarding these kinds of agencies.

The South Africa Chamber of Commerce and Industry (SACCI)[56] represents the interest of businesses by engaging with the government and regulators on matters that pertain to ensuring a conducive business environment for business owners, thereby protecting the interest of the business sector. SACCI's responsibility to entrepreneurs is to promote and lobby potential investors (e.g., the Government and other businesses) for conditions that enable the development of start-ups for youth entrepreneurs.[57]

The National African Federated Chamber of Commerce and Industry (NAFCOC),[58,59] in turn, is aimed at developing and promoting inclusive economic growth amongst existing and new businesses with memberships of about 5 million SMEs. NAFCOC has existing partnerships with various institutions, including governmental and educational institutions, and builds business relations with international business chambers.

The African Development Bank (AfDB),[60] in conjunction with the European Investment Bank,[61] has instituted an initiative referred to as Boost Africa Empowering Young Entrepreneurs. This initiative assesses possible funding for youth entrepreneurs at the earliest stages of their EA.

---

[55] Griffin-El (2015), Isenberg (2010).
[56] https://sacci.org.za/.
[57] NAFCOC (2021).
[58] Vuk'uzenzele (2021).
[59] https://nafcoc.org.za/.
[60] Crampton (2019), https://www.afdb.org/en.
[61] https://www.eib.org/en/index.htm.

3.6 Communities

The concept of 'communities' refers to the context in which youth entrepreneurs are embedded.[62] Communities can be both enabling and barrier factors within and for the youth entrepreneurial ecosystem. The notion of 'embeddedness' indicated earlier relates to both contextual and community influences that critically contribute to the formation of youth entrepreneurs' mental models (thinking and feeling). In other words, the spirit and culture of the embedded community can impact youths' shared values and norms, receptivity to education and mentorship, leadership and governance, and infrastructure. All these factors, in turn, impact the youths' EI (Fig. 3.8).

The embeddedness of community is also important for youth entrepreneurs in terms of how communities can provide an 'anchoring' that supports the healthy development of young people's inner domains. Indeed, an enabling community is most likely to contribute to shaping the youths' EA and encourage trust between role-players when co-initiating entrepreneurial ideas. The growth-effectiveness of youth entrepreneurship depends on a shared heart, mind, and will; hence, the need for positive community embeddedness.

While such embeddedness can be structural, cultural, political, and/or cognitive, cultural embeddedness most commonly impact youth entrepreneurs. Cultural embeddedness consists of the beliefs, values, ideologies, and norms that exist and develop within a given community (wherein a youth entrepreneur exists) and most often begins within the immediate family. General culture also influences the choice of a young person to become an entrepreneur and his or her response to information.[63]

With this understanding, it can be asserted that current embeddedness and culture run counter to the traditional South African notion of *ubuntu* (an African philosophy that values moral practice and the intention to act in a manner that is respectful and honest). In South Africa, *ubuntu* culture seeks to benefit society rather than just the individual.

---

[62] Shirokova et al. (2013).
[63] Ibid.

Fig. 3.8 The SHAPE YES Network for youth entrepreneurs—Communities

However, the practice of *ubuntu* is not widespread, and more effort is required for communities to benefit from this concept. South Africa, thus, needs to develop a pervading culture of *ubuntu* to provide collective benefits to and for all entrepreneurs, as such assistance could be crucial in bridging the current disconnect between existing individualistic and collectivist points of view.[64]

As the community spirit often starts with the immediate family, role-players can consist of parents, guardians, or siblings who form the

---

[64] Nel (2017).

primary support system and become the greatest influencers of youth entrepreneurs. Mentors in the broader community (adult allies) or peers are also great social influencers for youth entrepreneurs and can either create an enabling or a disabling environment. That is, youths often perceive especially their peers as trustworthy and relatable, which can create emotional support for youth entrepreneurs, particularly when those peers encourage their pursuits. Other community enabling aspects can include community organisations (e.g., social, sport, or cultural clubs), religious institutions, infrastructure, or facilities, and other public or private organisations located in direct geographical access to the community wherein a youth entrepreneur exists.[65] Conversely, many barriers to youth entrepreneurship occur as a result of a lack of (positive) community support. Without community support, many youths are left feeling hopeless and helpless in creating an entrepreneurial future for themselves.

When a facilitator in an educational institute co-initiates SHAPE, engagements will naturally occur with youths in the local community wherein they are pursuing their entrepreneurial education. Often, local communities consist of both community-based organisations and NGOs with whom local youth entrepreneurs interact. Local communities are also the principal consumers of the products and services rendered by youth entrepreneurs and form their infrastructure 'business friends'. In this way, local communities both receive value from and create value for youth entrepreneurs. Since these communities also tend to be the same as from where the youth entrepreneur hails, they also add pertinence to the link between 'community' and 'entrepreneurial development'. This link is particularly true in respect to how most South African youths are well-acquainted with the social ills (e.g., crime, corruption, violence, and the mismanagement of unemployment) that exist within their own communities[66] and, therefore, aim to address these ills practically through entrepreneurship.

---

[65] Shirokova et al. (2013).
[66] Van der Westhuizen (2016).

Youth entrepreneurial ability should, thus, begin at home and then proceed to higher education and training.[67] At the tertiary level, partnerships with local communities and SMEs can also better provide opportunities for youth entrepreneurs to form business friendships, thereby widening the scope for beneficial consultation and creating the potential for youth entrepreneurs and their business friends to move forward together in entrepreneurial activity.

The local communities act as support networks between youth entrepreneurs and the broader entrepreneurial process, thus, become an important supportive pillar in the SHAPE youth entrepreneurial ecosystem.

3.7 Small-and-Medium-Sized Enterprises (SMEs)

The terms 'entrepreneur' and 'SME owner' can be used synonymously in relation to their potential for serving as business friends to youth entrepreneurs, as most often, an SME owner is also an entrepreneur.[68] In the SHAPE strategy for youth entrepreneurial ecosystems, the emphasis is on youth entrepreneurs having an initial opportunity to try out social skills with existing entrepreneurs or business owner-managers through the processes of co-initiating, co-sensing, and co-inspiring. Further EA might result from these interactions by co-creating and co-evolving business ideas that occur together or individually (Fig. 3.9).

Normative, cognitive, and regulatory pillars are associated with the co-initiation phase between youth entrepreneurs and possible business friends, as facilitated through the education institute.[69] The normative pillar underpins social values, norms, and beliefs that govern individual and organisation behaviour. The cognitive pillar constitutes the 'shared logics of action' among youths and their ecosystem(s). These, in turn, can be used to interpret available information and formulate youths'

---

[67] Dhliwayo (2008, 329–340).
[68] Bagheri and Pihie (2011).
[69] Audretsch et al. (2021).

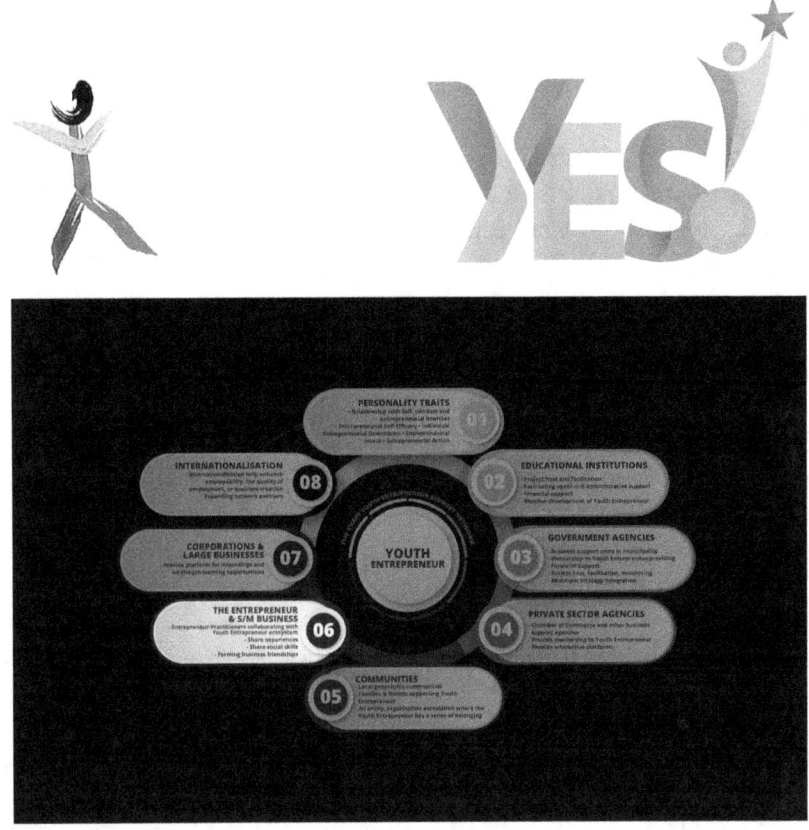

Fig. 3.9 The SHAPE YES Network for youth entrepreneurs—The entrepreneur & S/M business

expectations about the outcome of their entrepreneurial interactions. The regulatory pillar comprises regulations, laws, and other aspects that define the 'rules of co-value creation' and legal boundaries.[70]

Building on these three pillars, interactions of skills transfer, mentorship, and industry training from SME owners or existing entrepreneurs to youth entrepreneurs who are just beginning their EA are necessary to build an effective ecosystem and add value to socio-economic

---

[70] Ibid.

development. Possibly some of the most productive learning environments for youth entrepreneurs and their business friends occur when actions closely match the day-to-day realities of small-business leadership and networking.[71] Hands-on experience in actual business and industry environments for youths who would otherwise have little sense of the competitive pressures that face new entrants in a business field is also a crucial enabler aspect. The emphasis in these interactions between youth entrepreneurs and SME owners should, thus, primarily be on 'learning the business' by 'experiencing the business'. This process best occurs through the active performance of business operations in the course of an entrepreneurship initiative undertaken at an educational institute.

As part of the 'co' strategy, the possible collaboration between business friendship structures, youth entrepreneurs, and SME owner-managers is encouraged by facilitators of an educational institute. Possible emerging business friendships that can result from such collaboration include:

- Youth entrepreneurs who wish to co-create and co-evolve on their own and with their own business ideas become their own business friends.
- Business professionals (non-youth) who wish to draw on their participation in the youth entrepreneurial ecosystem to co-create and co-evolve on their own and with their own business ideas.
- Youth entrepreneurs who wish to co-create and co-evolve together with other youth entrepreneurs and with their own and/or joint business ideas.
- Youth entrepreneurs who wish to co-create and co-evolve together with other youth entrepreneurs *and* business professionals with their own or joint business ideas.
- Business professionals who wish to co-create and co-evolve together with other business professionals; professionals remain part of value creation within the youth entrepreneurial ecosystem.

Youth entrepreneurs who engage with initial EA benefit from their inner and external domain development through business friendships with

---

[71] Dhliwayo (2008).

SMEs that provide possible spin-off new ventures and creation opportunities. Business friendships also strengthen both the individual and the enterprise, especially in challenging business times.[72] Networks that youth entrepreneurs can access through business friendships include.

1. information networks, through which opportunities are identified, and resources are acquired (e.g., embracing information communication technology [ICT]);
2. networks for value-adding exchange (embracing competition and strengthening value chains); and
3. networks of social influence or status.

This last network type is especially important because youth entrepreneurs can boost their ESE to confidently overcome emotions associated with feeling helpless and/or hopeless about the future when they have social support. The ability of youth entrepreneurs to use existing networks within the ecosystem allows them to leverage over their competitors, both within the ecosystem and across other communities.

A possible way for a facilitator at an educational institute to bring youth entrepreneurs together with various potential business friends is to allocate industry mentors to youths. These mentors can provide guidance to their mentees, and the youth entrepreneurs can learn from these mentors' experiences and success stories. Industry mentorship between business friends and youth entrepreneurs can also enhance the collective learning capacity necessary to propel youths' creativity and innovativeness.[73]

---

[72] Mason and Brown (2014).
[73] Brown and Mason (2017).

3.8 Corporations and Large Businesses

Corporations and large businesses perform important functions in the development of the youth entrepreneurial ecosystem. These organisations generally specialise in attracting a pool of highly skilled individuals, many of whom are graduates with higher education qualifications from various disciplines.[74] In terms of contributing and adding value to the youth entrepreneurial ecosystem, educational institutes and corporations or large businesses can collaborate through both formal and informal agreements to support youth entrepreneurial development. A vibrant, value-adding youth entrepreneurial ecosystem essentially includes major businesses that help to cultivate said ecosystem (purposefully or otherwise).[75] Large businesses rooted locally instead of internationally are also likely to be the most successful in strengthening this ecosystem, as angel investors tend to be indigenous. Top management roles within local-based, larger organisations also tend to be more plentiful, ensuring that the company is generally well-connected within the community (Fig. 3.10).

Fewer and fewer jobs are available in the industrial sector due to technological advancements, which calls for new models of social innovation to facilitate youth entrepreneurship, along with new skills development for the new economy and opportunities for transforming resources and skills into value-creating endeavours.[76] Current wicked problems (also referred to as long-term unaddressed systemic problems that cause systemic crises), however, indicate that existing institutional arrangements are insufficient for adding value to socio-economic problem-solving, making innovations imperative.[77] An open innovation approach towards purposefully blending grassroots ideas, youth entrepreneurial innovations, and frugal innovations are still far from being actioned by most large businesses and corporations in South Africa. It is, therefore,

---

[74] Feldman et al. (2005).
[75] Isenberg (2011).
[76] Gupta et al. (2017).
[77] Ibid.

Fig. 3.10 The SHAPE YES Network for youth entrepreneurs—Corporations and large businesses

essential for a systemic disconnect to be overcome in order to effectively address wicked problems.

The youth entrepreneurial ecosystem could be a significant avenue for overcoming this disconnect, particularly if it is supported to create value through social, open innovations that connect corporations, communities, and educational institutes. Social innovation is a creative and connected solution that can be used to address unmet social needs, as it includes adding value and innovation *by* grassroots and youths *for* grassroots and youths. Through this approach, it becomes easier to co-create a healthy youth entrepreneurial ecosystem.[78]

Corporations and large businesses can further benefit youth entrepreneurs through mechanisms rooted in regulatory obligation. Corporate social investment (CSI), for instance, can provide skills development and mentorship to youth entrepreneurs. It is also crucial that corporations undertake talent recruitment programmes aimed at university graduates that assist with development. These larger businesses can also provide exhibitions to foster youth entrepreneurship and attract graduates. Similarly, skills development and training initiatives (e.g., the South African Skills Development Levy) can be promoted. Since most large businesses and corporations pay a tax towards the SETA to which they are registered, such funding can enable youth entrepreneurs to undergo industrial training and promote academic-industry collaboration with existing large businesses. In this way, youth entrepreneurs can be provided with valuable industry-specific skills.

Such vocational initiatives currently include 40% classroom training and 60% on-the-job training (also referred to as 'learnerships') when linked to obtaining a full accredited qualification. The regulatory pillar of learnership training and skills development similarly includes tri-party agreements between the youth, educational institutes, and large businesses or corporations. In these kinds of agreements, the corporation pays a skills development levy as tax to the industry-affiliated SETA.

CSI refers to business practices involving programmes that benefit the community, including youth development.[79] At both the mundo- (United Nations) and macrosystem levels (national government), CSI (also referred to as corporate social *responsibility*) can help with youth development and the training of youths in entrepreneurial activities. A business's CSI can encompass a wide variety of operations (e.g., assisting the broader socio-economic environment and/or helping people in the community grow through development programmes).

---

[78] Ibid.
[79] Caramela (2016).

As part of CSI, a business should assess its compliance with ethical and international norms and ensure that all its policies are in alignment. Sometimes, companies communicate these policies to better ensure that local communities benefit from these operations. It should be noted, however, that although these initiatives are usually perceived to be effective, they often lack necessary support and strategic management. The criteria for measuring their success also tend to be unclear and subjective, and one possible reason for companies to claim that they implement CSI programmes is to gain credibility and loyalty in the community, without much further substantiation to such a claim being required.

In case-study research, two South African retail banks were investigated to identify whether employees involved in CSI initiatives were supported by the programmes. These studies showed that the banks in question did not, in fact, support employees through CSI programmes and the programmes were, therefore, not effective. There, thus, needs to be better management of CSI programmes to improve their effectiveness and optimise their value for recipients.[80]

Similarly, work-integrated learning provides youths with the opportunity to learn within an industry. This approach can greatly increase EA within the youth by improving their skills and enabling them to gain experience. Inflexible and restrictive regulatory pillars for youths moving into work-integrated learning can, however, cause barriers. Therefore, there is a need to leave scope for flexibility. For example, the eligibility criteria imposed byeducational institutions when selecting youths for their programmes often do not include corporate representatives in reviewing the selection process. Corporations and large businesses must be more involved in work-integrated learning if they are to make a significant contribution to the entrepreneurial development of youths, address skills shortages, and promote graduate employability.[81]

The importance and effectiveness of educational institutes collaborating with industry to improve work-integrated learning are worth considering, as the investment of resources in this endeavour can learn to provide youths with skills and experiences that make them

---

[80] Penn and Thomas (2017).
[81] Dunn et al. (2016).

more entrepreneurial. Shared resources (e.g., facilities, equipment, and specialist expertise) enable all-round strength. Indeed, various case studies from developed countries show evidence that if major universities are supported by 10,000 companies, there are strong contributions from both universities and businesses. Studies from developing countries, conversely, show weak business contributions to work-integrated learning, which is problematic as youths are not provided with valuable work experience.

Despite the current lack of business contribution to work-integrated learning, there are some positive signs found within, particularly, the engineering sector of South Africa. Specifically, commitment and engagement appear to be higher for the work-integrated learning process when industries are financially invested in the process. South Africa could, thus, greatly improve work-integrated learning progress by partnering with both the community and industry to increase commitment from industry.[82]

Apprenticeships (also referred to as the internship method) are another way to link youths, large businesses, and educational institutes in a formal manner. To activate effective apprenticeships, designated representatives from large businesses and corporations should match interns with mentors who can manage their development and be accountable for internship outcomes. The interns' educational institutes, in turn, should assess these internship programmes to evaluate their effectiveness and ascertain whether tax incentives are providing a worthwhile return to the economy. Such monitoring could also ensure that when companies abuse these programmes, penalties can be enforced to ensure compliance.[83]

A wide-ranging study conducted in South Africa examined more than 20 South African tertiary education institutes and gathered data on whether the current education programmes include internships. This study found that there were positive outcomes for internships for ESE, IEO, and EI.[84]

---

[82] Reinhard et al. (2016).
[83] Naidoo and Hoque (2017).
[84] Botha and Bignotti (2016).

One further example of the importance of a strong partnership between government, industry, and educational institutes is illustrated in a one-year internship programme created by the Department of Science and Technology. Two hundred students from across five provinces studying mechanical, electrical, industrial, and civil engineering were provided with an opportunity to gain work experience in the industry. Along with the benefit to the youths who took part in this programme, the companies also benefitted by gaining an opportunity to boost their competitiveness by the acquisition of new talent, through the youth who completed the one-year internship and then went on to become permanent employees.[85]

Although many educational institutes in South Africa have educational programmes connected to industry, these programmes often lack resources and financial input from industry. Indeed, while institutions that provide work experience opportunities usually also offer to fund students in these programmes, the South African industry must show more commitment when financially investing in a work-experience programme. Since these programmes give students practical experience, youths who complete them tend to be more employable than youths who have not had work exposure.[86] Another possibility would be, therefore, to enable youths is to gain trade accreditation and incubation, facilitated by their educational institute and offered by relevant large businesses or corporations. Such accreditation could provide youths with the necessary knowledge to pursue entrepreneurial activities.[87]

The co-initiation between youth entrepreneurs, educational institutes, and corporations or large businesses is generally viewed through the lenses of two relevant tensions that underscore a systemic paradox, namely: the development tension (the inconsistent relationship between the youth entrepreneurial ecosystem and economic performance), and the policy tension (the unclear role of youth entrepreneurial ecosystem policies in respect to improving and adding value to socio-economic

---

[85] Zondi (2016).
[86] Reinhard et al. (2016).
[87] Melass (2015).

outcomes).[88] Radical social innovation is, therefore, necessary to bridge the current systemic disconnect and enable a future of possibilities for youth entrepreneurs.

3.9 Internationalisation

Internationalisation in Higher Education as a concept and strategic agenda in developing youth entrepreneurs is a relatively new, broad, and varied phenomenon driven by a dynamic combination of political, economic, sociocultural, and academic rationales and stakeholders. Its impact on regions, countries, and institutions varies according to their particular contexts[89] (Fig. 3.11).

One of the key reasons for the significance of internationalisation in Higher Education to support a YES Network is its role in promoting cultural exchange and global understanding. South African universities that embrace internationalisation create an environment that encourages interaction between local and international youth entrepreneurs. This enables the sharing of diverse cultural experiences, languages, and perspectives, enhancing intercultural competence and global awareness among these youth entrepreneurs. Such exposure nurtures open-mindedness, tolerance, and respect for different cultures, preparing youth to thrive in an interconnected and diverse world.[90]

Developing countries like *South Africa need to rethink and reimagine its socio-economic development-orientated problem-solving strategy when responding to developing an enabling environment to maximise the benefits of internationalisation in the context of the 'Knowledge Society' while serving its direct ecosystemic Youth Entrepreneur Support Network, while being part of the global community.*[91] *The Knowledge Society serves to facilitate the process where information translates into resources to enable youth entrepreneurs taking effective actions (it differs from the information society*

---

[88] Lafuente et al. (2018).
[89] De Wit and Altbach (2021).
[90] Hénard et al. (2012).
[91] Kishun (2007).

Fig. 3.11 The SHAPE YES Network for youth entrepreneurs—Internationalisation

that only creates and disseminates raw data). Therefore, translating output into outcomes.[92]

Internationalisation plays a central role in the Future World-of-Work strategy of higher education institutions in South Africa. It aims to 'Africanize' the purposes, functions, and curricula of universities, thereby creating a unique YES Network specifically tailored to the local ecosystem. However, young entrepreneurs require stronger support to

---

[92] Zhao et al. (2021).

establish these essential international relationships, which can contribute to their entrepreneurial journey and potentially facilitate the scaling-up of their initiatives. Traditionally, mobility was a key barrier to youth within the African context in internationalisation, where access to funds to enable mobility played a pivotal role. However, the digital transformation of the 'Knowledge Society' enables youth to access global networks, international funding opportunities, and cutting-edge technologies to support their entrepreneurial actions.[93]

In summary, internationalisation plays a multifaceted role in South African universities and beyond. It facilitates cultural exchange, broadens mental models of youth entrepreneurs, drives innovation and economic development, and elevates global competitiveness. Embracing internationalisation is vital for youth South African universities to provide youth entrepreneurs with an opportunity to remain competitive, foster global citizenship, and contribute to the socio-economic growth of the nation.

3.10 Synthesis

The key constructs outlined in this chapter translate into the different sections of the empirical investigation discussed in the following chapters. Furthermore, the identified key aspects were translated into factors for empirical investigation in each section of the investigation tool. Table 3.3 presents a summary of the youth entrepreneurship nexus.

3.11 Conclusion

This chapter also proposed the theoretical conceptualisation of the SHAPE ecosystem model for effective youth entrepreneurship. In this model, youth entrepreneurs feature as central agents, with their internal and external domain factors either enabling or hindering EA. A systematic literature review identified educational institutes as facilitating agents

---

[93] Altbach and de Wit (2021).

Table 3.3 Summary of the SHAPE youth entrepreneurship ecosystem

Factors	Aspects
Personal barriers in relation to systemic intermediaries (Chapter 2)	External aspects influencing the entrepreneurial personality traits of youth entrepreneurs; entrepreneurship education and training; financial support; collective creative thinking; support from intermediaries for youth entrepreneurs when making decisions in planning a new business; ability to work in teams
Educational institutions	Entrepreneurship training and skills development in higher education; entrepreneurship programmes to increase entrepreneurial self-confidence; support for entrepreneurship programmes in formal and supplementary tuition; entrepreneurial-orientated institutes; the importance of attendance
Governmental agencies	Governmental programmes or municipal support aimed at youth entrepreneurs and/or the youth entrepreneurial ecosystem(s); mentorship to youth entrepreneurs; policies related to entrepreneurship; funding for youth entrepreneurs
Private sector agencies	Growth services offered by private-sector agencies; distribution of information and entrepreneurship news; business development support; mentorship; private sector agencies' role and purpose to develop youth entrepreneurs; different types of private-sector agencies
Communities	Community support to create a culture of youth entrepreneurship; influence on business types; community entrepreneurial attitudes; entrepreneurial opportunities in the community; facilities and infrastructure
SMEs	SMEs' skills transfer and training for youth entrepreneurs; business development support; address high levels of crime; promote high levels of competition
Corporations and large businesses	Social innovation; CSI; corporate skills development and mentorship for youth entrepreneurs; other types of entrepreneurship support; talent recruitment programmes for university graduates
Internationalisation	Internationalisation helps to enhance employability, the quality of employment, or business creation; expanding network partners

in the youth entrepreneurial ecosystem, with emphasis on higher education institutes and especially universities. Findings from the literature also emphasised that there is a current systemic disconnect and lack of frugal social innovation to address wicked grassroots problems, which has created key barriers to the value chain and value creation aimed towards socio-economic development.

Since the microsystem is key for improving systems holistically and runs parallel with heartset, handset, and mindset development, involvement by youths and other role-players in their ecosystem is essential. The systematic literature review presented in this chapter also provided new insights into the role of educational institutes as facilitating agents responsible for co-initiating, co-sensing, co-creating, and co-evolving the youth entrepreneurial ecosystem. A limitation of the review was, however, that there is not much information available regarding the practical co-incorporation of youth entrepreneurs who are not affiliated with an educational institute in the ecosystem. Further research on this inclusivity is, therefore, still needed.

Of further note is that the proposed model is generic and flexible, thereby allowing for location-specific adaptation and movement in creating the architecture of the youth entrepreneurial ecosystem. The theoretical model was implemented in practice at a selected South African university over a period of time, and findings of the practical application are discussed in Chapters 4–8.

This chapter builds on the SHAPE project-supported research supported in part by the National Research Foundation of South Africa (Grant Number: 122002-Shape). These works include: Adelakun and Van der Westhuizen (2021), Awotunde and Van der Westhuizen (2021a), Awotunde and Van der Westhuizen (2021b), Nhleko and van der Westhuizen (2022), Ruba et al. (2021), Van der Westhuizen (2017a), Van der Westhuizen (2017b), Van der Westhuizen (2018a), Van der Westhuizen (2018b), Van der Westhuizen (2019), Van der Westhuizen, (2021).

References

Adelakun, Y., & Van der Westhuizen, T. (2021). Delineating government policies and individual entrepreneurial orientation. *Journal of Sociology and Social Anthropology, 12*(3–4), 106–117. https://doi.org/10.31901/24566764.2021/12.3-4.371

Altbach, P. G., & de Wit, H. (2021). The Boston College Center for international education and the emergence of a field of analysis, 1995–2020. In *Higher education in the next decade* (pp. 326–344). Brill.

Alvedalen, J., & Boschma, R. (2017). A critical review of entrepreneurial ecosystems research: Towards a future research agenda. *European Planning Studies, 25*(6), 887–903.

Audretsch, D. B., Belitski, M., & Cherkas, N. (2021). Entrepreneurial ecosystems in cities: The role of institutions. *PLoS ONE, 16*(3), e0247609.

Awotunde, O. M., & Van der Westhuizen, T. (2021a). Entrepreneurial self-efficacy development: An effective intervention for sustainable student entrepreneurial intentions. *International Journal of Innovation and Sustainable Development, 15*(4), 475–495.

Awotunde, O. M., & Van der Westhuizen, T. (2021b, September). Entrepreneurial self-efficacy and the SHAPE ideation model for university students. In *ECIE 2021 16th European Conference on Innovation and Entrepreneurship Vol 1* (p. 37).

Bagheri, A., & Pihie, Z. A. L. (2011). Entrepreneurial leadership: Towards a model for learning and development. *Human Resource Development International, 14*(4), 447–463.

Bolton, D. L., & Lane, M. D. (2012). Individual entrepreneurial orientation: Further investigation of a measurement instrument. *Academy of Entrepreneurship Journal, 18*(1), 91–98.

Botha, M., & Bignotti, A. (2016). Internships enhancing entrepreneurial intent and self-efficacy: Investigating tertiary-level entrepreneurship education programmes. *Southern African Journal of Entrepreneurship and Small Business Management, 8*(1), 1–15.

Brown, R., & Mason, C. (2017). Looking inside the spiky bits: A critical review and conceptualisation of entrepreneurial ecosystems. *Small Business Economics, 49*(1), 11–30.

Caramela, S. (2016). Understanding what Corporate Social Responsibility (CSR) is, and why it matters. *Imagine Tomorrow*.

Chia, R. (1996). Teaching paradigm shifting in management education: University business schools and the entrepreneurial imagination. *Journal of Management Studies, 33*(4), 409–428.

Chia, R. (2014). From relevance to relevate: How university-based business schools can remain seats of "higher" learning and still contribute effectively to business. *Journal of Management Development, 33*(5), 443–455.

CHIETA (Chemical Industries Education & Training Authority). 2021. *Who are we*. https://www.chieta.org.za/

Crampton, N. (2019). 26 of the richest people in South Africa. *Entrepreneur South Africa*. https://www.entrepreneur.com/article/327556

Danns, D. E., & Danns, G. K. (2019). Financing youth entrepreneurship in a developing country. *Quarterly Review of Business Disciplines, 6*(3), 193–217.

Davey, T., Hannon, P., & Penaluna, A. (2016). Entrepreneurship education and the role of universities in entrepreneurship: Introduction to the special issue. *Industry and Higher Education, 30*(3), 171–182.

De Wit, H., & Altbach, P. G. (2021). Chapter 15 Internationalization in higher education. In *Higher education in the next decade*. Brill. Available From: https://doi.org/10.1163/9789004462717_016. Accessed 13 July 2023.

Dhliwayo, S. (2008). Experiential learning in entrepreneurship education: A prospective model for South African tertiary institutions. *Education and Training, 50*(4), 329–340.

Dominici, G., & Gagnidze, I. (2021). Effectiveness of entrepreneurial universities: Experiences and challenges in digital era (a systemic approach). *Interdisciplinary Description of Complex Systems, 19*(1), 13–30.

DTI. (2017). *Department of small business development: Republic of South Africa*. Retrieved September 15, 2017, from www.dsbd.gov.za

Dunn, L. A., Schier, M. A., Hiller, J. E., & Harding, I. H. (2016). Eligibility requirements for work-integrated learning programs: Exploring the implications of using grade point averages for student participation. *Asia-Pacific Journal of Cooperative Education, 17*(3), 295–308.

EDHE (Entrepreneurship Development in Higher Education). (2021). *Background on the EDHE programme.* https://edhe.co.za/about/

eThekwini Municipality. 2017. *Welcome to the official website of the eThekwini Municipality.* Retrieved December 7, 2017, from www.durban.gov.za/

Feldman, M. A., Francis, J., & Bercovitz, J. (2005). Creating a cluster while building a firm: Entrepreneurs and the formation of industrial clusters. *Regional Studies, 39,* 129–141.

Garavan, T. N., & O'Cinneide, B. (1994). Entrepreneurship education and training programmes: A review and evaluation—Part 1: Literature review of problems associated with entrepreneurship education and training programmes. *Journal of European Industrial Training, 18*(8), 3–12.

Griffin-El, E. W. (2015). Network-based resources for the innovation process of South African micro-entrepreneurs: A conceptual framework. *South African Journal of Business Management, 46*(3), 79–89.

Gupta, A., Dey, A., & Singh, G. (2017). Connecting corporations and communities: Towards a theory of social inclusive open innovation. *Journal of Open Innovation: Technology, Market, and Complexity, 3*(3), 17.

Harrison, R. T., Leitch, C. M., & Chia, R. (2007). Developing paradigmatic awareness in university business schools: The challenge for executive education. *Academy of Management Learning & Education, 6*(3), 332–343.

Hénard, F., Diamond, L., & Roseveare, D. (2012). Approaches to internationalisation and their implications for strategic management and institutional practice. *IMHE Institutional Management in Higher Education, 11*(12), 2013.

Hernández-Chea, R., Mahdad, M., Minh, T. T., & Hjortsø, C. N. (2021). Moving beyond intermediation: How intermediary organizations shape collaboration dynamics in entrepreneurial ecosystems. *Technovation, 108,* 102332.

Isenberg, D. (2011). *The entrepreneurship ecosystem strategy as a new paradigm for economy policy: Principles for cultivating entrepreneurship.* Babson Entrepreneurship Ecosystem Project, Babson College.

Isenberg, D. J. (2010). How to start an entrepreneurial revolution. *Harvard Business Review, 88*(6), 40–50.

Kishun, R. (2007). The internationalisation of higher education in South Africa: Progress and challenges. *Journal of Studies in International Education, 11*(3–4), 455–469.

Lackéus, M. (2015). *Entrepreneurship in education: What, why, when, how.* Background paper. Organisation for Economic Co-operation and Development. https://www.oecd.org/cfe/leed/bgp_entrepreneurship-in-education.pdf

Lafuente, E., Szerb, L., & Ács, Z. J. (2018, November 29). The entrepreneurship paradox: More entrepreneurs are not always good for the economy—The role of the entrepreneurial ecosystem on economic performance in Africa. *Social Science Research Network.* https://papers.ssrn.com/sol3/papers.cfm?abstract_id=3307617

Maas, G. (2015). *Systemic entrepreneurship: Contemporary issues and case studies.* Springer.

Mason, C., & Brown, R. (2014). Entrepreneurial ecosystems and growth-oriented entrepreneurship. Background paper for the Entrepreneurial Ecosystems and Growth Oriented Entrepreneurship Workshop, organised by the OECD LEED Programme and the Dutch Ministry of Economic Affairs, The Hague, Netherlands, November 7, 2013. *Final Report, 30*(1), 77–102.

McIntyre-Mills, J. J. M. F. E. A., Kedibone, G. M., Arko-Achemfuor, A., & Njiro, E. (2014). Participatory approach to education: An action learning approach at the University of South Africa. *Participatory Educational Research, 1*(2), 106–132.

Melass, T. (2015). Feminine touch. *JSE Magazine: The Johannesburg Stock Exchange Quarterly Publication.* Retrieved January 15, 2018, from www.jsemagazine.co.za/smes/feminine-touch/

Mujahid, S., Mubarik, S., & Naghavi, N. (2019). Prioritizing dimensions of entrepreneurial ecosystem: A proposed framework. *Journal of Global Entrepreneurship Research, 9*(1), 1–21.

NAFCOC (National African Federated Chamber of Commerce and Industry). (2021). *Nafcoc's Vision 2023.* https://nafcoc.org.za/vision-2023/

Naidoo, M., & Hoque, M. E. (2017). Reducing youth unemployment beyond the youth wage subsidy: A study of Simtech apprentices. *SA Journal of Human Resource Management, 15*(1), 1–10.

Nel, J. A. (2017). Psychological ownership in corporate South Africa: An ubuntu and social identity perspective. In C. Olckers, L. Van Zyl, & L. Van der Vaart (Eds.), *Theoretical orientations and practical applications of psychological ownership.* Springer.

Nhleko, Y., & van der Westhuizen, T. (2022). The role of higher education institutions in introducing entrepreneurship education to meet the demands of industry 4.0. *Academy of Entrepreneurship Journal, 28*(1), 1–23.

Nonaka, I., Chia, R., Holt, R., & Peltokorpi, V. (2014). Wisdom, management and organization. *Management Learning, 45*(4), 365–376.

NYDA (National Youth Development Agency). (2021). *What is NYDA? Who are we?* http://www.nyda.gov.za/About-Us/What-is-NYDA

Oyugi, J. (2014). Effectiveness of the methods of teaching entrepreneurship courses to developing self-efficacy and intention among university students in Uganda. *International Journal of Social Sciences and Entrepreneurship, 1*(11), 491–513.

Parsons, T. (1951). *The social system.* The Free Press.

Paton, S., Chia, R., & Burt, G. (2014). Relevance or 'relevate'? How university business schools can add value through reflexively learning from strategic partnerships with business. *Management Learning, 45*(3), 267–288.

Penn, C., & Thomas, P. H. (2017). Bank employees' engagement in corporate social responsibility initiatives at a South African retail bank. *Acta Commercii, 17*(1), 1–10.

Pillay, K. (2015a, July 6). Learning and the illusion of solid and separate things: Troublesome knowledge and the curriculum. In *Edge Hill University Centre for Learning and Teaching University Learning and Teaching Day Conference.*

Pillay, K. (2015b, September 10–12). Unfolding wisdom: Theory U and the magic of nondual perception. In *Proceedings of the SAIMS 29th Annual Conference.*

Preedy, S., Jones, P., Maas, G., & Duckett, H. (2020). Examining the perceived value of extracurricular enterprise activities in relation to entrepreneurial learning processes. *Journal of Small Business and Enterprise Development, 27*(7), 1085–1105.

Rahimi, H., Amini, M., & Jahanbani, F. (2015). The place of entrepreneurial curriculum components in higher education. *International Journal of Academic Research in Business and Social Sciences, 5*(9), 263–279.

Reinhard, K., Pogrzeba, A., Townsend, R., & Pop, C. A. (2016). A comparative study of cooperative education and work-integrated learning in Germany, South Africa, and Namibia. *Asia-Pacific Journal of Cooperative Education, 17*(3), 249–263.

Remenyi, D., Grant, K. A., & Singh, S. (2019). *The University of the Future.* Academic Publishing International (ACPIL).

Röpke, J. (1998). *The entrepreneurial university: Innovation, academic knowledge creation and regional development in a globalized economy.* Philipps-Universitat.

Ruba, R. M., Van der Westhuizen, T., & Chiloane-Tsoka, G. E. (2021). Influence of entrepreneurial orientation on organisational performance: Evidence from Congolese Higher Education Institutions. *Journal of Contemporary Management, 18*(1), 243–269.

SA Institute for Entrepreneurship. (2021). *About us: Who are we?* http://www.entrepreneurship.co.za/contents/who-are-we/#OurVision

SACCI (South African Chamber of Commerce and Industry). (2021). *The voice of business.* https://sacci.org.za/

Sahay, A., & Nirjar, A. (2006). *Entrepreneurship: Education, research and practice.* Excel Books.

Sahay, A., & Nirjar, A. (2012). *Entrepreneurship: Education, research and practice.* Excel Books.

Scharmer, C. O. (2009). *Theory U: Learning from the future as it emerges.* Berrett-Koehler Publishers.

Scharmer, C. O. (2011). *Leading the future as it emerges* [MA Thesis]. Society of Organizational Learning, University of Cambridge.

Scharmer, C. O., & Käufer, K. (2013). *Leading from the emerging future: From ego-system to eco-system economies.* Berrett-Koehler Publishers.

SEFA (Small Enterprise Finance Agency). (2021). *About SEFA: Who are we.* https://www.sefa.org.za/about/history

Seta's South Africa. (2021). *About SETA South Africa: What is a SETA?* https://seta-southafrica.com/

Shirokova, G., Tsukanova, T., & Morris, M. (2013). The moderating role of national culture in the relationship between university offerings and students' start-up activities: Embeddedness perspective. *European Journal of International Management, 4*, 2–29.

Van der Westhuizen, T. (2016). *Developing Individual entrepreneurial orientation: A systemic approach through the lens of Theory U* [PhD thesis]. UKZN.

Van der Westhuizen, T. (2017a). The use of Theory U and individual entrepreneurial orientation to increase low youth entrepreneurship in South Africa. *Journal of Contemporary Management, 14*, 531–553.

Van der Westhuizen, T. (2017b). A systemic approach towards responsible and sustainable economic development: Entrepreneurship, systems theory and socio-economic momentum. In Z. Fields (Ed.), *Collective creativity for responsible and sustainable business practice.* IGI Global.

Van der Westhuizen, T. (2018a). The SHAPE project: Shifting hope, activating potential entrepreneurship. In D. Remenyi & D. A. Grant (Eds), *Incubators for Young entrepreneurs—20 case histories.* ACPIL.

Van der Westhuizen, T. (2018b). *Open heart, open mind and open will in transformative individual entrepreneurial orientation pedagogies* (pp. 443–448). Academic Conferences and Publishing International Limited.

Van der Westhuizen, T. (2019). Action! Methods to develop entrepreneurship. In *18th European Conference on Research Methodology for Business and Management Studies* (pp. 331–337).

Van der Westhuizen, T. (2021). Applying Theory U through shape to develop student's individual entrepreneurial orientation in a university eco-system. In O. Gunnlaugson & W. Brendel (Eds.), *Advances in pre-sensing Volume III: Collective approaches, in Theory U, Trifoss Business Press* (pp. 395–435).

Van der Westhuizen, T. (2022). *Effective youth entrepreneurship.* Sunbonani. https://omp.sunbonani.co.za/index.php/sunbonani/catalog/book/6

Vuk'uzenzele. (2021). *Support for youth.* https://www.vukuzenzele.gov.za/support-youth

Xavier, S., Kelley, D., Kew, J., Herrington, M., & Vorderwülbecke, A. (2013). *Global Entrepreneurship Monitor (GEM) 2012 Global Report.* GERA (Global Entrepreneurship Research Association), London Business School. https://www.gemconsortium.org/file/open?fileId=48545

Yeo, R. K., & Marquardt, M. J. (2015). (Re)interpreting action, learning, and experience: Integrating action learning and experiential learning for HRD. *Human Resource Development Quarterly, 26*(1), 81–107.

Zhao, Y., Llorente, A. M. P., & Gómez, M. C. S. (2021). Digital competence in higher education research: A systematic literature review. *Computers & Education, 168,* 104212.

Zondi, B. (2016). Industry internships gain momentum. *CSIR Science Scope, 9*(1), 104–105.

Open Access This chapter is licensed under the terms of the Creative Commons Attribution 4.0 International License (http://creativecommons.org/licenses/by/4.0/), which permits use, sharing, adaptation, distribution and reproduction in any medium or format, as long as you give appropriate credit to the original author(s) and the source, provide a link to the Creative Commons license and indicate if changes were made.

The images or other third party material in this chapter are included in the chapter's Creative Commons license, unless indicated otherwise in a credit line to the material. If material is not included in the chapter's Creative Commons license and your intended use is not permitted by statutory regulation or exceeds the permitted use, you will need to obtain permission directly from the copyright holder.

Part II

The SHAPE Lab: Tools for Enabling Youth Entrepreneurship

4

Toolkit—Tools to Shift Hope and Activate Potential Entrepreneurship

4.1 Introduction

This chapter provides practical tools and examples that youth entrepreneurs can apply to boost their entrepreneurial heartset, mindset, and handset and help bring their entrepreneurial dreams to life. It shares the entrepreneurial dream and outlines entrepreneurship as a career.

4.2 Our dream

Do we have a dream that sees us as the masters of our destiny? Will we be the generation that transforms the African economy? Are we dreaming a dream that allows us to take control of our finances and supply goods and services to our community and others on our continent? When we have such thoughts, we share the entrepreneurial dream.

The entrepreneurial dream is simply the desire and ability to change the world around us into a place where individuals and communities grow and prosper.

To bring our dream into action: we shift our hope and activate our potential through entrepreneurship (Fig. 4.1).

Fig. 4.1 Entrepreneurial dream

The entrepreneurial dream is a journey that encourages its participants to (a) find their purpose, life-calling, or passion; (b) analyse their attitudes to work and life in general; (c) analyse their skills; and (d) translate their ideas into action.[1]

---

[1] Steenberg (2017).

While many entrepreneurs begin their dreams with a strong desire to make it come true, we need to use our abilities to get the business idea off the ground. Hence the action-based nature of our theme: SHAPE—Shifting Hope, Activating Potential Entrepreneurship.

Otto Scharmer, whose ideas have been an important inspiration for this book, argues that our capacity to pay attention 'co-shapes' the world.[2] What stops us from giving our full attention to situations we encounter (including business situations) is that we are not fully aware of the 'interior places' within ourselves that our attention and actions spring from. Scharmer calls this lack of awareness our 'blind spot'. He sheds light on this blind spot in business leadership and suggests processes, principles, and practices that will help change-makers to eliminate the blind spot. His ideas help to identify some of the deep personal factors that we can draw on for the guidance, energies, and inspiration that will help propel us along the path of entrepreneurship. This book brings together some of these ideas and presents what we call the 'SHAPE entrepreneurial discovery'.

All the essential processes that an entrepreneur goes through involve collaboration: A collaboration with other people, but also, more deeply, collaboration with one's own deeper self. So, we get (as shown in Fig. 4.2) co-initiating, co-sensing, co-inspiring, co-creating, and co-evolving.[3] This builds on the Theory U approach discussed earlier in the book (Chapter 3).

4.3 Co-initiating: Uncovering our Intent

Entrepreneurial attitude starts with that profound wish that we all must make a success of our lives. This 'heartset' leads to 'mindset' (really putting our mind to the issues, figuring out all the issues) and then acting on what we know and doing the actual work needed, which we will call

---

[2] Scharmer and Käufer (2013).
[3] Scharmer and Käufer (2013).

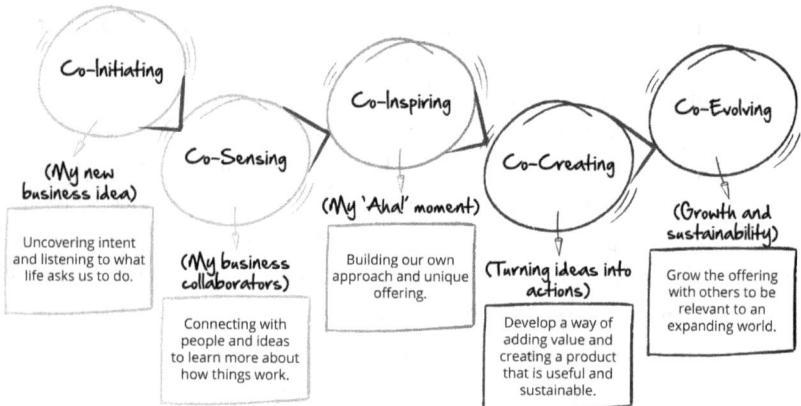

Fig. 4.2 The SHAPE major entrepreneurial discovery processes (a Theory U approach) (*Source* Van der Westhuizen and Steenberg, 2022)

Fig. 4.3 Basic SHAPE entrepreneurial ability model (*Source* Van der Westhuizen, 2022)

the entrepreneurial 'handset'. These three stages form the basic SHAPE Entrepreneurial Ability Model (Fig. 4.3).

These stages relate to processes through which we can shift our entrepreneurial hope and activate our entrepreneurial abilities; they usually involve more than just the entrepreneur working alone. Most successful entrepreneurs draw important support from groups of people that they have built around them. They also need to have potential customers, and they also need a conducive working environment,

Fig. 4.4 Life, purpose, and passion

called a business 'ecosystem', which includes suppliers, distributors, customers, competitors, government agencies, and so on. All of these will be involved in the delivery of the entrepreneur's product or service (Fig. 4.4).

4.4 Finding a Life Purpose and Passion

Entrepreneurship is both a journey and a destination: As soon as we think we have arrived, we discover a new beginning that brings new opportunities every day.

However, it is not easy to decide what our life purpose is when we do not understand all the options and consequences of our choices. It seems that to be successful today, we need to have an idea that is different from what is happening around us. It also seems that there is always a 'Bigger Picture'—a better hustle and another choice that changes the possibilities. Many would-be entrepreneurs never take the necessary action because there always seems to be a better idea than the one they are working with now. The Bigger Picture describes the way that human beings—individually and collectively—fit into a world that includes family, friends, community, city, region, a country, and surrounding countries.[4]

While for us as entrepreneurs, there is a Bigger Picture; our potential customers have had the same needs for a long time. What are the things that people spend money on? There is a business producing those things, and the possibility is always open for us to start supplying those services to the potential customers around us.

When our business connects with the needs of people in the big world, and we draw on the support of the entrepreneurial ecosystem, we start 'co-creating' towards a common goal that contributes to the achievement of the objectives of sustainable socio-economic development. The aim of socio-economic development is to harmonise the three pillars of sustainable development: economic development, protection of the environment, and social upliftment. It does this by promoting a prosperous, innovative, knowledge-rich, competitive, and eco-efficient economy that provides high standards of living and high-quality employment opportunities.

The individual inner journey of an entrepreneur involves deep self-reflection on their life purpose and passion. The entrepreneur's reflective journey often follows the five stages of the SHAPE diagram shown in Fig. 4.2: Co-initiating, co-sensing, co-inspiring, co-creating, and co-evolving. Sharing a business idea with others, and discovering that idea within our own ecosystem, is more achievable when we, as entrepreneurs, have self-direction. These five processes guide us to better apply self-leadership and empower ourselves first from within before seeking to co-develop within our ecosystem.

After our self-reflection, we might find that we are well on the journey already and that our next stage is much closer to where we need to be.

As we begin to understand the social and economic problems surrounding us—the Bigger Picture—we can begin to apply our skills and knowledge gained through teaching, learning, and first-hand experiences to start generating solutions to real-world problems. When we solve problems for people, this is the first practical step to creating a product. Understanding the Bigger Picture points us in the direction of

---

[4] Van Zomeren and Dovidio (2017).

the skills and knowledge that we need to solve real-world problems and towards the opportunities out there for us to become entrepreneurial.[5]

With more exposure and experience, we can develop better solutions.[6] We can enhance our exposure and experience in many ways: By travelling to other towns or cities, other provinces or countries; participating in student exchange programmes; reading up on ways that other people do things; visiting companies (they often arrange tours for students or the public); visiting the local municipality's business support unit, visiting the local chamber of commerce; and speaking to role models, for example, our parents or successful family members, and to existing business owners.

People often start out with a specific interest and, as they grow in knowledge and experience, they may change direction a few times through exposure to new opportunities and through meeting new people.[7] Many successful entrepreneurs changed their industry or focus area completely while undergoing 'growing pains' as individuals and businesspeople.

To find our life's calling, we need to reflect on four areas: the things we love, the things we are good at, what the world needs, and what we can get paid to do.[8] This reflection informs our passion, vision, mission, and vocation.

4.5 Competencies and Abilities for Entrepreneurs

The SHAPE Model for Entrepreneurial Competencies captures the abilities needed by an entrepreneur.

Anyone can develop these competencies over time by owning a business. A story is told that an entrepreneur was shown a model, like the competency model shown in Fig. 4.5, and was asked if it was correct.

---

[5] Steenberg (2017), Van der Westhuizen (2016).
[6] Schwartz and Bar-El (2015).
[7] Steenberg (2017).
[8] Steenberg (2017).

She confirmed that each of these things is necessary to run a business and that she did, in fact, have these competencies. The researcher then asked her how she got these skills, and she answered, 'through osmosis'—the physical process by which something is acquired by absorption, independent of action. The researcher asked her which skills she had when she started her business. She answered that she needed to make money to stay alive (this was her attitude). The rest she learnt over time by being in business. The moral of this story is that we will learn about all aspects of running a business while we are running the business, and we do not have to get stuck on knowing everything about business before we start. The skills that we do not have, we can get from others through cooperation or employment; or by listening to others talk about them, or by reading.

The most important skills are having an entrepreneurial spirit and developing an entrepreneurial attitude. We then move from the heartset to the mindset and the handset of the SHAPE journey.

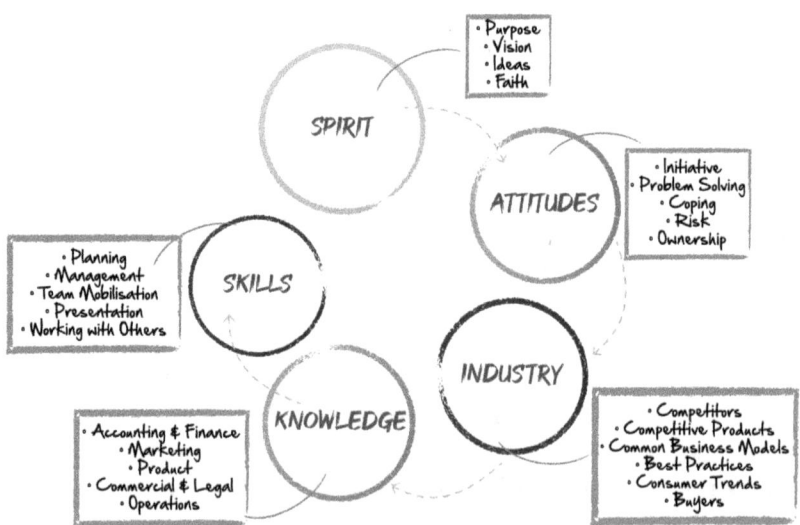

Fig. 4.5 The SHAPE model for entrepreneurial competencies (*Source* Steenberg and van der Westhuizen, 2022)

4.6 Introspection: Thinking About Hopes and Dreams

Introspection means self-examination, analysing yourself, looking at your personality and actions, and considering your motivations. An example of introspection is when you meditate to try to understand your feelings. An aspect of the entrepreneurial mindset is determination and self-leadership to sustain the initial business dream.

Our first question then is: Why do we want to start a business? This question can be very important to determine the type of business we should start.

If we only want to make some extra money, maybe we should start something 'on the side', along with what we are already doing. Or, perhaps we are looking for more freedom, not having a 'boss looking over our shoulder' all the time. If this is the case, it may be time to leave our eight-to-five job to start something new, or we could possibly do better by asking for a raise or getting a better job (Fig. 4.6).

If we want to do something in the community, maybe joining or starting an NGO (non-governmental organisation) or NPO (non-profit organisation) could be a solution.

Fig. 4.6 Entrepreneurial hopes and dreams

Once we have our reason for starting a business, we ought to consider what skills we possess to start and run that business.

Table 4.1 shows some topics that we might reflect on before starting out.

We need to be brutally honest with ourselves when thinking about these issues because the decision to start our own business will have an enormous impact on our lives. We need to know that we are doing what we really want to do.

Table 4.1 Topics for reflection before starting out

Toolbox

01 Our skills and abilities, and how we have exercised these skills up to now

02 Our skills and abilities – the things that other people tell us we're good at

03 How long can we survive without earning an income – helps us decide whether we should stick to our current day-job (if any), and how long it will take before our ideas start to make money

04 Start-up capital required – related to how much money we have in our savings and how long this will keep us going while the business starts up

05 Be ready to put in the 'hard yards' – be willing to make short-term sacrifices for longer-term rewards

06 Our life's 'passion' and calling – these are the things that excite us and get us going at the start of the day

07 Our financial resources – determines how big we can start and whether we need to look beyond our savings for start-up finance

08 Plan B if our ideas fail – helps us to think through the potential obstacles and pitfalls, to plan and expect what could go wrong

09 Our idea and vision for the type of lifestyle we want to lead – corporate executive or running our own show?

4.6.1 The SHAPE process of discovering our business idea

Figure 4.7 shows how the SHAPE Start-up 'ENTREVOLUTION' Process can be applied in discovering our business idea.

'ENTREVOLUTION'

The SHAPE Start-up 'Entrevolution' Process outlines the typical process of moving from being a person with no EI to creating a business that's moving out of the start-up phase.

As with most careers, no one is 'born' as an entrepreneur and simply starts running a business. We become aware of the potential to be an entrepreneur through many different influences. It may come from discovering our passion, listening to the stories of successful people, or questioning why something is happening in our life.

When looking at people's follow-through on their business intentions, it was found that only 50% of people who have an intention to start a business will do something about it.[9] In Fig. 4.8, the outer circles show what factors influence their big decision.

To move from intending to start a business to doing it; four major factors come into the picture:

1. We need to want to start a business ('own attitude'). The biggest supporter or criticiser or motivator or deal-closer or inspiration or smack-down when one is an entrepreneur is oneself. Our attitudes, beliefs, and self-motivation will be the driver of action on business passions and will bring ideas to life.
2. The five people closest to us will be required to support our idea ('attitude of those around us').

---

[9] See Ajzen (1991).

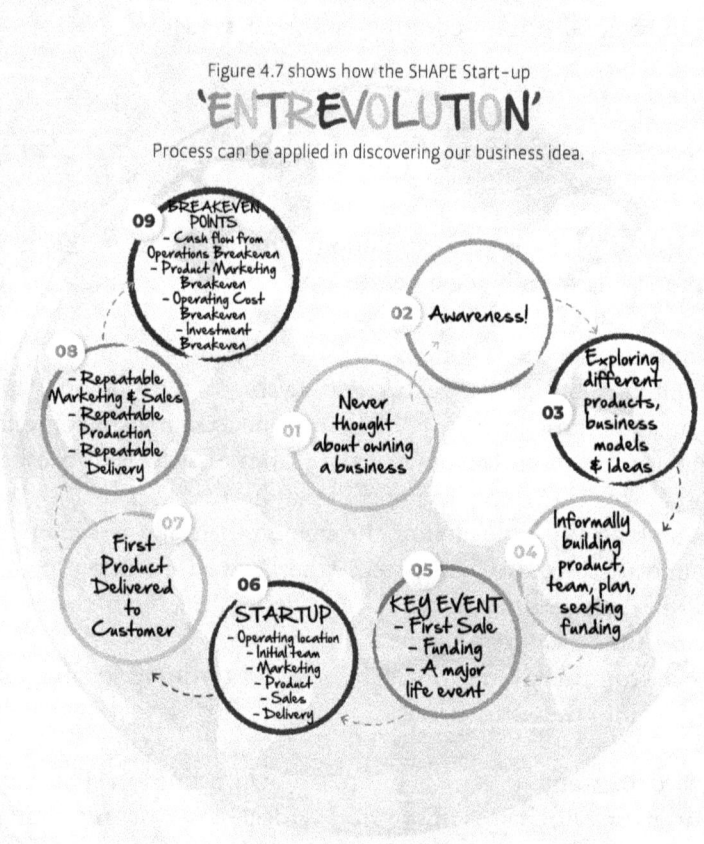

Fig. 4.7 The SHAPE start-up 'Entrevolution' process (*Source* Steenberg & van der Westhuizen, 2022)

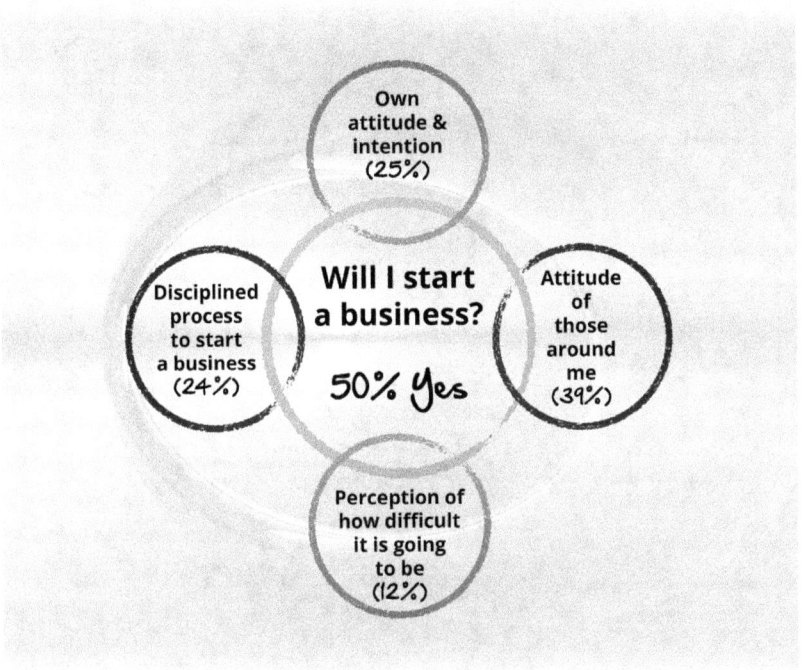

Fig. 4.8 SHAPE intention influence factors (*Source* Steenberg & van der Westhuizen, 2022)

3. We must decide whether we believe it will be difficult to do ('planned behaviour construct').
4. We need to follow a structured process to start our business.

Entrepreneurs come in all shapes and sizes.[10] They come from different backgrounds and age groups, and they all have their own different experiences and skillsets. The SHAPE Self-Assessment Tool on Entrepreneurial Attitudes, as set out in Table 4.2, is a useful tool for helping to 'SHAPE' ourselves and doing self-reflection to improve our self-leadership abilities.

---

[10] Ngwenya (2014).

Table 4.2 SHAPE Self-assessment tool on entrepreneurial attitudes

THE ENTREPRENEUR'S SELF-CONFIDENCE TAKES CARE OF ANY DOUBTS THEY MAY HAVE	DESCRIPTOR	10 = TOTALLY ME 0 = NOT ME AT ALL
CURIOUS — We know how to do things.	Entrepreneurs like to know how things work. They spend time investigating the unknown.	
IMAGINATIVE — We can see how it can work.	Entrepreneurs are creative. They imagine solutions to problems. This prompts them to generate new ideas and create new products.	
PERSISTENT — We do not give up, even when everyone pushes us to abandon the idea.	True entrepreneurs face up to bureaucracy; they make mistakes, accept criticism, and deal with money, family or stress problems. But they still stick to their dreams of seeing the venture succeed.	
GOAL SETTING — We always work out what to do next	Entrepreneurs are motivated by the excitement of starting a new business and watching it grow. Once achieved, they seek out new goals or ventures to try.	
HARDWORKING — We have lots of energy and can push ourselves	Entrepreneurs need a lot of energy to see a venture start and succeed. Yet, they are not discouraged by the long hours needed to achieve their goal.	
SELF-CONFIDENT	We believe in ourselves and have people around us that support us.	
FLEXIBLE — We move fast	Entrepreneurs need to be flexible in order to adapt to changing trends, markets, technologies, rules and economic environments.	
WORKS WELL WITH OTHERS — We mobilise others, build trust, inspire others.	Entrepreneurs must be able to manage and motivate others; they love learning from others and from experience.	
INDEPENDENT — We are independent of others	We believe in ourselves and have people around us that support us.	

The table lists some of the most important entrepreneurial qualities. We do not all have all of these qualities, or we may not have had the opportunity to show some of these qualities. But most of them are important for someone who hopes to start a business. In the last column, rate yourself from 0 (Not me at all!) to 10 (Totally me!).

Did you score between 70 and 100? If this is you, then you have only a few areas to work on. Did you score less than 70? You may want to reflect on the areas you marked less than five and think about how you can surround yourself with people to support you in bringing these aspects into your business.

4.7 Supporting our Entrepreneurial Dream—The Five People Around Us

Research has suggested that the five people closest to us strongly influence our chance of entrepreneurial success. The people who give us advice and whom we surround ourselves with inspire us with ideas. They move us to action by holding us accountable, organising us into structured action, helping with the work that needs to be done, and promoting our message (Fig 4.9).

If we want to change our lives, we need to change whom we take advice from and look carefully at our role in our own scheme. Are we being our own best promoters? Do we do the required work while also organising everything? Who do we look towards for ideas and to push us into action? As entrepreneurs, we need to be ready to play these roles for ourselves.

4.8 Entrepreneurship is a Career

When someone starts a business, they are deciding to develop a career path for themselves.

Just imagine for a moment that we decide to attend our class's twentieth reunion. What will we tell our friends from high school who have not seen us for twenty years? Will we tell them about a life of adventure

Fig. 4.9 Five people around you (*Source* Steenberg & van der Westhuizen, 2022)

in which we tried various things, succeeded, and failed, until one day we figured it all out and made millions? Or are we going to tell them a story of not having failed because we never really tried anything new?

Everyone is good at something, and we can use that knowledge and skill within ourselves to help others. Not everybody is an entrepreneur, of course, but if we are, it may be our greatest asset. So, be all we can be and change the world around us. Let us 'Shift Hope and Activate Potential Entrepreneurship'!

We may ask: What does the life of an entrepreneur offer us that our day job does not?

This is perhaps an answer to that question:

- It increases our skillset much faster (entrepreneurs can escape the corporate challenges that slow down personal and skills progression).

- It offers personal development (a good platform for our self-development and can also be for the world at large).
- We see our vigorous work changing the lives of others (our offering gets to change the lives of the people who consume it).
- There is the possibility of unlimited income (as entrepreneurs, our income is related to our efforts and the success of our business, meaning the harder we work, the higher our income will be).

4.9 Conclusion

This chapter has outlined the requirements shaped by an attitude and desire to succeed in the world of work that points to an entrepreneurial mindset. This is a process of 'uncovering intent and listening to what life asks us to do'. Entrepreneurs are not born; they are made, moulded by an environment they have, in part, created for themselves. The chapter helps us think about whether we are journeying down the right path to entrepreneurship, and it then gives us tools to help us decide on the capabilities and attitudes that we need to develop if we are going to be successful as entrepreneurs.

References

Ajzen, I. (1991). The theory of planned behavior. *Organizational Behavior and Human Decision Processes, 50*(2), 179–211.

Ngwenya, L. K. (2014, March 10). My entrepreneurship. *University of Johannesburg*. https://www.slideshare.net/KWANDANGWENYA/my-entrepreneurship. Retrieved 4 August 2020.

Scharmer, C. O., & Käufer, K. (2013). *Leading from the emerging future: From ego-system to eco-system economies*. Berrett-Koehler Publishers.

Schwartz, D., & Bar-El, R. (2015). The role of a local industry association as a catalyst for building an innovation ecosystem: An experiment in the state of Ceara in Brazil. *Innovation, 17*(3), 383–399.

Steenberg, R. (2017). The Entrepreneurial spirit—Towards an education model for entrepreneurial success in South African entrepreneurs. PhD thesis. Georgetown, Texila American University in association with the University of Central Nicaragua.

Van der Westhuizen, T. (2016). Developing individual entrepreneurial orientation: A systemic approach through the lens of Theory U. PhD thesis, UKZN.

Van der Westhuizen, T. (2022). *Effective youth entrepreneurship*. Sunbonani. Available at: https://omp.sunbonani.co.za/index.php/sunbonani/catalog/book/6

Van Zomeren, M., & Dovidio, J. F. (2017). Human essence in conclusion: Why psychology needs a bigger picture and some suggestions on how to get there. In M. Van Zomeren & J. F. Dovidio (eds). *The Oxford handbook of the human essence*. Oxford University Press.

Open Access This chapter is licensed under the terms of the Creative Commons Attribution 4.0 International License (http://creativecommons.org/licenses/by/4.0/), which permits use, sharing, adaptation, distribution and reproduction in any medium or format, as long as you give appropriate credit to the original author(s) and the source, provide a link to the Creative Commons license and indicate if changes were made.

The images or other third party material in this chapter are included in the chapter's Creative Commons license, unless indicated otherwise in a credit line to the material. If material is not included in the chapter's Creative Commons license and your intended use is not permitted by statutory regulation or exceeds the permitted use, you will need to obtain permission directly from the copyright holder.

5

Toolkit—Enabling Tools for Entrepreneurship in South Africa

5.1 Introduction

Entrepreneurship is an increasingly important factor in the well-being of individuals and society.

Entrepreneurship is a way to tackle head-on the constantly changing business environment of the twenty-first century: building sustainable development, supporting the economic growth of countries, creating new job opportunities for young graduates, and promoting societal well-being in general.

Entrepreneurship and business creation are increasingly important alternatives in many countries for young people facing a labour market with double-digit unemployment rates. Supporting the future of business in developing countries requires sustainable businesses that are innovation driven. One way to do this is through co-sensing.

Co-sensing entails observing—Observe! Observe! Connect with different people and different places to get a sense of the overall ecosystem and discover mutual opportunities for business development.

'Co-sensing' is about connecting with people and ideas to learn more about how things work. This chapter looks at building a business model that will show us what our business could be and do. In doing this, we will look at where opportunities could be located.

5.2 Inspired Action

People from every walk of life take up the challenge of starting a business and building a successful future. The future of South Africa—and all of Africa—depends on the ability of young people to shape our future economies by harnessing the forces of the Entrepreneurial Revolution—the 'Entrevolution'—as it came to be called at the Entrepreneurship Development in Higher Education (EDHE) Lekgotla held in Durban in June 2019, where some of the 'movers and shakers' told their stories of business start-ups.

5.3 Opportunities

When we think about starting our business, we should ask ourselves four questions:

1. Which sector or sectors are we interested in?
2. How does this sector supply services to other sectors?
3. Which sectors supply the sector that we are interested in?
4. How can we use what we are currently learning (our current knowledge and skills) to enter this sector?

5.3.1 Economic Sectors in South Africa

In any country, the businesses that sustain the economy can be sorted into different sets of sectors or industries. Whatever business a new entrepreneur starts up will fall into one of these categories, as illustrated in Fig. 5.1.

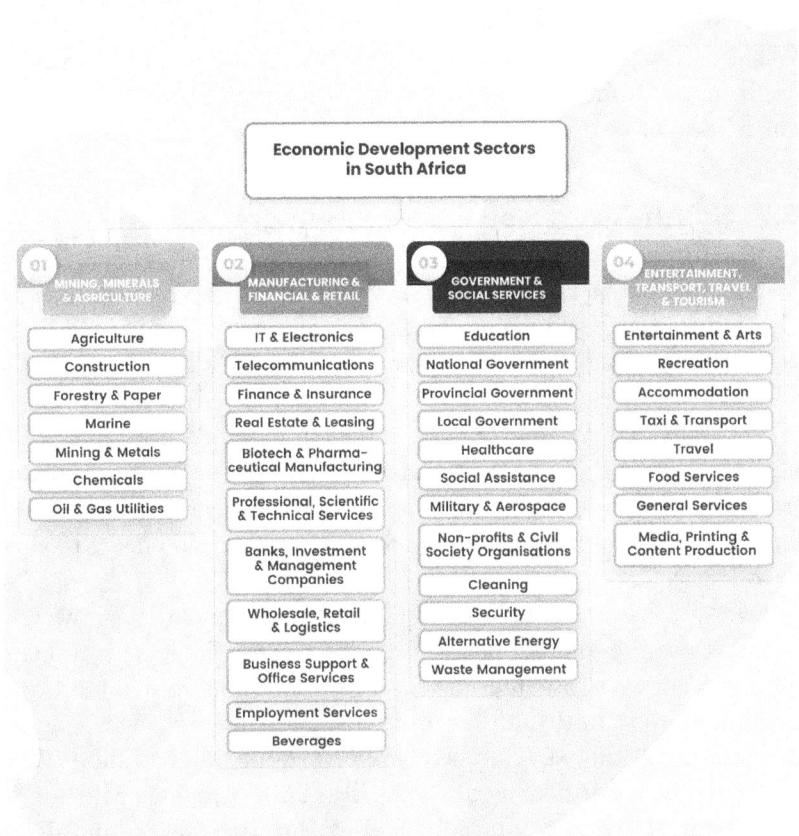

Fig. 5.1 Economic development sectors in the South African economy (Adapted for South African indexing from the North American Industry Classification System)

Understanding the sector that our business fits into will make it easier to identify the people we need to work with or collaborate with or who can give us the most useful support.

Table 5.1, which shows business turnover by industry, can help us identify opportunities in the economic sectors where there may be a niche market or evidence of potential profits that could be made.

5.3.2 South Africa Needs Entrepreneurs

The unemployment rate among the youth in South Africa is staggeringly high. The official unemployment rate among youths (15–34 years) was 46,3% in Quarter 1 2021. The rate was 9.3% among university graduates.

This means that two out of every three job seekers cannot find work, not even counting the people who have simply given up looking. In addition, many people have jobs that do not pay well, and there is much potential in the South African economy for more entrepreneurs to enter the workspace.

One of the first places to look is in 'import replacement'. Can we start a business making and supplying a product or service currently being imported from overseas? In doing so, we will not only fulfil a local need but also help to stem the outflow of valuable foreign exchange.

In South Africa, we currently import about R1.3 trillion (US$ 88,037 million) worth of goods annually. This is mainly paid for by the demanding work of our miners and through the export of our natural resources. It is time that we started asking ourselves why we are not producing more products for the African continent, instead of making money for international companies who seem to understand our customer needs better than we do.

In the textile industry, for example, the country's protracted struggle with low economic growth and falling incomes, recently exacerbated by the coronavirus outbreak and national lockdown, have restrained consumer spending. In the textile manufacturing sector, production and employment have stagnated, and many producers are uncompetitive relative to the cheap Asian imports.

Table 5.1 Business turnover (income) by industry sector (2019) (*Source* Statistics SA [2020])

ECONOMIC SECTOR	NUMBER OF BUSINESSES	TURNOVER (Rm)	CONTRIBUTION (%)
Forestry and fishing	1 437	41 416	0.3
Mining and quarrying	2 824	817 503	7.1
Manufacturing	49 776	2 960 996	27.3
Electricity, gas and water supply	1 451	286 770	2.4
Construction	39 108	504 870	4.6
Trade	101 660	3 917 970	36.5
Transport, storage and communication	16 748	951 558	8.6
Financial services and real estate	102 751	1 244 364	10.2
Community, social and personal services	28 821	303 664	2.9
Total / Average	344 576	11 057 842	100

5.3.3 We Can Succeed as Well

As shown in Table 5.1, there were 344,576 businesses in South Africa in 2019, and the owners of these businesses—over time—do much better than the average employee. We, too, can succeed in our own business.

As a prospective start-up, it is important to look at the businesses around us and ask ourselves, can we do something similar? Can we do it better?

While it is true that we cannot go blindly into setting up a business without some understanding of how a business works, it is still perfectly possible for anyone with sufficient common sense to run their own business. Starting and running a business can be a tremendously rewarding experience.

5.3.4 Addressing a Niche

Addressing a niche—a gap—is all about the ability to identify opportunities, the willingness to take risks, and being able to innovate. There are plenty of stories of entrepreneurs who started small businesses during their schooldays by selling basic products (snacks, stationery, t-shirts, homemade jewellery, cooked meals, etc.) to other school kids or their parents. The same is true of people who started businesses at their universities and colleges or even workplaces. If we can find things that people need, we can address a niche in a market.

Many of these small businesses survive, and their founders go on to develop the skills that help them serve larger customer segments and bigger markets. Indeed, some of the biggest businesses were started when their founders were on campus: Google, Microsoft, and Facebook, which were all begun by student entrepreneurs. In South Africa, Internet Solutions is another good example. Students created these ideas while they were at university and transformed them from humble beginnings into mega-corporations known all around the world.

The skills that we need to run a small business, which could just be selling cold drinks from a cooler box or selling advertising by developing a following on YouTube, are the same skills needed to run a large multinational corporation. All businesses are made up of processes that include managing suppliers, getting customers, and delivering a quality product. When we put these processes together to meet a need, we are on our way to running a business (Fig. 5.2).

'Laptop-preneurs' are creating an 'Entrevolution' in the way that new businesses start-up. Building a business from your cell phone is a perfectly workable possibility; these days, you can do just about everything on a smartphone. But despite the apps and great technologies, we need a little bit more than a cell phone to start and run a good business.

A cell phone can be used to:

- Buy products from various local and international suppliers
- Market those products to other people
- Organise payments; and
- Arrange the delivery of products.

Fig. 5.2 Digital ecosystem for 'laptop-preneurs' (*Source* Van der Westhuizen, 2022)

A tech-savvy entrepreneur might need nothing more than just their smartphone and the right apps to operate an entire business, which could be an online business or traditionally office-based.

5.3.5 What About Exporting?

Going beyond our own backyard: A way of harnessing potential markets is to sell our unique products to foreign markets. South Africa is known for its precious metals, but we are also gaining a share in other areas. When we develop a product that can be exported, we can earn money that makes our country wealthier by supporting our balance of payments. There is a massive market for South African goods in other African countries (Table 5.2).

5.3.6 What Are We Importing?

We also import many goods that can—and should—be produced locally. Importing these items may be an ideal market to enter.

Table 5.3 shows total South African imports from all foreign markets (2019).

The combined BRICS countries (Brazil, Russia, India, China, and South Africa) need to create a million businesses annually in the years to come, each employing more than five people, to sustain the rate at which jobs need to be created. We all need to think seriously about running our businesses and using the skills that we have developed to find workable markets and grow the economy of South Africa in a global context. Each of the markets we currently import from is a major potential market for locally manufactured goods.

Table 5.2 Total South African exports to all foreign markets (2019) (*Source* Wits, 2019)

PRODUCT GROUP: EXPORTS	EXPORT PRODUCT SHARE (%)
Intermediate goods	34.3
Raw materials	28.84
Consumer goods	22.45
Stone & glass	17.28
Minerals	15.21
Capital goods	14.13
Transportation	13.64
Metals	11
Fuels	9.82
Machinery & electrical	8.06
Chemicals	6.07
Vegetable	5.66
Food products	4.39
Other	8.87

Table 5.3 Total South African imports from all foreign markets (2019) (*Source* Wits, 2019)

PRODUCT GROUP: IMPORTS	IMPORT PRODUCT SHARE (%)
Consumer goods	31.33
Capital goods	27.66
Machinery & Electronics	22.41
Intermediate goods	18.06
Fuels	16.86
Raw materials	14.5
Chemicals	10.63
Miscellaneous	12.79

5.4 Financial Returns for Entrepreneurs Versus Employees

In this country, a successful business owner can make as much as ten times more than an average employee over their working lifetime.

Entrepreneurship is all about creating something new and introducing change because of innovation. The effort is profit-driven, obviously, but entrepreneurship can also bring about dramatic changes and create major new influences in the world. Entrepreneurs' incomes tend to be higher than those of their corporate counterparts. Financial growth for an entrepreneur tends to be greater than that of an employee because the employee is constrained by a salary or a wage that usually gets reviewed only once a year, whereas the entrepreneur's income is limited only by how hard he or she works.

Entrepreneurs do not earn market-related salaries; they earn returns on selling products to customers and employing others to enhance those returns. When thinking of the choice between becoming an entrepreneur or working for a company, earning potential—how much money you can earn now and, in the future, is a major consideration. But the choice is also between working for yourself or somebody else.

These are some salary indicators based on estimated figures: Let's say that the average salary of a school-leaving employee in South Africa is approximately R7 500 per month. This means that you could earn around R90,000 per year if you got a job as a matriculated school-leaver working in a company. The median starting salary of a recent graduate in South Africa in 2020 was estimated at about R220,000 per year. This may sound great, but an entrepreneur can earn even more (Fig. 5.3).

Also, remember that while university graduates have a better earning potential than matriculants, graduates earn little or nothing during the three or four years of studying. They also often have huge study loans to repay as soon as they graduate or over the following years.

However, for most entrepreneurs, salaries are a secondary consideration. Many entrepreneurs are driven by factors other than money, including impacting the world. This is called an 'anchor'. It may be good for us to spend some time reflecting on what our anchor is and what will make us get out of bed every day to make a difference in the world. If

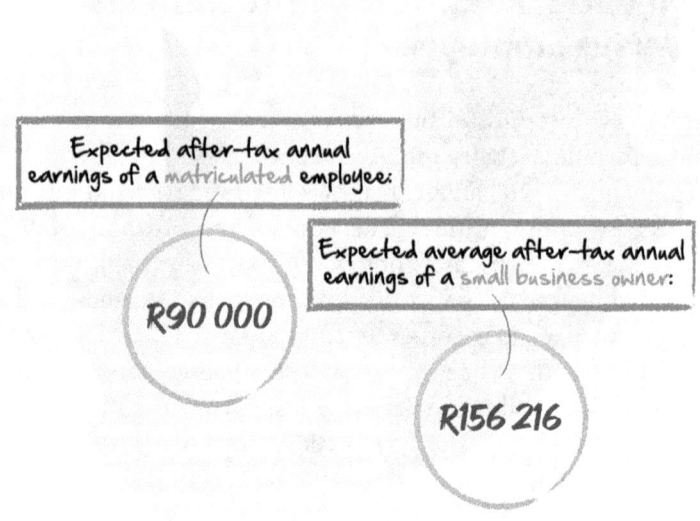

Fig. 5.3 Example (*Source* Authors)

we can find this anchor, our heart-spirit will grow, and we will work to make the difference that the world needs us to make.

5.5 A Youth Entrepreneur Development Tool

Questions of internal and external domains, collaboration with stakeholders, and linking sources of inspiration with the discovery of entrepreneurial passion are all concepts that should be explored, developed, and encouraged in entrepreneurial education and business friendship interrelationships.

Youth entrepreneurs can use the tools shown in Fig. 5.4 to map the entrepreneurial actions that will be necessary to develop themselves and their new venture idea and ultimately contribute to socio-economic development (Harrington (2016, 2017).

5 Toolkit—Enabling Tools for Entrepreneurship …

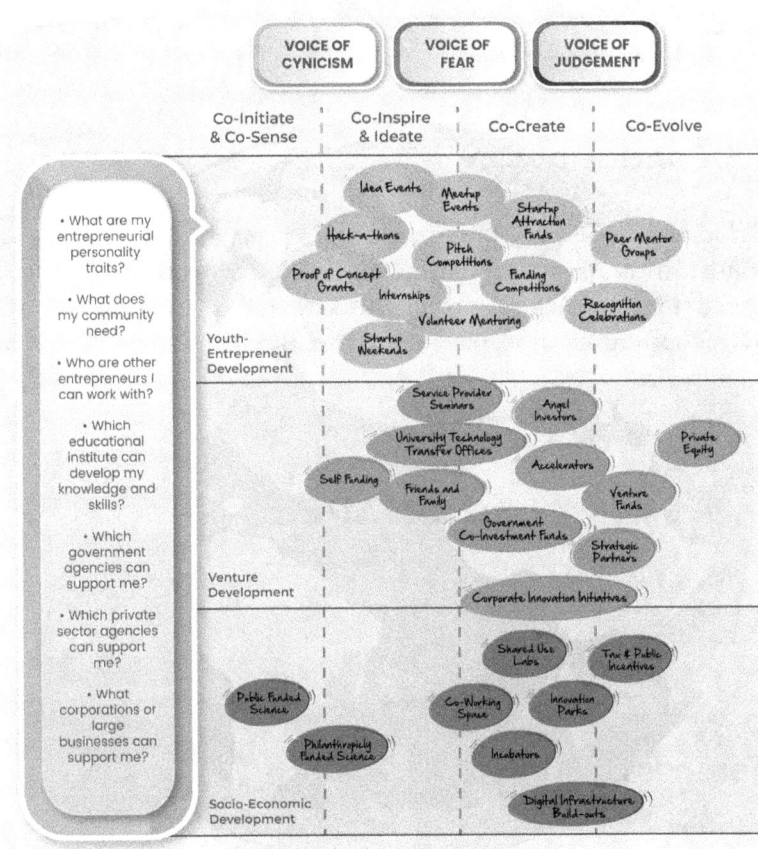

Fig. 5.4 A toolbox for enabling ecosystemic interpersonal actions (*Source* Adapted from Harrington (2016, 2017); Scharmer & Käufer, 2013)

For youths who can take charge of their personal development and continuously take action to resolve perceived barriers and collaborate with the ecosystem to discover enabling business factors, these abilities might hold the key to reconstructing the most important systemic role-player: the microsystem.

5.6 Conclusion

This chapter has looked at the opportunities available to the entrepreneur in South Africa, particularly in the area of import substitution. It also described the industry sectors in this country to indicate the scope of the opportunities available and sectors that entrepreneurs may not have considered.

References

Harrington. (2016). Is your entrepreneurial ecosystem scaling? An approach to inventorying and measuring a region's innovation momentum. *Innovations: Technology, Governance, Globalization, 11*(1–2), 126–142.

Harrington, K. (2017). Entrepreneurial ecosystem momentum and maturity the important role of entrepreneur development organizations and their activities. Available at SSRN 3030886.

Scharmer, C. O., & Käufer, K. (2013). *Leading from the emerging future: From ego-system to eco-system economies*. Berrett-Koehler Publishers.

Statistics South Africa. (2020). *Annual Financial Statistics (AFS) 2019*. https://www.statssa.gov.za/publications/P0021/P00212019.pdf

Steenberg, R. (2017). *The Entrepreneurial spirit—Towards an education model for entrepreneurial success in South African entrepreneurs*. PhD thesis. Texila American University in association with the University of Central Nicaragua.

Van der Westhuizen, T. (2022). *Effective Youth Entrepreneurship*. Sunbonani. Available at: https://omp.sunbonani.co.za/index.php/sunbonani/catalog/book/6

WITS (World Integrated Trade Solution). (2019). *South Africa Product exports and imports 2019*. https://wits.worldbank.org/CountryProfile/en/Country/ZAF/Year/2019/TradeFlow/EXPIMP/Partner/WLD/Product/All-Groups

Open Access This chapter is licensed under the terms of the Creative Commons Attribution 4.0 International License (http://creativecommons.org/licenses/by/4.0/), which permits use, sharing, adaptation, distribution and reproduction in any medium or format, as long as you give appropriate credit to the original author(s) and the source, provide a link to the Creative Commons license and indicate if changes were made.

The images or other third party material in this chapter are included in the chapter's Creative Commons license, unless indicated otherwise in a credit line to the material. If material is not included in the chapter's Creative Commons license and your intended use is not permitted by statutory regulation or exceeds the permitted use, you will need to obtain permission directly from the copyright holder.

6

Toolkit—Tools to Assist in Making the Move into Entrepreneurship

6.1 Introduction

Continuing with the co-sensing idea of 'connecting with people and ideas to learn more about how things work', entrepreneurs need to act quickly and continuously. But first, as entrepreneurs, we need to know what we are going to do, what to start with, and what to do next. We need to plan our priorities. Although a lengthy business plan does not guarantee that the business will succeed, it is important to have a clear outline of its vision and action steps. This is where it helps to create a business model canvas. This chapter describes aspects relating to the SHAPE Four-Quadrant Business Model Canvas and shows how we can put our ideas into entrepreneurial action.

6.2 Strategy

Business strategy is the art of deciding when the company will do what and which part of the organisation should be involved in its various activities. A strategy is mostly concerned with the new initiatives undertaken to improve the market share and growth of the business.

Most businesses revise their strategy regularly, annually, or quarterly, or perhaps even monthly, depending on the type of business. This involves some type of strategic review. A strategic review looks at results achieved in the previous period and designs high-level plans to address the next review period.

Most strategy systems recognise that strategy changes happen more frequently than annually and that plans need to be refined regularly in response to the possible rapid changes in the business environment. The COVID-19 pandemic is a good example of the need to re-strategise when occasion demands it.

Businesses often document the outcomes of their strategy processes as a strategic plan.

6.3 Innovation

A business that stagnates or fails to innovate (fails to think in a fresh way about their product, service, markets, etc.) will eventually be replaced by businesses that innovate and change with the times.

It is tempting to think that a business can continue to innovate indefinitely, but as the business matures, innovation tends to become more expensive with a smaller impact on growth. This is called the business lifecycle.

Innovation is about finding new and more productive ways of interrelating all aspects of the business and may involve looking for:

- new markets
- new products
- new production methods
- new management methods
- new business models; and
- faster processes.

Innovation-driven enterprises create more jobs than enterprises that are not innovation-oriented. By constantly seeking socio-economic value propositions and exceptional customer value, businesses can create major transformations over time. Larger companies that constantly innovate can create exceptional value for their shareholders, especially if they have investment capital that can 'change the game'.

The Internet as a business tool is a good example of innovation in business. Entrepreneurs lead busy lives, but Fig. 6.1 (derived from an online search and not validated in any scholarly literature) demonstrates what happens in only one minute on the Internet.

Whatever business we see ourselves starting, it is highly likely to use the Internet. The Internet provides both ideas and opportunities to create new businesses that may not have been thought of before.

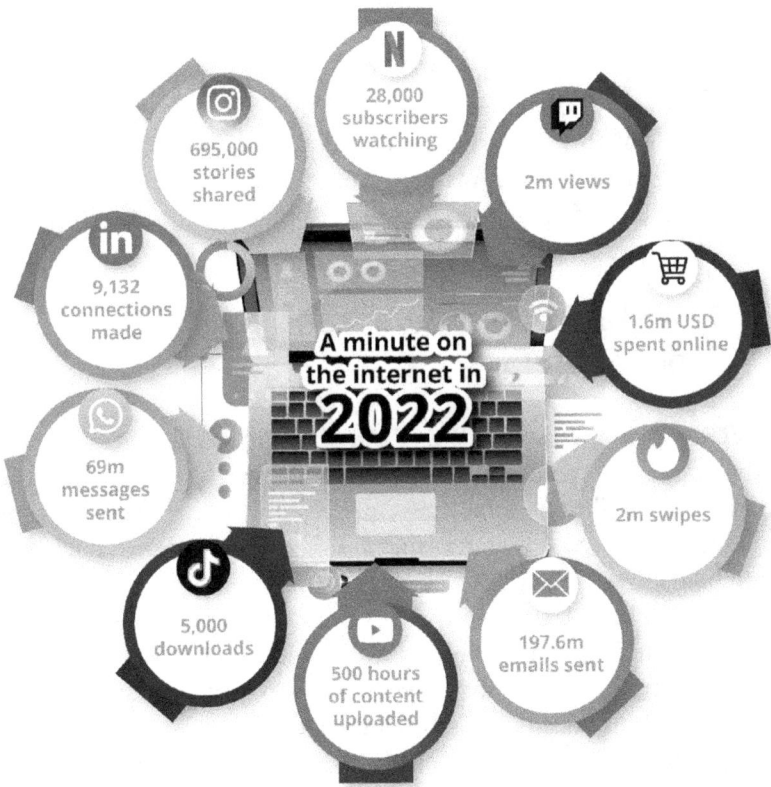

Fig. 6.1 What happens in an internet minute (*Source* Lori Lewis via AllAccess)

6.4 Developing a Business Model

When a business starts, it needs a product, a customer, and a business model that shows how the business will operate. Initially, all of these points may be unknown. We may not know yet if there is a market for our idea. We may not have the necessary partnerships, platforms, and systems to support any of this. In developing a business plan, the SHAPE Business Model Canvas (BMC) is a great tool to help us think through every aspect of the nascent business idea.

Businesses work well when we can find and service a large customer group or market that has similar needs and these customers seek a product that is similar to that supplied by our business; when we use an effective sales pitch and convince these customers to buy from us; when delighted customers promote our business by word of mouth; and when we can mobilise the needed resources.

To make all of this work, it's a good idea to register on social media such as Facebook or Google Ads right from the start and use catchy posts to build a big following that, over time, will translate into real profits.

6.5 The SHAPE Four-Quadrant Business Model Canvas

The SHAPE Four-Quadrant BMC is a strategic management tool for quickly and easily defining and communicating a business idea or concept. It is built on a business model canvas that Thea van der Westhuizen has used in mentoring and training sessions for young entrepreneurs over eight years (Fig. 6.2).

The SHAPE Four-Quadrant BMC is a one-page document that works through the fundamental elements of a business or product to give it a coherent structure. It sets out how the business intends to create and deliver value economically, socially, and culturally.

Entrepreneurs have found it useful because it gives the general structure of a business plan without going into too much detail. For this reason, it is sometimes called the 20-minute business plan. It also helps

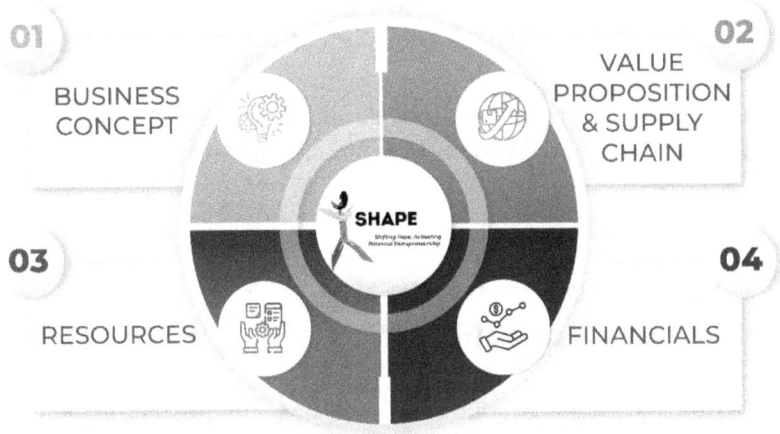

Fig. 6.2 The SHAPE Four-Quadrant Business Model Canvas (*Source* Van der Westhuizen, 2022)

to identify potential strengths and weaknesses in a business at an early stage so that the necessary corrections can be made.

We can put our product together using a tool such as the SHAPE BMC. Over seven years, Thea van der Westhuizen has mentored several hundred student entrepreneurs in the SHAPE social technology that has helped them explore the best ways to map out a business. The SHAPE canvas is not a replacement for the traditional business plan, but it is a good way to map out the business in simple, easy-to-understand terms.

Any business aims to put a product or service on the market; at this stage of developing the business model, experimenting and learning are essential to a company's development. By testing our ideas with our customers and analysing this data to get validation of our assumptions, we can build a business based on learning from our customers and validating their needs.

Riaan Steenberg recommends that before we even start trying to sell anything, we should speak to at least eighty people about our product without expecting them to buy it. This is likely to refine our idea of the product and our idea of what people want and expect. It will also give us better insight into how to approach the design and sale of our product.

Steenberg found that initial sales that used this approach were at least four times better than those of products where customer input was not taken into consideration during the design.

Ideas may be simple, but few people make money just from an idea. Putting a business concept behind the idea is what turns it into an actual business.

6.6   Where to Start with the SHAPE Four-Quadrant BMC

Completing the SHAPE Four-Quadrant BMC is not essential, but a useful way to start is to follow the steps set out below.

First, print out this list, or project it onto a whiteboard to make sure you capture your ideas and put them into words.

> Step 1: Fill in the Concept and Value Propositions blocks (the business purpose).
> Step 2: Complete the Value Chain and Customer block.
> Step 3: Fill in the Resources block.
> Step 4: Complete the Cost Structure and Revenue Streams block (financial block).

Once you have completed these steps, you have created a basic business plan.

6.7   Conclusion

Traditional lengthy business plans do have a purpose and place for youth entrepreneurs when planning and developing business. Business plan templates can easily be downloaded from the Internet through a quick Google search. The value contribution of a lengthy and verbose written business plan can still be debated. It often serves as a good direction, action map, and description of the enterprise's vision, mission, ethical foundation, and action plans. However, creating a succinct business model canvas through dividing four quadrants of describing the business concept, outlining the value proposition and value chain, what resources are needed to enable the enterprise and financial planning will assist the youth entrepreneur in having a broader sense of purpose and direction for the venture in a focused manner.

Reference

Van der Westhuizen, T. (2022). *Effective youth entrepreneurship*. Sunbonani. https://omp.sunbonani.co.za/index.php/sunbonani/catalog/book/6

Open Access This chapter is licensed under the terms of the Creative Commons Attribution 4.0 International License (http://creativecommons.org/licenses/by/4.0/), which permits use, sharing, adaptation, distribution and reproduction in any medium or format, as long as you give appropriate credit to the original author(s) and the source, provide a link to the Creative Commons license and indicate if changes were made.

The images or other third party material in this chapter are included in the chapter's Creative Commons license, unless indicated otherwise in a credit line to the material. If material is not included in the chapter's Creative Commons license and your intended use is not permitted by statutory regulation or exceeds the permitted use, you will need to obtain permission directly from the copyright holder.

7

Toolkit—New Customers and Product Development

7.1 Introduction

This chapter gets down to the nitty–gritty of what we are going to do: How we are going to develop a way of adding value and creating a product or service that is useful and sustainable. The key issue in the chapter is to be truly creative. The chapter discusses innovation and how our unique business offering is going to make money. So, we need to think about market research and the difference between marketing and sales. The chapter also discusses three ways to get into the market: business tendering, starting a business with no products ('drop-shipping'), and starting a business with no money.

To start a business, we sell a product to a customer. The SHAPE Lean Model highlights the importance of working out what people want; we then sell it to them and build an organisation that can continue doing this (Fig. 7.1).

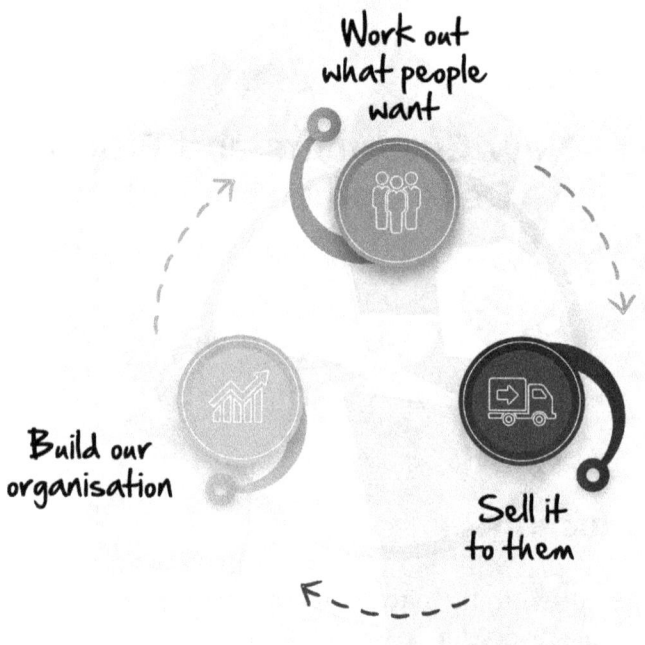

Fig. 7.1 The SHAPE lean model (*Source* Steenberg, 2017)

7.2 The 'New' for Our New Business

It has been said that every ninety days, we live in a 'new' world. This may be an exaggeration; it simply means that many things around us change rapidly. For example, we don't use the same type of phone that our parents used when they were young, and cars today don't look or work the same way they used to. Many of the products that existed when we were children are no longer available, like the iPhone Bluetooth headset Apple discontinued in 2009.

The world is moving forward more and more rapidly, and any business that wants to stay relevant and in business needs to look at new ways to do things. This is called 'innovation'.

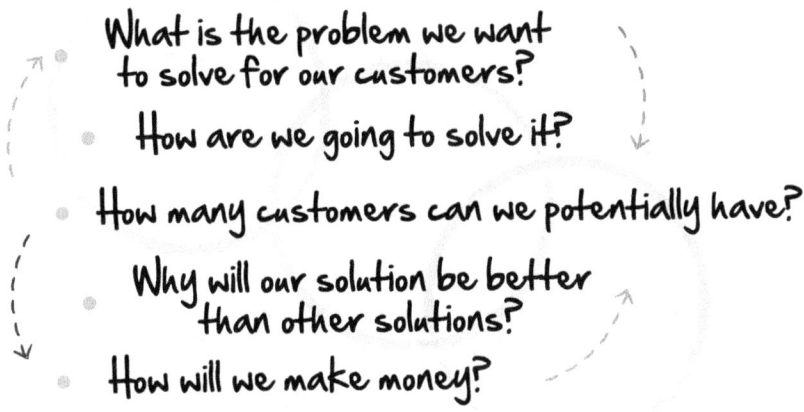

Fig. 7.2 Five key questions for innovative thinking

The owner of a business must ensure that the business has something to offer the customer that will set it apart from its competition in the short, medium, and long term. A business that fails to innovate will lose customers to businesses that do innovate.

When thinking about innovating, we need to ask these five key questions (Fig. 7.2):

7.3 Cost of Finding Customers

One of the highest costs for any business is finding new customers. Advertising can be expensive, and not every advert or hit on a website or app download will make us a profit. We need to understand the cost of acquiring a single customer (cost of customer acquisition) and also work out how much money we make from each customer (lifetime value of customer). If we can get to a point where we make more money from a customer than we spend getting a new customer, we start making profits.

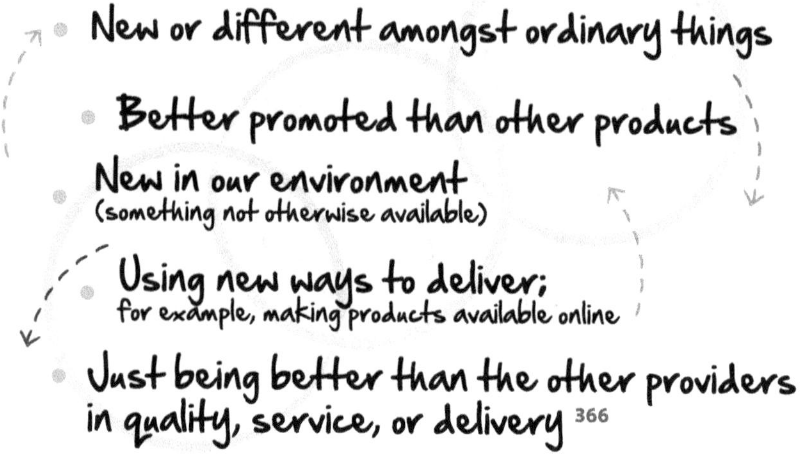

- **New or different amongst ordinary things**
- **Better promoted than other products**
- **New in our environment** (something not otherwise available)
- **Using new ways to deliver;** for example, making products available online
- **Just being better than the other providers in quality, service, or delivery** [366]

Fig. 7.3 Key questions for personal differentiation

7.4 Building a Reputation

By having good products and developing a reputation for quality and service, we can reduce the cost of finding new customers and work on ways to sell more to customers we already have.

7.5 Expressing Our Uniqueness

To be unique, we could position our product in a way that we appear to be (Fig. 7.3).

7.6 Doing Market Research

The best people to ask what they want to buy from us are potential customers.

If we produce a product that is too radical, we may be the only person who understands it or sees its potential. We also need to know if anyone else is already in this type of business. If no one is doing what we are planning to do, we may also need to ask why not. Perhaps there is no demand for this product or service.

To start researching the market, we need to draw up a brief description of our product or service, with some questions that will give us insight into what customers are looking for. The best way to find out what customers want is to ask them, rather than fooling ourselves that we already know what they want.

Here are some questions that could be useful to ask a potential customer (Fig. 7.4):

It is not too difficult to conduct telephonic or face-to-face meetings with potential customers to get this information. Once we have held between twenty and eighty such interviews, we can use the feedback about our product or service and design something that will work for most of our customers.

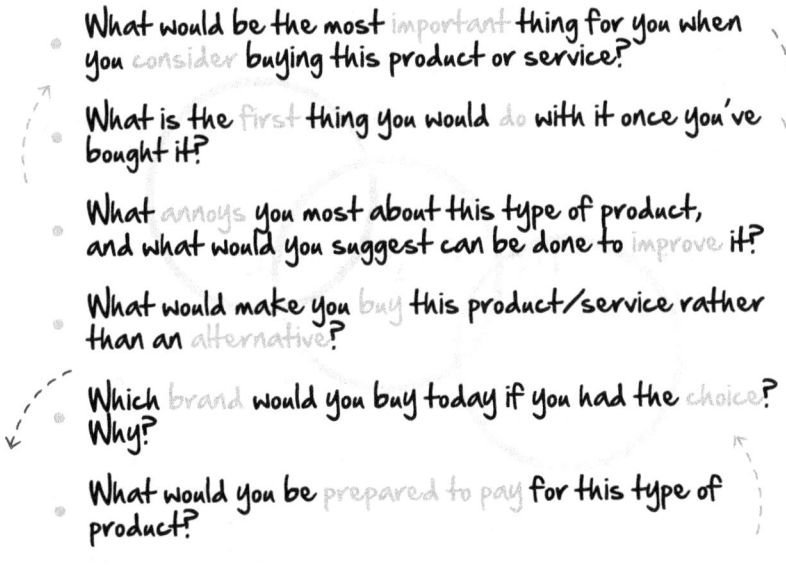

- What would be the most important thing for you when you consider buying this product or service?
- What is the first thing you would do with it once you've bought it?
- What annoys you most about this type of product, and what would you suggest can be done to improve it?
- What would make you buy this product/service rather than an alternative?
- Which brand would you buy today if you had the choice? Why?
- What would you be prepared to pay for this type of product?

Fig. 7.4 Market research questions

It is extremely valuable to speak to potential users of the product (and not just our family and friends). If we find out that our customers will not like an aspect of our planned product or service, we can improve the offering, and then more of them will like it.

We may read an article on the Internet which says that 'Demand for Product X will be so many billion by 20xx'. But this does not mean that the people we can reach will buy Product X. What is really important is to do our own market research.

7.7 What Does Our Business Sell?

Too many start-ups begin with an idea for a product they think people want. Then they spend months, sometimes years, perfecting that product without ever showing the product, even in a basic form, to the prospective customer. When a product fails to reach broad acceptance from customers, it is often because the product developers never spoke to prospective customers to determine whether the product was interesting. When customers finally communicate—through their lack of interest—that they do not care about the idea, the start-up fails.

Entrepreneurs may find it useful to apply the SHAPE Lean Product Development Cycle while ideating their business value proposition (Fig. 7.5).

7.8 Sales and Marketing: Two Sides of the Same Coin

The marketing function needs to bring leads to the table, and the sales function needs to take those leads and convert them into customers. Salespeople usually complain about the quality of leads, and those concerned with marketing complain that the salespeople are not sending out the correct message to the target market they have sourced.

When we start a business, we need customers. To get customers, we might build a website with relevant content, listing our products and

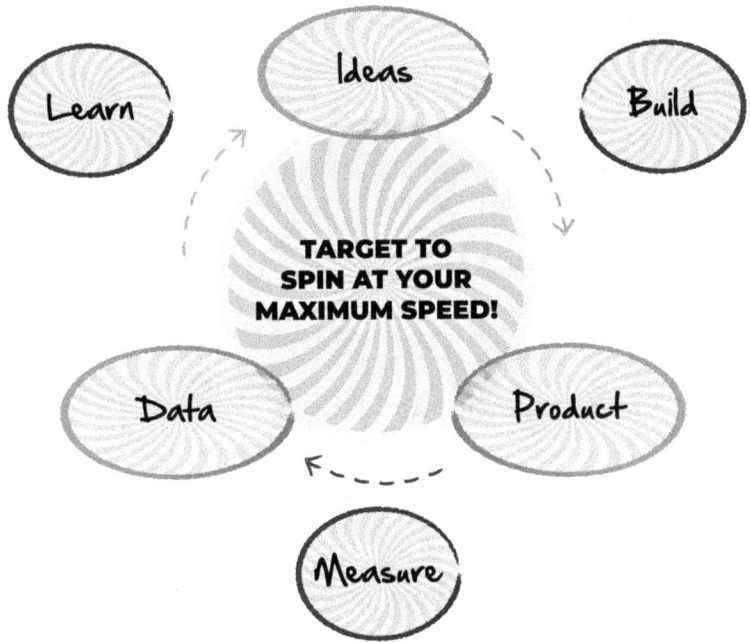

Fig. 7.5 The SHAPE lean product development cycle (*Source* Steenberg, 2017)

services and using pay-per-click (PPC) advertising (via Google or Facebook, for example) and other strategies to ensure that we get people to phone us.

As entrepreneurs, we often overestimate how interested people may be in our product.

All contacts, form submissions, and phone calls generated by marketing campaigns, using search engine optimisation (SEO), PPC, email, and display advertising, among others., are generally lumped together by those involved in marketing and called 'leads'.

Doing this is a mistake because not everyone who interacts with our business is a potential buyer of our product. Even when someone phones in response to an advert in a newspaper, it does not necessarily mean that they are interested in our product. They may just have found the ad interesting and wanted to find out more. Because a person submitted a form on Facebook, it does not mean they will come to our event.

Form submissions and phone calls could be leads, but they could also be (Fig. 7.6):

Thoroughly validating all leads by separating genuine sales inquiries from irrelevant inquiries ensures that we target the right people and follow up on them correctly. Sifting through form and phone inquiries to separate true sales leads from non-leads (like the ones listed above) is called 'lead qualification'.

It is well worth the effort to qualify all leads since typically, as many as 45% of all inquiries are not true sales leads.

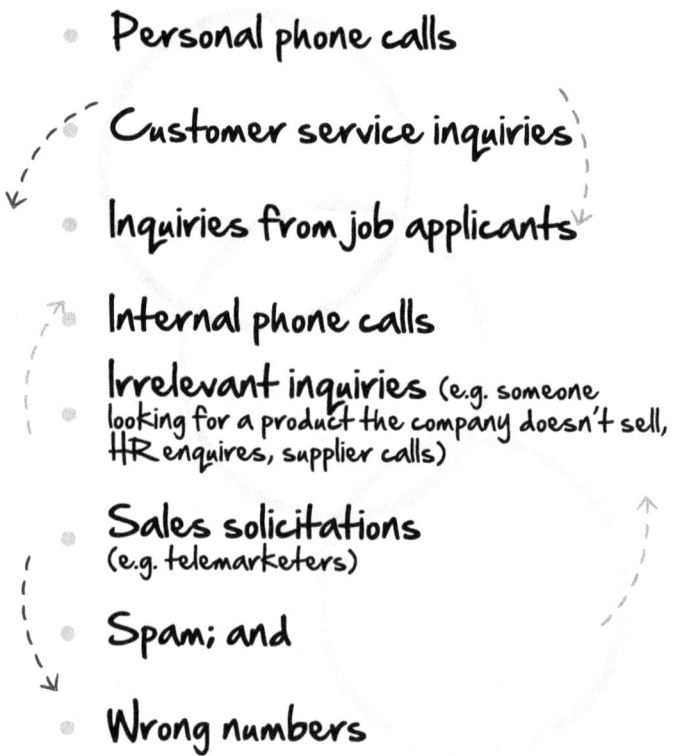

- Personal phone calls
- Customer service inquiries
- Inquiries from job applicants
- Internal phone calls
- Irrelevant inquiries (e.g. someone looking for a product the company doesn't sell, HR enquires, supplier calls)
- Sales solicitations (e.g. telemarketers)
- Spam; and
- Wrong numbers

Fig. 7.6 Validating leads

7.9 Marketing to Get People Interested

How will people find out about our business? Where are the people who will buy from us? Marketing aims to get our message out to people who could potentially buy from us. Once we understand who those people are, we need to let them know what we offer.

A key part of building a new business is understanding the market we are servicing. Especially when it comes to digital marketing, we want to ensure that the leads coming in are potential customers.

We use the data in the 'persona' that we design (see Sect. 7.12) to target people on digital platforms. This allows us to be specific and get exactly the clients we're looking for.

7.10 What to Do with a Qualified Lead?

A qualified lead is someone that we can start selling to. To do this, we need to present the product to the customer, highlighting its features and benefits, and at the same time work out what the customer's potential objections may be to buying the product, buying it right now, and buying it from us.

If we can answer the customer's objections, we can bring that customer to the decision point where he or she decides to proceed with the purchase; we then give the customer the necessary information to make payment for it.

7.11 Marketing Funnel

Most businesses have a marketing/sales funnel like the diagram in Fig. 7.7. Many software packages can help us to manage our sales funnel.

When we design our sales process, we observe that not every person who will visit a website will be interested in our product and would thus not be a lead. So, not all leads are qualified leads, and not all qualified leads will become customers. So, it is important to work backwards and work out how much of a drop-off we will have at each stage to ensure

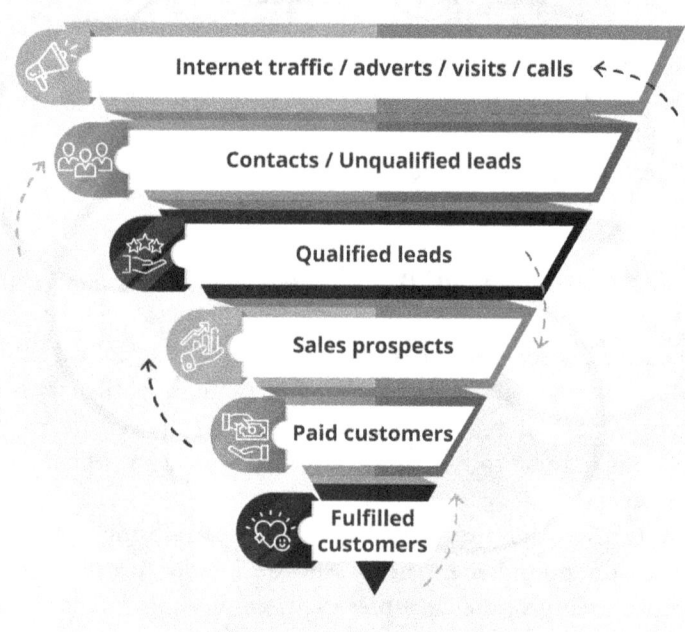

Fig. 7.7 The SHAPE marketing and sales funnel (*Source* Steenberg, 2017)

that we do enough to market to our potential customers so that we get enough customers.

As an indication, as few as between 1 and 3% of unqualified leads turn into paying customers. This means that for every 100 people who walk through the door, no more than three of them may buy. To get one person to walk through our door (whether a physical shop or on the Internet), we need to spend money. Taking care of our customers is one of the pillars of business success because each potential customer has indirect cost implications for the business. Money has to be spent on marketing and public relations to hook potential and existing customers.

In making sales projections, it is advisable to determine how many people need to enter the funnel and how much we will have to pay to have one person click on our website. Once we have determined this, we will have a good idea of how to set up our sales process.

7.12 The Buyer 'Persona'

With internet advertising, we can target our potential target market very specifically. We call the buyer that we are looking for the buyer 'persona'.

Getting as much information as we can about who potentially buys our product (our end-user) will enable us to increase the number of people with exactly those characteristics who walk through the front door. In this way, we can pinpoint a narrowly defined subset of potential customers with similar characteristics and needs.

Do not be afraid to go out and speak to real potential customers. Do good, direct customer research now, and it will pay off later. It might seem that not all of this customer information is relevant, but it is certainly better to have too much information than too little. With issues like gender, for example, we want to know the percentage split between our male and female customer base.

Here are some suggestions on how to map a segment of the market. Look especially for characteristics that would make this end-user unique, characteristics that differentiate them from non-target users.

Characteristics that we could map include (Fig. 7.8):

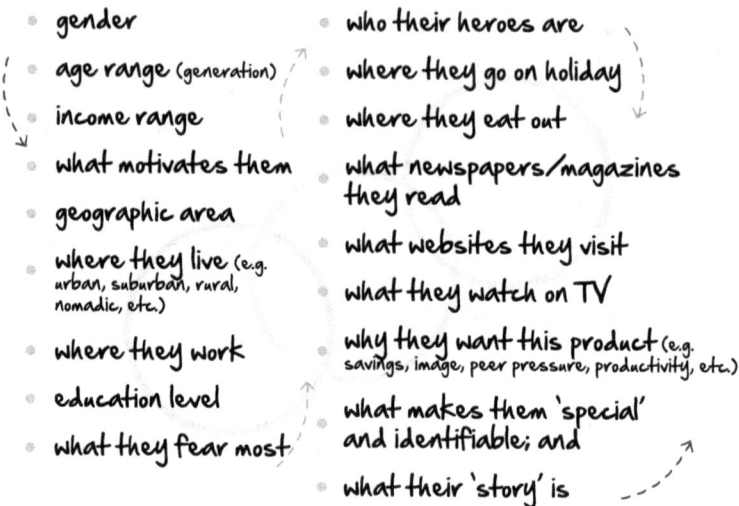

Fig. 7.8 End-user characteristics

Once we have a broad segment, we should define it more narrowly to create a persona, a portrait of one specific end-user. Table 7.1 lists some suggestions. What we are trying to aim at is to identify those characteristics that make this buyer's persona unique.

The information can be used to target these buyers specifically, and a well-trained sales team will be able to respond specifically to the needs of a given *persona*.

Building a correct sales strategy is important so that the business can accurately plan how many leads it needs to get to reach the required revenue. Not everyone who walks in the front door of a business is going to buy, and every business needs to understand the importance of this.

7.13 Sales Activity

We are all desperate to create more jobs and to make money. It is tempting to think that there is a simple formula that is guaranteed to make this happen. The only sustainable way to make money is to decide what to sell to customers, find a way to do that and then use the proceeds

7 Toolkit—New Customers and Product Development

Table 7.1 Example of a persona map

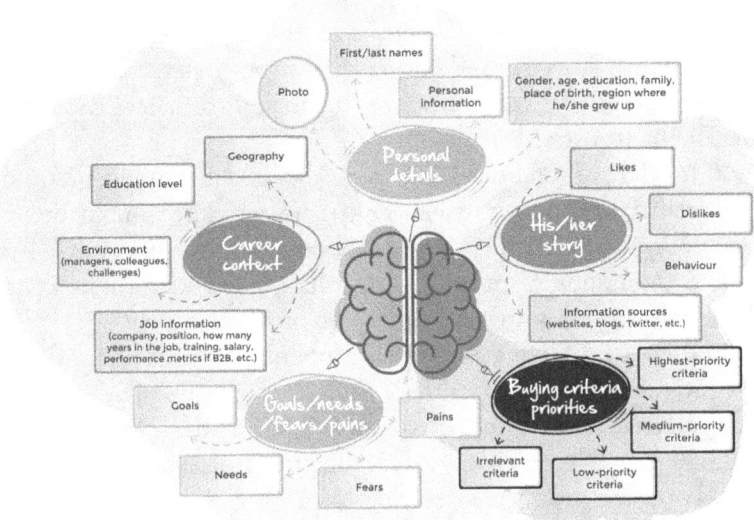

to allow us to sell to more customers. If we do this successfully, we will grow and expand our business while making money, creating jobs, and satisfying customers.

Even if we create a business that works for us, it may not work for everyone. If everyone does the same thing, there will be too many businesses in competition with each other.

7.14 Brochures and Prototypes

Once we have mapped out the types of things that people are looking for in our product ('features' and 'benefits'), we can put this information into something like a brochure, a web page, or Facebook.

Most of us buy things from adverts and brochures that tell us what the product does. By creating a brochure, we create a physical representation of the product.

A lean start-up business has three basic pillars: prototyping, experimenting, and pivoting. By putting a product out into the market (prototyping), getting feedback (experimenting), and then adapting the product or its delivery before we push out the next product (pivoting), we can constantly improve and ensure that we stay relevant.[1]

For a prototype, we may only need to make just a few copies of a product, perhaps just one.

Speak to eighty potential customers about our product. Without trying to sell the product to them, ask them why they might buy the product? Why wouldn't they buy the product? If we plan to sell our product to thousands of people, it may be a good idea to speak to a couple of them before starting to build the product!

Group the features that customers are looking for most often. Can we create a product with these features?

Once you have decided that it is feasible to create the specific product, you manufacture a prototype—a type of proof that we can create the product. For some products or services, a prototype is a massive undertaking and may involve computer models, production models, and complex engineering challenges. For other products, it may be something that we can do in writing, on paper, or very practically. If we can create a prototype, we have already proven to potentially interested parties that it can be done.

Statistically, if we can get to the point where we have a clear brochure and prototype (even if it's only a representation), we're more likely to achieve sales than the 60% of people who believe they will be required to first write a detailed business plan.

7.15 Sales are About Getting People to Buy

Just because someone says they are interested does not mean they will take money out of their pocket to buy your product.

---

[1] Ries (2011).

7 Toolkit—New Customers and Product Development

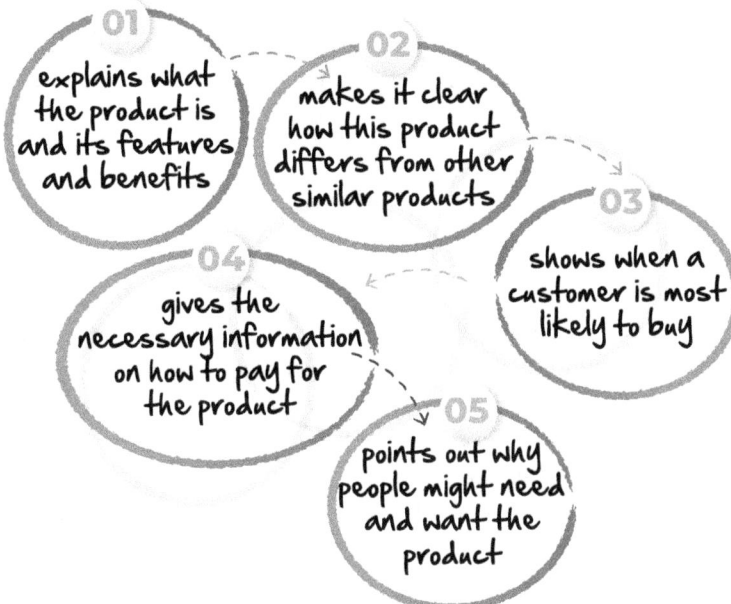

Fig. 7.9 Five-step sales process

7.15.1 The Sales Process

The sales process fills in the gaps in a person's understanding of why they should buy this product at this time. The sales process (Fig. 7.9):

7.15.2 After-Sales Revenue

In most cases, just because we have sold the product to an individual does not mean that the relationship with the customer has ended. With many products, the relationship only starts when we have concluded the sale.

It is important to maintain our relationship with the customer after the sale, support their purchase with after-sales service, sell additional products in the future, and maximise the word-of-mouth advertising and sales that flow from a satisfied customer.

The total cost of getting a new customer (COCA) is usually quite high. The challenging part is to maximise the lifetime value (LTV) of the client. A lot of time and energy goes into getting each new customer, so it is important to ensure you keep your customers and work hard to do that.

7.16 B2C Versus B2B Trade

A lot of the business that's done with large organisations: government, semi-government entities (public schools or universities, Eskom, Transnet, etc.), municipalities, big corporations, and suchlike, is done through tendering, where even quite small entrepreneurs can apply. This is called tendering for business.

Tenders are usually advertised (in newspapers or online), and smart entrepreneurs watch for opportunities to apply for business in this way. Here are some examples of organisations that invite tenders:

- National Departments of government such as SA National Roads Agency, Department of Correctional Services, etc.
- Provincial Departments of government such as Departments of Education KZN, Health Eastern Cape, Human Settlements Free State, etc.
- Local Government Departments such as City of Cape Town, Johannesburg, eThekwini, etc.
- Parastatal organisations such as the state-owned enterprises include Eskom, Transnet, etc.
- Local and international NGOs (non-government organisations), for example, World Vision, Doctors Without Borders, etc.
- Certain large corporates such as Anglo Incorporated, Oil companies, Unilever, etc.

There are also commercial tender service databases worth knowing about that scan the government and business world for open bids, e.g., tradeworld.sap.com and ZapMeta.

7.17 Starting a Business with No Products: Drop-Shipping

It is possible to start up a business without any funding (except maybe the cost of your smartphone). Yes, it is. One interesting example is drop-shipping, a type of e-commerce (conducting business electronically on the Internet). The merchant entrepreneur sells a product online, but instead of buying the product and storing it in a warehouse or storeroom before shipping it to the customer, the product is shipped directly from the manufacturer to the end customer. Although the wholesaler could be a manufacturer, distributor, or another supplier, he or she may never meet the distributor or even the end-user. Virtually any type of product may be sold in this way. The key is to provide a smooth supply chain from an online store to the manufacturer, distributor, and customer.[2]

The beauty of drop-shipping is in the simplicity of the model. If the partnership between retailer and distributor works well and the retailer builds an effective online marketing platform, there is no need to outlay any expense on buying, storing, or even manufacturing products upfront. All we must do is make sure our orders are fulfilled and delivered smoothly.

7.17.1 Tools to Make Drop-Shipping Work for Start-Ups

Drop-shipping entrepreneurs' only responsibility is to provide an effective link between customers looking for a particular product and manufacturers or distributors who can supply that product. The drop-shipper is in every sense a 'middleman', working online. It is simple, hands-off sales, without the packing, delivery, or warehousing of product. The sequence is as follows (Fig. 7.10):

---

[2] Adapted from https://www.3dcart.com/.

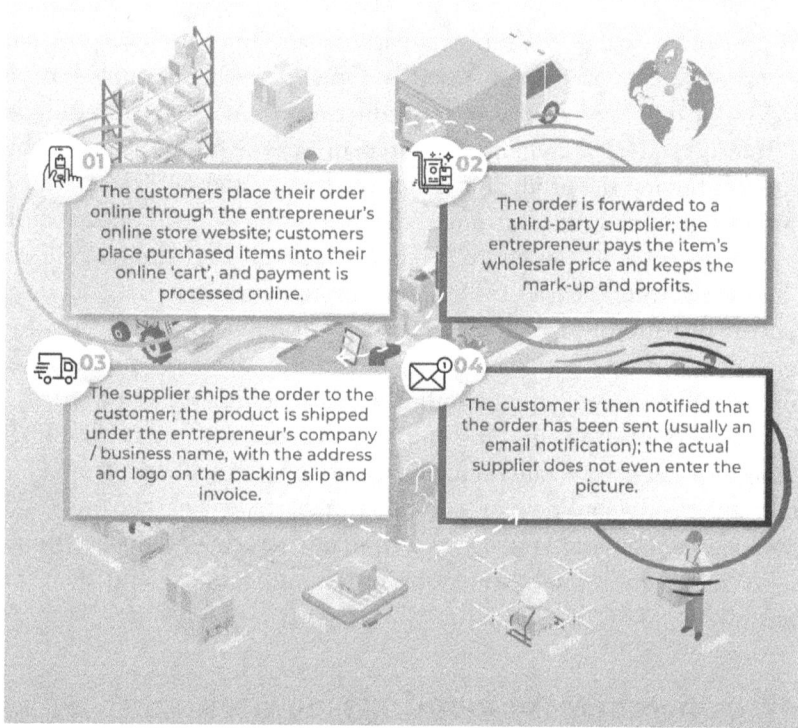

Fig. 7.10 Drop-shipping four steps (*Source* Van der Westhuizen, 2022)

7.17.2 Pros and Cons of Drop-Shipping

Drop-shipping sounds like a good idea, but before launching an online store based on this business model, it is wise to look at its strengths and weaknesses.

7.17.2.1 Advantages of Drop-Shipping

There are numerous advantages to drop-shipping (Fig. 7.11):

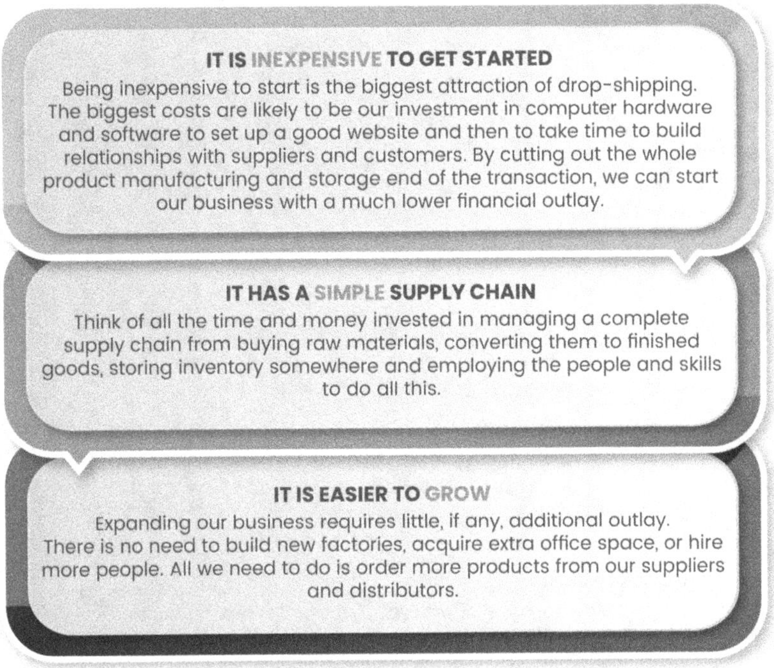

7 Toolkit—New Customers and Product Development

> **IT IS INEXPENSIVE TO GET STARTED**
> Being inexpensive to start is the biggest attraction of drop-shipping. The biggest costs are likely to be our investment in computer hardware and software to set up a good website and then to take time to build relationships with suppliers and customers. By cutting out the whole product manufacturing and storage end of the transaction, we can start our business with a much lower financial outlay.

> **IT HAS A SIMPLE SUPPLY CHAIN**
> Think of all the time and money invested in managing a complete supply chain from buying raw materials, converting them to finished goods, storing inventory somewhere and employing the people and skills to do all this.

> **IT IS EASIER TO GROW**
> Expanding our business requires little, if any, additional outlay. There is no need to build new factories, acquire extra office space, or hire more people. All we need to do is order more products from our suppliers and distributors.

Fig. 7.11 Advantages of drop-shipping

7.17.2.2 Disadvantages of Drop-Shipping

What are some of the downside issues for the drop-shipping model as our e-commerce business? (Fig. 7.12).

Despite these potential drawbacks, drop-shipping is one way of starting a business with little start-up expense and no products. Virtually any product, anywhere in the world, has the potential to be sold through drop-shipping. All we need to do is market it successfully and keep the customers happy by ensuring the quality of products and delivery and attending promptly to any complaints.

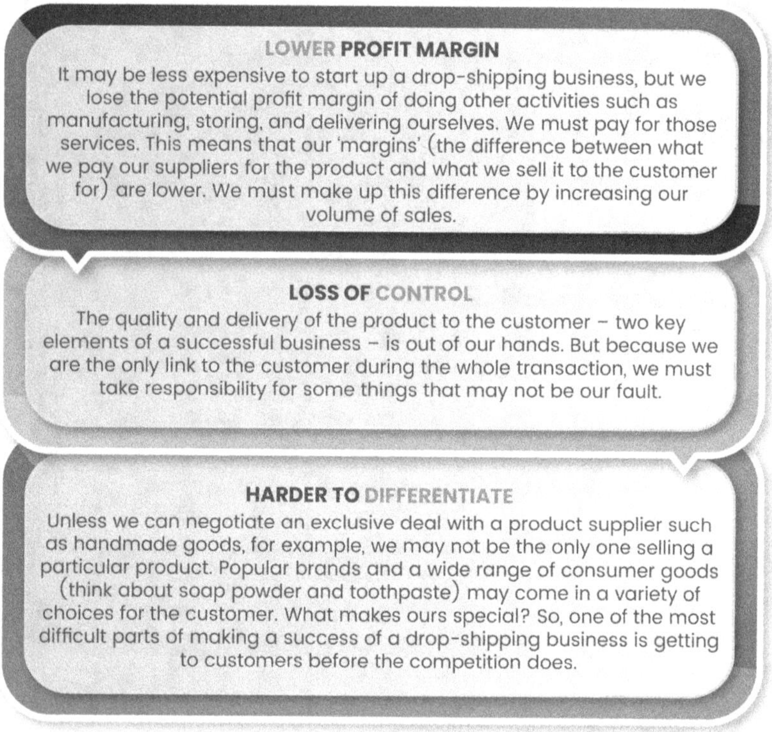

LOWER PROFIT MARGIN
It may be less expensive to start up a drop-shipping business, but we lose the potential profit margin of doing other activities such as manufacturing, storing, and delivering ourselves. We must pay for those services. This means that our 'margins' (the difference between what we pay our suppliers for the product and what we sell it to the customer for) are lower. We must make up this difference by increasing our volume of sales.

LOSS OF CONTROL
The quality and delivery of the product to the customer – two key elements of a successful business – is out of our hands. But because we are the only link to the customer during the whole transaction, we must take responsibility for some things that may not be our fault.

HARDER TO DIFFERENTIATE
Unless we can negotiate an exclusive deal with a product supplier such as handmade goods, for example, we may not be the only one selling a particular product. Popular brands and a wide range of consumer goods (think about soap powder and toothpaste) may come in a variety of choices for the customer. What makes ours special? So, one of the most difficult parts of making a success of a drop-shipping business is getting to customers before the competition does.

Fig. 7.12 Disadvantages of drop-shipping

7.18 Tools to Starting a Business with No Money[3]

It is possible to start a business with no money. Many services only require a person to be present and do something for someone else.

All this requires is to find a way to advertise ourselves.

Can we walk dogs for someone or babysit? Can we buy groceries for someone or drive them to the shops once a week to do their grocery

---

[3] Adapted from Bose (2018).

shopping? Each of these is something that can be done for a fee, and through careful investment, we can build towards bigger and better initiatives over time.

7.18.1 Businesses That Can Be Started with Little or No Capital

The following are some businesses that require little or no capital to start. There are many more (Fig. 7.13).

- CV writing service
- Personal shopper
- Clothes repair
- Children's party service
- Cupcake bakery
- Personal cooking service
- Food delivery
- Singing/music lessons
- Arts and crafts instructor
- Dog walker/pet sitter; and
- Babysitting.

Fig. 7.13 Businesses that can be started with little or no capital

7.18.2 Businesses Requiring a Low Initial Investment

The following are some of the businesses that require low initial investment. There are many more (Fig. 7.14).

- Lawn care
- Day-care/crèche
- Proof-reader
- Bookkeeper
- Real estate agent
- Freelance writer
- Childbirth assistant
- Drop-shipper
- Blogger
- Photographer
- Virtual assistant
- Exercise centre
- Personal trainer; and
- Personal sales.

Fig. 7.14 Businesses requiring a low initial investment

7.19 Tools in Applying the Transaction Model: How Are We Going to Get Money from the Customer?

Buying a house and renting a house is not the same thing. The difference between these two ideas is the model to show how a transaction (or sale) may be concluded. There are various possibilities in terms of the transaction model for our business.

The transaction model defines how we get money from the customer. This could, for example, be through a cash payment, electronic fund transfer (EFT), card payment, or cryptocurrency.

As we have seen, we do not need to register a business to start a business. If we have something that others want to buy, and they are prepared to pay us for it, then it is a business, and a business has three essential components (Fig. 7.15):

Fig. 7.15 Applying the transactional model

7.20 Conclusion

By now, we should have a good idea of what opportunities are out there, how to set about drafting a business plan that will convince all those we show it to that we have a viable business proposal, and where to start looking to bring our proposal to life. At this stage, it is all about marketing, marketing ourselves and marketing our product or service.

If we can find our way through the paperwork and have the skills and resources, tendering might be a good way to get our foot in the door. Drop-shipping is a great way to start with a minimum of start-up capital outlay, provided we can target a product and market and bring them together. Then there are a host of opportunities out there that require little or no funding to get going. All that is required is our imagination and perseverance.

References

Bose, S. (2018). Checklist: How to start a business with no money. *Small Business Trends*. Retrieved August 8, 2020, from https://smallbiztrends.com/2016/05/start-abusiness-with-no-money.html

Ries, E. (2011). *The lean startup: How today's entrepreneurs use continuous innovation to create radically successful businesses*. Crown Publishing Group.

Steenberg, R. (2017). *The entrepreneurial spirit—Towards an education model for entrepreneurial success in South African entrepreneurs* [PhD thesis]. Texila American University in association with the University of Central Nicaragua.

Van der Westhuizen, T. (2022). Effective youth entrepreneurship. *Sunbonani*. Available at https://omp.sunbonani.co.za/index.php/sunbonani/catalog/book/6

Open Access This chapter is licensed under the terms of the Creative Commons Attribution 4.0 International License (http://creativecommons.org/licenses/by/4.0/), which permits use, sharing, adaptation, distribution and reproduction in any medium or format, as long as you give appropriate credit to the original author(s) and the source, provide a link to the Creative Commons license and indicate if changes were made.

The images or other third party material in this chapter are included in the chapter's Creative Commons license, unless indicated otherwise in a credit line to the material. If material is not included in the chapter's Creative Commons license and your intended use is not permitted by statutory regulation or exceeds the permitted use, you will need to obtain permission directly from the copyright holder.

8

Toolkit—Tools to Develop Core Business, Growth, and Sustainability

8.1 Introduction

'Co-evolving' brings with it the idea of growing our business with others to be relevant to an expanding world. If our business idea is not relevant, it is unsustainable. It is like the seed thrown on stony ground; it will fail. All businesses need resources to feed on to thrive. In economic terms, these are sometimes called the 'factors of production': land, labour, capital, and entrepreneurship.[1] Labour refers to what we today call human resources, and capital is the money or financing required to keep the business afloat, pay suppliers and employees, and reinvest in the business so that it can grow and prosper for its owners and shareholders. Our last resource, entrepreneurship, is us, the people with the drive, attitude, and innovation to start and run a successful business.

The third quadrant of the SHAPE Business Model Canvas is a tool to help entrepreneurs to think about their business's resources and operational needs.

---

[1] Land, by the way, is not just property, buildings, etc., but includes any natural resource used to produce goods and services.

Any asset that can be transformed or consumed to produce a particular benefit can be considered a resource. In this chapter, a business resource refers to any tool or asset the entrepreneur uses to establish, manage or support the organisation's operations. This can be a human or any other type of resource or asset, both tangible and intangible, that is mobilised by the entrepreneur in the process of building a business, organisation, or another initiative. The effectiveness of each resource varies depending on the way we—the entrepreneur or owner—employ it in our business operations, as well as on our knowledge and understanding of the resource.

This chapter classifies resources into human, information, physical, financial, and space and time that are seen as critical for our business. But the important question is: What resources do our business need?

8.2 Work on Our Business

When we start to grow, we need to work 'on' our business, and not just 'in' our business.

After the initial survival stage, the owner's objectives could be, among others, to (Fig. 8.1).

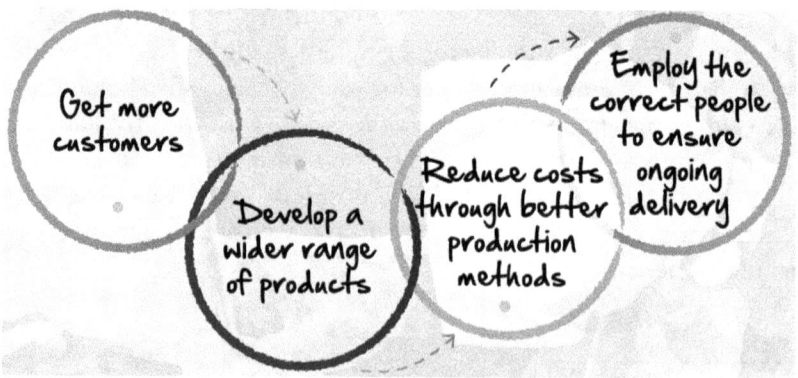

Fig. 8.1 Business owner objectives

These things require us to work on the business by bringing in the right people and motivating them to do the right things. From time to time, we may still need to get on the phone and search for customers, meet with suppliers, and get involved in the actual production of a large order. But we need to learn to hand over work to others, delegate, and hold them accountable for achieving that work.

8.3 When It's Not Working: Tools to Pivot or Persevere

Trying to keep a business going when it does not make a profit is like banging your head on a brick wall. At some stage, we need to admit that we need to do something else; change our strategy, or maybe even throw in the towel altogether and try some other business. Since businesses do not usually succeed overnight, we need to recognise when it is time to change. We also need to be careful not to throw away some aspects of our business that might be worth saving.

To 'pivot' means to change direction. We don't throw everything away and start over again; we build on what we've learned so far. The tricky part is knowing when to pivot. Usually, when we see that a product experiment or an unproductive product development is not bearing fruit by way of additional sales and customer enthusiasm, it may be time to pivot.

It takes courage to pivot. In some ways, it is admitting that some aspect of the business has failed, and no one likes to do that. So, we try to keep going with the same strategy, only to get the same results. Ultimately, some companies fail because they are hesitant to change direction.

We need to take a long cool look at our business before deciding when or if to pivot. This usually entails getting our product development and business leadership teams together for a meeting (or three) to discuss what is going wrong and ways to put the business, or part of it, back on track. These meetings must be presented with hard facts: data that tells a story about which products or business units are doing well and which are not. Has the business lost sight of its core customers and their needs?

This type of strategic meeting is useful from time to time, no matter the size of our business.

Eric Ries lists what he calls a 'catalogue of pivots'.[2] Table 8.1 shows descriptions of different ways to change direction. There is no set formula to follow; different pivoting strategies will apply at different stages of the business lifecycle.

As is evident in the table, there are many ways to pivot; the important thing is the strategy behind the pivot: Why are we doing it? Every situation is different, so there are no rules about the best strategies to adopt. Whichever strategy we choose, a pivot needs to be carefully considered and will need the resources: manpower, money, machinery, whatever, to make it work.

8.4 Tools to Apply the SHAPE Start-Up Strategies for Funding

One of the first things a business must do is raise money. But as every new business owner soon discovers, this is not as easy as simply applying for a bank loan (although that may be one strategy). Businesses need cash to start up. There are several sources to consider when looking for financing, and it is important to explore all the options before deciding.

8.4.1 Bootstrap from Sales

If we are just selling something to others, we need to buy our first stock of raw materials or supplies. The good news is that if we have a decent margin, we could double the amount of stock we buy after the third or fourth cycle of selling it. So, the idea is that we keep selling until we have enough money to invest in more stock and then buy more stock. Marketing is important, and it is also important that we do not take more cash out of the business than we need to keep buying stock.

---

[2] Ries (2011).

Table 8.1 Pivoting strategies (*Source* Van der Westhuizen, 2022)

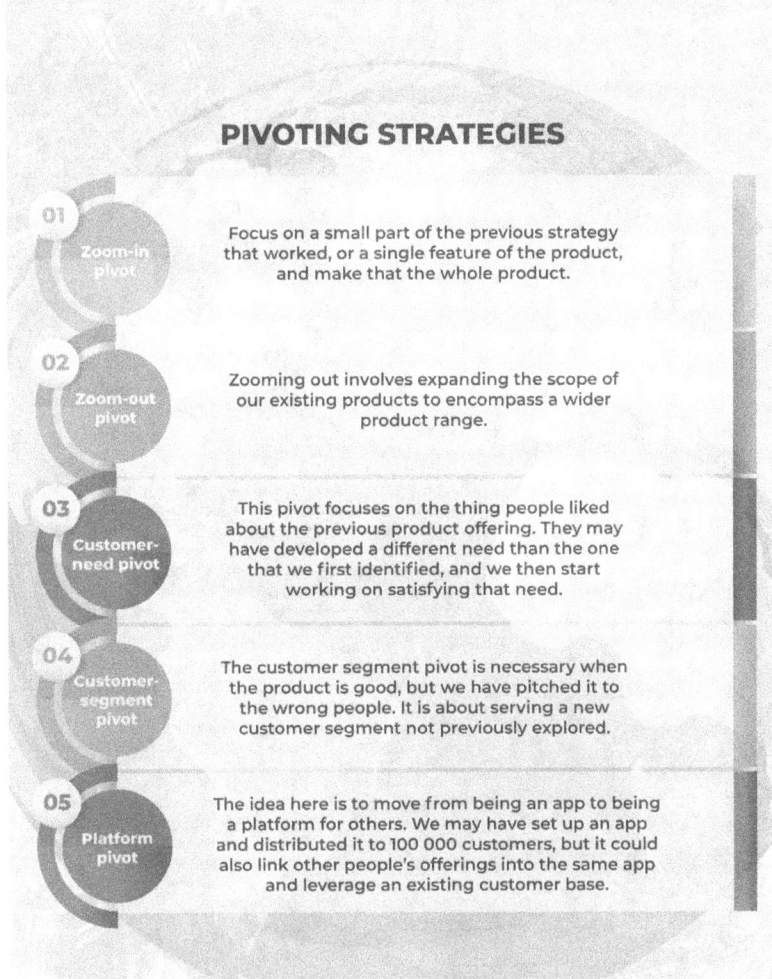

(continued)

Table 8.1 (continued)

PIVOTING STRATEGIES

 **06 Business-architect pivot** — We may change from high margin/low volume to low margin/high volume or B2B to B2C. These changes may be because of the time it takes to sell, the complexity of sales, and competitive forces.

 **07 Value-capture pivot** — By changing what is monetised (what people pay for), a business can add or remove features that change the value of what is being sold. By offering a standard or even a free model, we can build distribution, but by making a much-desired feature more attractive, we may make more money. The trick is to judge the correct features to monetise.

 **08 Engine-of-growth pivot** — This strategy is looking for faster or more profitable growth. There may be a part of the business that makes us more money, and we may have to kill off or severely limit another part of the business that is less profitable. For example, we may make more money from advertising on our platform than we do from subscriptions. So, we drop the subscriptions and focus on advertising.

 **09 Channel pivot** — If we struggle to sell our product on one channel, we may look at a different channel to sell it. For example, we may be selling car tracking devices to consumers, which is a tough and competitive market. To change the channel may be to install our devices upfront in purchased vehicles. The consumer still benefits, but now it is part of the upfront price of the car.

 **10 Technology pivot** — A new technology or outsourcing agreement may significantly change the complexity of what we need to deliver. We may build a factory but find a great new technology done by someone else that reduces the cost significantly. We can still satisfy our customers, but with a very different overhead structure. Technology can have a major impact on the way new businesses view their delivery requirements.

Source Steenberg (2017)

This simple arrangement works well for many businesses that start as a side business.

The good part about 'bootstrapping' our business is that we will be in control of the business from the start, and we do not need external funding except to buy our initial stock.

8.4.2 Fund from Savings

We can save to start our own business. Just remember that we may need as much as six to nine months of operating costs to begin a business before it starts to turn a profit. If we currently have a good budget and a stable income, we can prioritise saving for our business and start it when we have as much as we need according to our plan.

8.4.3 Pitch Our Needs to Friends and Family

Asking for a loan from friends and family should be approached professionally, and we will most likely be more successful if we present them with a good case for the business: what the risks are and what we will do to repay the money.

8.4.4 Access Small Business Funding

Most banks, the Small Enterprise Development Agency (Seda), and institutions such as the Industrial Development Corporation (IDC), National Youth Development Agency (NYDA), and others can offer funding and loans for potential businesses. We should familiarise ourselves with the requirements and processes for accessing this funding.

8.4.5 Crowdfunding

Crowdfunding is a way to raise online capital for a new idea or business. Once we start looking, we'll find there are many crowdfunding resources and strategies. KickStarter and Indiegogo are two international sites for starting a campaign, and Thundafund is a local SA crowdfunding site. Our business strategies need to be very clear to potential funders, and we'll be required to provide them with real benefits at the different stages of a crowdfunding campaign.

8.4.6 Angel Investors

There are local groups such as Gust and AngelList listed online. These platforms help us to network with potential investors who may be interested in our business proposal.

8.4.7 Venture Capital Investors

If our business idea gets bigger and we need to bring on more staff or assemble a team with a proven track record, a venture capital investor may be the right place to look for funding. Venture capital investors are interested in the uniqueness of an idea and the track record of the team that will run the business.

8.4.8 Start-Up Incubator or Accelerator

Start-up incubators and accelerators offer free or relatively cheap resources that may include office facilities and consulting, along with networking opportunities. They could also pitch events (organised opportunities) to sell our business ideas and products to groups of people. Some incubators may also provide seed funding or assist in the fundraising process. When entering an incubator, it is important to have realistic expectations about what they can do to assist you and not end up with massive debts if your business fails.

8.4.9 Pre-contracting

A good strategy for funding is to negotiate a buying commitment, order or advance payment from a customer or strategic partner. If there is a real demand for our product or service, someone will be willing to order it in advance, which could start the ball rolling. Some entrepreneurs have done this through pre-orders for their product, early licensing of their product, giving a strategic customer a stake in the business in exchange for funding, or offering to make a version of a product for one customer while preparing it to be sold to a wider target market.

8.4.10 Bartering

If we have a product that is interesting to specific clients, we could offer our product in exchange for rent, advertising, or other services.

8.4.11 Bank Loans or Lines of Credit

If we have the right type of collateral and potential orders, we may qualify for secure or unsecured lending, depending on various factors. If we are looking for money, it is important to speak to our bank to find out what services they offer to small businesses.

8.5 People as Resources: Start Building Our Team

The people in our ecosystem are the most valuable resource we could have. Our collaboration: co-initiating, co-sensing, co-inspiring, co-creating, and co-evolving will greatly determine the sustainability of our business.

To scale our business, we must give responsibilities to other people. This is called delegation. In other words, we need to start building a team.

Forming a team may mean bringing in a partner, employing one or more people to assist, or hiring a freelancer with the skills that we need. These three tips can help us find the right mix (Fig. 8.2).

> Be clear about your business goals. From the start, ensure that the team understands the vision we have for our business and their part in making it happen.

Follow good employment policies and procedures. The website www.labour.gov.za *(click on the hyperlink for access)* provides all the guidelines needed for us to keep within the labour laws of the country. When hiring employees, we need to follow these guidelines, ask the right questions, and fill in the required forms to avoid ending up with a labour dispute. These are not difficult to source, but it is important to follow them to ensure that we are legally covered.

> Establish a strong company culture. We do this by introducing each new employee to the company's vision, mission, goals, and shared values (called 'company induction'), building a shared vision and involving the employees at every step. People want to be part of something great. However, this is only achieved if they are engaged as part of the process.

Fig. 8.2 Forming our team

We need to know what we can do personally and what we need others to do. If we need a team, should we contract people or outsource them online through a freelancing service?

The concept of 'staff on demand' is becoming a lot more common, even in large organisations. We could perhaps ask ourselves if it is better to pay someone to do it once (for example, a cleaning service to come in to clean our offices), or is it worthwhile to hire someone on the company payroll to keep on doing it?[3]

Here are some technology businesses that specialise in offering needed services to small businesses:

- Fiverr.com (can be used to quickly design a logo)
- Dice (for programmers)

---

[3] Ismael et al. (2014).

- EnvatoStudio (for creative work such as artists, actors, and designers)
- Freelancer.com (project workers)
- Guru.com (freelance talent globally)
- RecruitMyMom (work-at-home moms)
- MediaBistro (freelance media such as writers, designers, editors, ad-sales, and other positions)
- PeoplePerHour.com (talent and jobs, paid by the hour)
- Upwork (contractors in all categories across the globe)
- Sologig.com (experienced IT and engineering professionals).

8.6　Understanding Our Value Chain

Many inputs are needed to deliver a product or a service. These inputs are called supplies or raw materials, and the people we get them from are called suppliers. Traditional value chain approaches sometimes do not consider the follow-up services required to support a product after it has been sold (Fig. 8.3).

At this point, we should look at the cost of each step in the value chain and work it back to a cost per product. This will allow us to get an idea of the product cost. By adding the margin, we will have an idea of the price at which we need to sell the product to avoid losing money.

The second layer of the value chain (support activities) looks at how the company supports each step of the primary production activities through procurement (the buying or purchasing function), technology, human resources, and organisational infrastructure. For most small businesses, at the start, the entrepreneur is all of these things, but over time, as the business grows, other people get added to the team.

We can do the above value chain analysis by examining the functions under each aspect listed below.

- The buying processes that will support each of these stages (inbound logistics, operations, outbound logistics, marketing, and sales, service).

Figure 13.1: The SHAPE Value Chain Model.
Source: Steenberg, 2022.

The main aspects of the model are:

1. Source – Who will be our suppliers, and what products or components do they supply?
2. Market – We need potential buyers, and we use marketing to let them know that we have the product.
3. Sell – We engage in selling to our potential targets. This may involve activating supply, manufacture, and delivery processes.
4. Supply – Once we have the potential clients, we need to supply from the source that we engaged with earlier.
5. Manufacture – We may need to engage in a manufacturing process to ensure that the product is ready to be delivered.
6. Deliver – What will the process and experience be of delivering the product to the customer?
7. Follow-up service – What else will the customer need once they have purchased our product or service? How can we build this service and continue to maintain a relationship with these customers?

Fig. 8.3 The SHAPE value chain model (*Source* Steenberg, 2017)

- The technology that can be used to facilitate the flow of information, how these technologies are integrated, and the competencies of the people who will operate these systems.
- The human resources (people) that are required for each of these stages of the customer journey. It is especially important to ensure that sales and service staff are prioritised early on in a business.

The infrastructure (management, premises, transport, and so on) needs to be put in place. The aim is to have the minimum infrastructure to deliver the product and service and look carefully at how to expand into the future.

8.7 Experimenting to Improve

Most entrepreneurs use trial and error to find solutions that will work best for them. But we can increase our likelihood of success if we rationally and systematically decide on the best strategy for our start-up.[4] This requires us to think of our business as an experiment in which we constantly test our assumptions and make sure that they work for our customers. If we can attend to all the issues that our customers have with our business, we will make massive progress towards giving them a product that they want to buy.

8.7.1 There Is an App for That—Use for Free Until We Need to Pay

Some of the services that we may need offer free accounts until a certain limit or other constraint is reached.

Free tech services that can support our business are:

- HubSpot (free CRM—customer relationship management)
- Google Ads (free keyword planner)

---

[4] Aulet (2013) and Ries (2011).

- OpenOffice (free office software)
- TaskQue (free task management software)
- GrowthBot (free chatbot software)
- Buffer (schedule social media posts)
- Canva (cool presentations)
- Doodle (simple scheduling)
- Grasshopper (international phone reception desk)
- Slack (team collaboration)
- Evernote (notetaking)
- Wave (expense tracking)
- MailChimp (free emailer software)
- Wordpress.com (free blog sites)
- Wix (free website)
- Shopify (low-cost e-commerce site)
- Zoho (integrated business management system).

8.7.2 Free Accounting Services

Many banks have accounting platforms already built into a business account that can assist with payroll, VAT, and other management accounts without extra charges. We may be able to do our own accounting without having to do more than opening a bank account. This can save thousands in monthly accounting fees. We will need to log in and get the business going. In time, this may change to an outsourced accounting function, and later we may run a whole finance department, all depending on how the business grows.

If we do not want to use the bank to do our accounting, other tech-driven accounting tools have free options. The following are some of the most popular accounting tools we could use:

- XERO
- QuickBooks
- Microsoft Dynamics
- Zipbooks
- Wave

- GnuCash
- TurboCASH
- Akaunting.

8.7.3 Free Prototyping

Prototyping our business concept can be done without incurring costs on platforms or apps such as:

- proto.io
- pidoco.com
- Figma.com
- Prototypr.io
- Marvelapp.com.

8.7.4 Free Online Supply Chain

Drop-shipping, as discussed in Sect. 8.15 above, uses technology to take orders from customers and ship a product to them directly from the supplier. These services do not come free; some examples are:

- Shopify
- aceonline.co.za
- dropified.com
- Buyfast
- computerwholesaler.co.za
- ChinaBrands.com.

There are many other resources that can be accessed for free or at a low cost. It is important to leverage these resources as this allows us to focus on what we'll be required to do to make the business a success.

Many of these services can be used on a trial or free basis. If we try an idea and it works, then that's great, and it costs nothing.

8.8 Start Getting Some Sales

Sales are the lifeblood of any business, and we need to live by the mantra, always be selling. We are constantly selling our business to customers, staff, suppliers, banks, and our friends and family. We need to always be positive about our business because if we are not, no one else will be. Even if times are tough, we need to remain optimistic.

The staff that we employ to sell should have clear targets more than what we pay them. We should work out a commission structure that motivates them to perform.

We should focus on the following (Fig. 8.4).

- Always listen to our customers.
- Understand what our salespeople are selling to our customers, and make sure that it is something that we can deliver.
- Create clear product information that emphasises the features and benefits of our product.
- Make sure that we follow up on potential customers and ask for commitment and timeframes for buying.

Fig. 8.4 Start getting some sales

8.9 Experimentation and Expanding the Product Range

Once we have started to sell our product or service, we may realise that our customers have other needs. This should encourage us to experiment and slowly but surely transform our business to become more relevant to our customers.

We can introduce new features to existing products, new products to existing customers, or try to make products 'on paper' and get people to buy them before we even produce them. By testing new variations, we can select the ones that perform best and make more of those.

The same goes for our marketing. We may find that social media works well for marketing our product, but also try a print advert and see what the response is from that. We will be required to do more of what works, and less of what does not work or does not work as well.

8.10 Conclusion

The top two barriers identified by youth entrepreneurs relate to access funding and own personality traits. It can be argued that developing personality traits of creativity, innovation, resilience, and ability to take risks and proactively search for, and act on opportunities, are key to changing the view youths perceive funding needs for enabling entrepreneurial action. With many free services and support being offered by role-players in the youth entrepreneurial ecosystem, as well as online resources, the perceived obstacle of the need for funding can be mitigated. The ability to understand problem-solving solutions to pivot business ideas when flexibility is required relates to the development of internal domains. The current and relevant situation where the world of work is moving towards requires fewer physical resources like office space and a full range of office equipment. Digital developments enable youth entrepreneurs to enable their entrepreneurial initiatives by integrating various online platforms with electronic devices like laptops and phones and replacing costs that would have been spent on a traditional office setup. Creative and innovative abilities are the new currency driving access to funds.

References

Aulet, B. (2013). *Disciplined entrepreneurship: 24 steps to a successful startup.* Wiley.

Ismael, S., Malone, M., & Van Geest, Y. (2014). *Exponential organizations: Why new organizations are ten times better, faster, and cheaper than yours (and what to do about it).* Diversion Books.

Ries, E. (2011). *The lean startup: How today's entrepreneurs use continuous innovation to create radically successful businesses.* Crown Publishing Group.

Steenberg, R. (2017). *The entrepreneurial spirit—Towards an education model for entrepreneurial success in South African entrepreneurs* (PhD thesis). Georgetown, Guyana: Texila American University in association with the University of Central Nicaragua.

Van der Westhuizen, T. (2022). *Effective youth entrepreneurship.* Sunbonani. https://omp.sunbonani.co.za/index.php/sunbonani/catalog/book/6

Open Access This chapter is licensed under the terms of the Creative Commons Attribution 4.0 International License (http://creativecommons.org/licenses/by/4.0/), which permits use, sharing, adaptation, distribution and reproduction in any medium or format, as long as you give appropriate credit to the original author(s) and the source, provide a link to the Creative Commons license and indicate if changes were made.

The images or other third party material in this chapter are included in the chapter's Creative Commons license, unless indicated otherwise in a credit line to the material. If material is not included in the chapter's Creative Commons license and your intended use is not permitted by statutory regulation or exceeds the permitted use, you will need to obtain permission directly from the copyright holder.

Part III

Journaling of the Author on Working as a Youth Entrepreneur: Self-Reflections Pre-, During & Post-SHAPE

9

En Route: A Self-Reflective Lens as a Case Study

9.1 Introduction

In keeping with the stated paradigm for this research, namely, that the practitioner-researcher and the participants learn jointly from their past and current experiences, I provide the following autobiographical case study, in which I reflect on the experiences in my own life (entrepreneurial experiences in particular) that I believe qualified me to lead the SHAPE systemic action learning and action research (SALAR) project.

9.1.1 My Journey Leading to the SHAPE Project

I know what it feels like to be a youth entrepreneur and have been entrepreneurially active for over 20 years. My experience of being an entrepreneur began at age five when I was collecting silkworms, and the neighbouring children caught on to the trend. My parents used to give me a limited amount of pocket money and told me, from a very early age, that if I needed more money, I should make a plan and work for it. So, I started selling both silkworms and the silk they produced to my schoolmates and people at my church. I developed an eye for trends that appealed to other kids, and all through my primary school years, I sold items of one kind or another like stationery, homemade cookies, and lemonade, that gave me a small profit.

In due course, shortly after graduating from North-West University with a cum laude M.Com degree, I co-authored a book titled *Guesthouse Management in South Africa*, in which my contribution dealt with aspects of strategic planning and business development.

Moving to Mossel Bay at age 23, I launched two businesses, using the skills derived from my academic education to create the business model in each case. The first of these was Tesen Tourism Planning, which provided strategic planning and business development services to the Garden Route Municipality and various private clients. The biggest business success was the development of a four-storey beachfront building, owned by Petroleum South Africa, into an arts and craft centre, which is still in existence. The other business was the Garden Route Tourism Academy, which provided training to several hundred people in the tourism industry along the Garden Route.

Both Tesen Tourism Planning and the Garden Route Tourism Academy drew on the set of intermediaries outlined in Dhliwayo's model as described in Chapter 1, I was not aware at that time of any existing model of potential sources of support for an entrepreneur. However, I intuitively sensed that this was what was required to bring about the networking that would help grow my businesses. This, I regard as the inner source from which I acted, as set out in Scharmer's Theory U.

In running my two businesses, I worked hard, put in long hours, made many sacrifices, and often was left with little profit for myself. Much of the time, I seemed to be sorting out problems rather than having any fun. But I also learned life lessons from dealing with a diversity of personalities and cultures as a business owner in South Africa, which prepared me for doing business in the Middle East, where I then decided to relocate.

A quick impression of my overseas entrepreneurial career can best be conveyed by listing the highlights of my early professional activities in the Middle East:

9 En Route: A Self-Reflective Lens as a Case Study   211

- *Innovating and developing a human resource performance appraisal system for SABIS International, one of the world's largest privately owned education systems.*
- *Becoming business development manager for Al Masah International, a large property development group, where I was responsible for developing the Abu Dhabi branch from scratch to the stage where it was a profitable business dealing with multi-million-dollar accounts.*

Making a switch to higher education when the global recession hit Dubai, I saw alternative opportunities in an industry that was showing statistical growth and was not being affected by the global downturn. My professional achievements in this new sector (new for me) in the Middle East included several innovations. As a result, I was named by Deputy Prime Minister Sheikh Hamdan bin Zayed as Best Business Lecturer in the Western Region of Abu Dhabi for innovative approaches in taking learning outside the classroom into the field of action.

- *Being part of a core team, which launched the first-ever water sports festival in the Western Region of Abu Dhabi (a water sports festival in the desert!), attracting over 76,000 visitors over two weeks; the Al Gharbia Water Sports Festival continues as an annual event.*
- Initiating the first shopping festival in the Western Region of Abu Dhabi, hosted by women for women, which continues as an annual event to this day.
- *Initiating the first entrepreneurship conference to be held in the Western Region of Abu Dhabi; and*
- Together with my students, being named winners of the Lion's Den Business Plan Competition in an award made by the British Ambassador to the UAE.

None of these successes would have been possible without the knowledge and experience gained during my undergraduate and postgraduate degrees and from my hands-on activity as an entrepreneur in South Africa.

Despite all the awards and achievements, there were long periods, sometimes lasting up to ten months, where I was unemployed and had to come up with a plan to take care of myself to survive. It was a time of continuous trial and error before the awards and successes emerged.

After intense corporate involvement over ten years, including visits to more than twenty countries, I felt that I needed a break from business, and I relocated back to South Africa, choosing Durban as a place to 'settle down' as a staff member at the UKZN.

In this sequence of personal experiences, I have repeatedly undergone the cycles of Theory U for myself, not only passing from a reactive to a generative response field in the social emergence curve of Lion's Den Business Plan Competition but also spiralling several times through the social pathology curve, sometimes even to the point of aborting various ideas. Passages of social pathology have been accompanied by feelings of severe anxiety, fear, and stress when it was far from clear how I would cope with this or that predicament.

How is it then that I have managed to keep bouncing back to the level of social emergence, continuously trying to go from left to right through that U-curve? The way it appears to me is that after an interlude of 'processing thought' regarding the challenge at hand, a new idea or a new way out emerges in my head. When the solution presents itself, I feel it resonates within me; I experience a 'rush'. I often get asked by my friends, 'Thea, why do you always need to be so persistent?' Is it my Christian belief that God will provide? Or is it my fear of failure that I might not survive financially if I don't come up with a new plan?

These dynamics in my own life and what I observe from young people around me inspired me to take on this project and the research it involves. I wish to investigate why some young people lack the drive to pursue their own goals and aspirations. Why do some young people have low self-confidence about being entrepreneurial? Why are young people not as entrepreneurially oriented as they may think they are, and why do their entrepreneurial activities lack sustainability? Could a programme be devised to address these challenges?

In the time I have been enrolled for my Ph.D. I have continued to encounter challenges, both professional and personal, that correspond with stages in the spiral dynamics of Theory U; moments when the temptation to abandon my goal is countered by a strong emotional drive that keeps me going; an Inner Source from which I act. I keep a journal of these life experiences and actions in my blog at www.theavander.com.

9.1.2 Pre-SHAPE

My episteme and 'ontos' took me to the point where I was able to 'lead from the emerging future' to move from what had been only project conceptualisation to project development and implementation. Without the experience that I gained over 15 years professionally, plus 36 years of personal experiences, both in South Africa and internationally, I would probably never have ended up in Durban, at UKZN, or have decided to tackle the SHAPE project. Life resulted in me being in Durban at this point and engaging in my current activities; God led me to Durban.

Throughout my life, both friends and colleagues used to describe me as a 'go-getter', 'self-driven', 'inspiring', 'determined', 'pushy', or 'extroverted'. However, I have perceived my actions throughout my life as having been driven mostly by fear of failure. Even more, I think I was fearful that I would not survive on my own. I saw myself as an introvert, having a public face and a Thea-true face. I was unsure what my purpose was, how I saw success, and what I was constantly driven to. There was always just this drive towards something. A 'something' that wasn't yet crystallised in my mind and heart.

I realised that I first needed to make changes within myself before I could start to explore how to bring about the changes I desired concerning student entrepreneurs, systemic levels, and ultimately socio-economic development in South Africa. I needed to introspectively question my viewpoints and feelings regarding myself versus Self and my work versus Work. The observer of this research, which is me, is thus being observed by me through me. The inner journey made me need to think and feel with an open mind, heart, and will to bring the change I want to see. I was confronted with Scharmer's three enemies: 'voice of judgement', 'voice of cynicism' and 'voice of fear' and needed to find ways to fight the inner enemies that might block my open mind, heart and will.

Before the SHAPE project phases were begun, I prepared myself spiritually and mentally. I needed to make peace with the inner enemies that confronted me. I needed to find more clarity on the two central questions: What is my Self? What is my Work? To help me progress on my spiritual journey and try to find a sense of peace and purpose, I took certain steps. Firstly, I attended a course with the theme of 'Church: Freedom in Christ'. This course changed me profoundly and led me through several inner journeys of letting go of the past and letting in the new. Secondly, my PhD supervisor, Professor Kriben Pillay, sponsored me to fly to Cape Town to attend a Theory U beginners' workshop to familiarise myself with Theory U practices. Thirdly, I attended a course in Johannesburg, presented by a neurologist on psychoneuroendocrinology, to gain an understanding of how the functions of an individual's mind, body, and soul operate as an integrative whole in relation to all systemic levels: what could be understood as an individual's reality. It taught me that an individual's mind, body, and soul cannot be separated from the Whole and gave me an added sense of the significance of nondualism.

After attending the Freedom in Christ course, the Theory U workshop, and the psychoneuroendocrinology course, I felt I had a sense of purpose. Persistent and deep-rooted feelings of anxiety made way for an inner calm knowing that God would provide; that the future would emerge as it should because everything is a nondual whole, and this whole is real and reality at the same time, and that our mind, body, and soul are a conjoined Whole.

It was the first time in almost sixteen years that I had had such a sense of peace and purpose. I felt liberated and free; I felt like a new Me. Essentially, I had travelled through the U-curve's conceptual framework and was profoundly changed.

9.1.3 During SHAPE

I felt as if my radical presencing moments had occurred in the pre-SHAPE stage. I also frequently experienced smaller presencing moments as I co-created and co-evolved with SHAPE. I was able to identify open-heartedly with the reflections of the student entrepreneurs because

9 En Route: A Self-Reflective Lens as a Case Study 215

I had had those same emotions and experiences in my life when I was a young entrepreneur. I was also able to identify with the feelings and experiences of the other intermediaries of the student entrepreneurs because I had similar experiences with similar systemic relationships in my own life, both in South Africa and while living in the Middle East.

Although SHAPE brought with it several pressures, I felt equipped to deal with challenges as they arose.

It felt as if I could crystallise, prototype, and bring forward solutions to project challenges.

It felt as if my emotions and feelings were in balance, and I did not experience big emotional highs or lows. I did not have the sense of fear or anxiety which I had experienced before my radical change in the pre-SHAPE stage.

It was as if I had gone into an instinctual project management mode in the 'during-SHAPE' project stage because the project was time-consuming and kept me very busy. This intuitive project management mode drew on all the experiences and skills that formed my own episteme, which was, in return, guided by my ontos and, therefore, enabled me to lead intuitively from the emerging future. The 'changed me' was filled with enthusiasm, energy, positivity, and readiness to co-initiate, co-sense, co-inspire, co-create, and co-evolve with other individuals. The way I saw other individuals also changed. I used to see others as potential business partners, stakeholders, or investors. My newfound experiences led me to perceive others as potential business friends with whom business friendships could be formed; alliances with like-minded, like-hearted, and like-willed individuals, and not merely as partners with money-making as a primary aim. There was a vision of a much bigger and more beautiful picture inspired by social emergence that had the potential to lead to economies of creation.

Although the SHAPE project lacked sufficient funding for its operations at this stage, I had calm, inner confidence that funding would come and the journey would proceed. Then, unexpectedly and unasked for, some funding was offered by the local municipality, in the form of a 'municipality mentor' who would serve as an intermediary to the youth entrepreneurs. The financial support from the municipality was eventuated after the mentor actively participated in the project's pre-SHAPE stage. Maybe the municipality mentor felt co-inspired too?

I saw this as a sign from God or the Whole that all was on track, and I shouldn't be fearful. I was READY to start leading from the emerging future, which was now evolving into the during-SHAPE stage.

9.1.4 Post-SHAPE

One of the primary reasons I chose to tackle the SALAR, SHAPE, was because I wanted to contribute to a deeper and more radical change in young people that would help develop their entrepreneurial orientation and their levels of entrepreneurial self-confidence. In doing so, I was hoping to contribute to developments in the microsystem, which I hoped would, in turn, lead to positive development in meso- and macrosystems, ultimately contributing, in the long term, to socio-economic development in South Africa.

As the SHAPE participants moved through the U-curve, they experienced change and the development of their entrepreneurial disposition. I also underwent a personal change in my movements through the U-curve. The U-curve that I experienced had several repetitive cycles where I moved from the left to the right, re-entered the left phase, and moved to the right phase, repeatedly. It felt as if I was experiencing the same emotions and feelings as the participants but in relation to them, not myself. It was as if my senses and open heart strongly empathised with the motions of the participants.

Also, I felt an open heart towards the systemic challenges being experienced in the support structure for the participants (municipality mentors, chamber of commerce mentors, LED tutors, existing entrepreneurs and operational support staff from UKZN). Repeated site visits to the offices of these intermediaries enabled me to observe the daily systemic struggles these intermediaries face. I empathised with their vision of advancing systemic change, the systemic challenges they experience in actualising their vision, and their perseverance in pursuing their vision for a better South Africa. It was as if a strong emotional link of business friendship and camaraderie had been formed since we all shared the same vision and were working together to bring this shared vision to reality.

I also developed a sense of 'maternal' responsibility towards the Aspiring Young Entrepreneurs, looking into possible ways to help them achieve their hopes and aspirations. It was as if I felt and sensed their fears and anxieties as well as sharing their enthusiasms and elations. This openhearted empathy with all the role-players and participants in SHAPE often brought me to an emotional state in which I found myself crying when I withdrew to somewhere quiet to reflect on events. I'm still not sure what type of tears they were; I think it was tears of empathy. Often after such an emotional moment, I was filled with renewed energy and a new vision of hope for leading this project to further heights.

At last, as reflected above in the pre-SHAPE stage, the SHAPE as a SALAR initiative started with minimum funding, but as indicated, I never lost hope that funding would emerge. At this stage, our hopes were answered by the National Research Foundation, which generously allocated a Thuthuka grant to the research, thereby opening doors to take this research further.

As I cycled through the project's first iteration and observed the barriers and opportunities to youth entrepreneurship, I reflected on my past. I had experienced the same barriers and opportunities on my entrepreneurial journey as the participants of the SHAPE project were themselves experiencing. As the responses of many of the participants, my reaction when encountering a barrier was usually to take a knock in my self-efficacy and inspiration to continue. But from a source deep within, deep energy emerges to bridge barriers and grasp opportunities. If youths can have a deep shift within their entrepreneurial personality traits, then the biggest barrier is conquered.

Open Access This chapter is licensed under the terms of the Creative Commons Attribution 4.0 International License (http://creativecommons.org/licenses/by/4.0/), which permits use, sharing, adaptation, distribution and reproduction in any medium or format, as long as you give appropriate credit to the original author(s) and the source, provide a link to the Creative Commons license and indicate if changes were made.

The images or other third party material in this chapter are included in the chapter's Creative Commons license, unless indicated otherwise in a credit line to the material. If material is not included in the chapter's Creative Commons license and your intended use is not permitted by statutory regulation or exceeds the permitted use, you will need to obtain permission directly from the copyright holder.

Index

A

Abilities 42, 74, 77, 123, 129, 150, 204
African Development Bank (AfDB) 88

B

B2B trade 176
B2C trade 176
Barriers xii–xiv, 4, 19–21, 23, 32, 41, 44, 50, 51, 57, 61, 91, 99, 106, 203, 217
Barriers to Entrepreneurship xii
BRICS (Brazil, Russia, India, China, and South Africa) 144
Brochures and prototypes 173
Business ideas 14, 21, 42, 92, 94, 122, 127, 156, 194, 203

Business model 47, 71, 153, 154, 156, 178, 210
Business turnover 140
Buyer 'persona' 171

C

Case study 209
Co-initiating 9, 12, 39, 50, 64, 66, 68, 74, 75, 89, 92, 106, 119, 122
Communities 14, 20, 21, 72, 89–92, 95, 97, 99, 117
Competencies xiv, 77, 78, 123, 124, 199
Core business 187
Corporates 72, 176
Corporate social investment (CSI) 98

Corporations 15, 21, 42, 96–101, 142, 176

D

Develop 10, 40, 48, 60, 61, 72, 73, 77, 78, 81–83, 85, 89, 90, 122, 123, 131, 133, 142, 144, 148, 161, 216
Drop-shipping 161, 177–180, 184, 201
During-SHAPE 214–216

E

Economy 5–7, 9, 40, 43, 58, 70, 96, 100, 140, 144
Ecosystem xiii, 57, 58, 61–63, 65, 68, 71, 73–75, 77–79, 83, 93–97, 101, 104, 106
Educational institutes 52, 69, 71, 74, 75, 77, 79, 83, 85, 87, 96, 97, 99–101, 104, 106
Educational institutions 88, 99
Enablers xiii, 4, 19, 21, 32, 57
Entrepreneurial action (EA) 9, 36, 49, 148, 153, 203
Entrepreneurial dream 117, 131
Entrepreneurial heartset, mindset and handset xiii, xiv, 12, 13, 21, 23, 32, 35–37, 39, 43, 44, 51
Entrepreneurial Intention (EI) 13, 32, 35, 48, 49, 60
Entrepreneurial self-efficacy (ESE) 10, 35, 37, 61
Entrepreneur(s) xvi, 8, 9, 11, 14, 16, 17, 21, 23, 31, 38, 41, 42, 45–47, 50, 62–66, 69, 73–75, 80, 89, 91, 92, 102, 117, 119, 121, 123, 127, 129, 132, 133, 138, 140, 142, 144, 147, 148, 150, 153, 155–159, 166, 176, 177, 187, 188, 195, 197, 199, 203, 209–211, 214–216
Entrepreneurship 3, 4, 8, 9, 11–14, 17–19, 21, 32, 39, 40, 42–44, 46, 52, 58–63, 66, 70, 71, 73–76, 78, 81–86, 89, 91, 94, 98, 104, 105, 117, 119, 121, 131–133, 137, 138, 147, 187, 211, 217
Entrepreneurship Development in Higher Education (EDHE) programme 70, 81, 138
Entrepreneurship Frameworks and Models 18
Experimenting 50, 157, 174, 199
Exports 145

F

Financial returns 147
Foreign markets 144–146
Framework(s) 12, 13, 18, 38, 44, 62, 214

G

Government agencies 14, 21, 52, 72, 80, 83
Growth xii, 3, 9, 13, 23, 42–45, 61, 65, 66, 85, 86, 88, 89, 104, 153, 154, 211

H

Handset 48, 50, 63, 78, 106, 120

Index

Heartset 12, 33, 36, 46–50, 63, 78, 106, 119

I

Imports 140
Individual entrepreneurial orientation (IEO) xviii, 8, 32, 40, 60, 61
Industry sector 141
Innovation 8–12, 15, 21, 32, 35, 39, 40, 42–44, 47, 50, 65, 96–98, 102, 104, 106, 137, 147, 154, 155, 161, 162, 187, 203, 211
Inspired action 138
Intermediaries xiv
Internal domains 31, 33, 36, 40, 61
Introspection 125

L

Large businesses 15, 21, 72, 96–101
Life purpose 121

M

Marketing 166, 167, 169–171, 177, 184, 190, 203
Marketing funnel 169
Market research 46, 164–166
Mindset 12
Model(s) 12, 21, 23, 40, 57, 61, 63, 71, 77, 78, 84, 89, 96, 104, 106, 120, 123, 124, 161, 162, 174, 177, 179, 183, 187, 198, 210
Models of entrepreneurship 20

N

New customers 163, 164
Nexus xii, 46, 48, 61, 104
North American Industry Classification System 139

O

Open heart 78, 216
Open mind 78, 213
Open will 78
Opportunities xii, 10, 14, 17, 21, 32, 37, 38, 44–47, 50, 60, 65, 74, 76, 79, 85, 86, 92, 95, 96, 101, 121–123, 137, 138, 140, 142, 150, 155, 176, 184, 194, 203, 211, 217

P

Passion 49, 118, 121, 123, 127, 148
Persona map 173
Post-SHAPE 216
Pre-SHAPE 213–217
Private sector agencies 72, 86–88
Product development 189
Product range 203

Q

Qualified leads 169

R

Reputation 164
Resources xv, 16, 45, 65, 74, 77, 79, 82, 83, 87, 95, 96, 99–102, 140, 156, 158, 184, 187, 188, 190, 193, 195, 201, 203

Risk 41, 47, 51
Risk-taking 8, 41, 47

S

SALAR 13, 58, 76, 209, 216, 217
Sales 158, 168–172, 174, 175, 177, 189, 190, 197, 199, 202
SHAPE Four-Quadrant Business Model Canvas (BMC) 153, 156–158
SHAPE YES Network xv
Shifting Hope, Activating Potential Entrepreneurship (SHAPE) xi, xvi, 4, 12–15, 18, 20, 21, 23, 31, 35, 38, 40, 49, 52, 58, 62, 63, 65, 66, 68, 79, 80, 87, 90–93, 97, 103–105, 119, 120, 122, 124, 127–130, 156, 157, 166, 167, 170, 187, 190, 198, 209, 213–217
Small-and-medium-sized enterprise (SME) 60, 92
Small Enterprise Development Agency (Seda) 193
Social technology xi, xv, xvi, 66
Socio-economic development 4, 7, 12, 23, 40–42, 44, 50, 52, 58, 63, 65, 66, 75, 81, 106, 122, 148, 213, 216
South Africa xviii, 3, 9–13, 15, 21, 43, 58–60, 62, 66, 80, 81, 85, 88–90, 96, 100–102, 138, 140, 142, 144, 147, 150, 210–213, 215, 216
Starting a business 126, 138, 161, 177, 180
Strategy 3, 4, 9, 12–14, 23, 31, 35, 39, 40, 49, 52, 60, 65, 68, 79, 81, 83, 92, 102, 103, 153, 154, 172, 189, 190, 194, 199
Student Entrepreneurs xvi
Sustainability 4, 7, 12, 13, 42, 44, 48, 61, 81, 195, 212
Synthesis 104
Systemic Action Learning and Action Research (SALAR) xvi
Systemic Approach xvi
Systemic Levels xvii
System(s) xvii, 4–7, 11, 13, 23, 32, 36, 40, 41, 43, 58, 60, 63, 68, 73, 76, 78, 79, 86, 88, 91, 106, 154, 156, 199, 200, 211
Systems Thinking xvii

T

Taxonomy 66, 67
Tools 9, 77, 104, 117, 129, 130, 133, 148, 155–157, 183, 187–190, 200
Transaction model 183
Triple H of Entrepreneurship xvii, xviii, 10, 32, 34,
Typologies of Youth Entrepreneurs 16

U

Uniqueness 164, 194

V

Value chain 86, 95, 106, 158, 197
Voice of cynicism 213
Voice of fear 213
Voice of judgement 213

Y
Youth entrepreneur development process 11
Youth Entrepreneurs xviii
Youth Entrepreneurship xviii
Youth Entrepreneurship: Enablers and Barriers 19
Youth Entrepreneurship Programmes xix

GPSR Compliance
The European Union's (EU) General Product Safety Regulation (GPSR) is a set of rules that requires consumer products to be safe and our obligations to ensure this.

If you have any concerns about our products, you can contact us on

ProductSafety@springernature.com

In case Publisher is established outside the EU, the EU authorized representative is:

Springer Nature Customer Service Center GmbH
Europaplatz 3
69115 Heidelberg, Germany

www.ingramcontent.com/pod-product-compliance
Lightning Source LLC
LaVergne TN
LVHW021335080526
838202LV00004B/188